MODERN CANTERBURY PILGRIMS

MODERN
CANTERBURY PILGRIMS

*And Why They Chose
the Episcopal Church*

John H. Hallowell
W. H. Auden
Antonio D. Marquez
Donald Slesinger
D. R. Davies
Theodore O. Wedel
W. G. Peck
Joseph Wittkofski
Samuel J. Wylie
Kathleen Bliss
Owen C. Thomas

Emani Sambayya
William A. Spurrier, III
Eduard Heimann
Michael Allen
Enrico C. S. Molnar
Hoxie Neale Fairchild
William H. Baar
Michael Budzanoski
Chad Walsh
Howard A. Johnson
William G. Pollard

Edited, with an essay, by
JAMES A. PIKE

MOREHOUSE-GORHAM CO.

New York   1956

FOREWORD

THERE should be no such book as this. That there is, is a reflection of the fact that our Lord's will for His Church—"that they all may be one"—has been thwarted, by the sin and blindness of men. But the disunity of the Church, the brokenness of the Body of Christ, is a fact, just as was the maltreatment—unto death—of the Body of Christ when He came among us in the flesh. Thus it is that a man must decide—if he is to have a part in the life of the visible Church at all—what *part* of the Church shall command his working allegiance. For many this decision is by default: they simply remain what they were born. (The many who find this approach commendable could hardly justify Missions: it would apply to a totem pole worshipper as well!) The decision has been the result of conscious reflection on the part of others, especially those who have been converted to the Christian Faith in adult life or who have conscientiously and thoughtfully returned to it after a period of agnosticism, and then have the additional burden of deciding where in the Christian scene they belong.

Visitors to Kent will have observed that there are a number of different roads into Canterbury. So too the richness and breadth of the Anglican heritage are such that the primary attraction differs widely among the many thousands of adult converts who find their way to us each year. Equally varied is the ecclesiastical, sociological, and personal background of those who make the pilgrimage. The aim of portraying this very diversity in place of departure, route of travel, and point of entry has dominated the process of

7

selection, and hence it hardly need be conceded that there are hundreds of others who could have written essays equal in illumination and sincerity to those here presented. It is to be hoped that the selection has been sufficiently comprehensive that many of these others will find themselves here represented in fact if not by name. (Speaking of comprehensiveness, in choosing the subtitle, "And Why They Chose the Episcopal Church," brevity won over complete accuracy: four of the essayists are from other branches of the Anglican Communion.)

There will be those who feel that the issuance of such a work is divisive, uncharitable, and unecumenical. This has been far from the intent of the publisher, the editor, and the essayists, as the tone of the essays by and large will display. A sound Christian unity will not come from minimizing differences but from clear and explicit statement of differences and with increased mutual understanding of respective positions. Happily this approach is a basic premise of the Ecumenical Movement today. It is founded in the hope that the Coming Great Church, to use Canon Wedel's fine phrase, will be the richer for the incorporation of all of the positive insights of the respective traditions, rather than "swept and garnished" because of a premature sacrifice of religious emphases and practices which have been meaningful and dear to Christians in the various Churches.

Thus it is hoped that these essays will tend toward the better understanding of the Anglican heritage—not only by those within the Church (who do not always fully understand or appreciate it) but by other Christians as well—and thus perhaps make a small contribution to the fulfillment of our Lord's high priestly prayer, "that they may be one, that men may know that thou hast sent me." Come that day, such a book as this will have no place, nor for that matter will Anglicanism itself, as all men worship and work together in the Holy Catholic Church of Christ.

JAMES A. PIKE

The Deanery, New York City
Feast of St. Augustine of Canterbury
1955

CONTENTS

MODERN CANTERBURY PILGRIMS

1

JOHN H. HALLOWELL

A political philosopher of the first rank, Dr. John H. Hallowell is Professor of Political Science at Duke University. Born in 1913, he graduated from Harvard and did graduate study at Duke (Master of Arts) and Princeton (Doctor of Philosophy). He began his teaching at the University of California at Los Angeles. Dr. Hallowell has served as a visiting professor at Stanford University and was the Charles R. Walgreen Foundation lecturer at the University of Chicago. This year, he is serving as a Fulbright professor at the University of Munich, also having been awarded a Guggenheim Fellowship.

Professor Hallowell is author of three important books: The Decline of Liberalism as an Ideology: With Particular Reference to German Politico-Legal Thought, Main Currents in Modern Political Thought, *and* The Moral Foundation of Democracy. *He was a contributor to* Religious Perspectives in College Teaching *and is author of a "Faculty Paper,"* Communism and Christianity, *issued by the National Council of the Episcopal Church, and of articles in various reviews. He is married and has three children.*

JOHN H. HALLOWELL

IT HAS sometimes been said that there is no such thing as an intellectual conversion to Christianity. Yet as I look back upon my own "conversion" it appears, at least at first, to have been largely motivated by intellectual considerations. I hesitate to use the word conversion to describe my own experience, for my return to Christianity was marked by no dramatic incidents and, as I am coming more and more to recognize, the process of conversion is a matter at least of a lifetime. There is no precise time, moreover, to which I can point and say, "At that time I was converted." My return to Christianity was the result of a long maturing conviction that Christianity explained the meaning of life better than any rival religion or philosophy.

I was baptized in the Church of the New Jerusalem, the Church to which my parents belonged and which was founded upon the teachings of Emmanuel Swedenborg. I attended Sunday School there until I was of high school age, when I lost interest. My father was not a regular churchgoer but he was a man of strong religious faith. Both his faith in the ultimate goodness and sovereignty of God and that of my grandmother made a strong impression upon me as a child. Although confined to her room by physical infirmities, my grandmother never complained of her lot but waited with patient serenity for the death that would release her from the vicissitudes of old age. The Bible was her constant companion and although she never forced it upon me, she frequently talked to me of the faith which it inspired.

It was in the 1930's that I went away to college (Harvard) and like many college students then and now I drifted further

and further away from Christianity. I had long since ceased
going to church with any regularity and since few of my
friends in college ever went to church I did not go either. The
intellectual atmosphere in the classrooms was exciting and, as
I felt then, liberating. As my intellectual horizons widened
and as I became more and more sophisticated, I became more
and more impatient with religion in any form. Impatient,
perhaps, is not quite the right word, for the truth of the matter is that I gave very little attention to it. And since religion,
for the most part, was ignored in the classroom, I had no
occasion to think seriously about it.

I gathered from my history courses that the Middle Ages
were notable principally for the prevalence of superstition
and intolerance. The Church was mentioned as figuring
prominently in political intrigues, as an obstinate barrier to
intellectual enlightenment, and as a stronghold of hypocrisy.
My own reading of history had led me to similar conclusions
and the classroom only served to confirm with greater intellectual authority conclusions which I had arrived at inde-
pendently. From my psychology courses I acquired a
completely new vocabulary that enabled me to explain my
own and my friends' behavior with an ingenuity and seeming profundity that was the mark of an "educated" man. I
could at last put away my childish beliefs and face up with
the language of the most sophisticated of my contemporaries to the "realities" of human existence. I learned that
man was simply a complex animal organism and that the
observation of the behavior of rats in a maze was contribut-
ing important new knowledge about the behavior of man.
From the history of philosophy I acquired a general skepticism about the possibility of knowing the truth about anything. My professor in this course was a genial skeptic
whose intellectual gymnastics were a joy to observe. The first

half hour he would do his utmost to defend the position of
the philosopher under consideration and the second half
hour would be devoted to an equally brilliant demolition.
Each lecture would close with slightly perceptible raised
eyebrows and a smile of intellectual triumph. The course
started with Plato (who impressed me greatly), skipped,
of course, the backward Middle Ages, to confront us with
the redoubtable Descartes, and continued to what was presumably the most enlightened of all philosophical systems—
American pragmatism. But my genial professor, a true
skeptic to the last, closed the course, as he began it, with
a quizzical smile, and while I came away admiring his
dialectical skill, I also came away with a sense of the intellectual futility of seeking answers to the most basic questions.

It was not until my senior year when I encountered the
equally brilliant but more constructive mind of Professor
Alfred North Whitehead that the philosophical quest for
truth appeared once again as a valid and exciting pursuit. As
I listened to him lecture in the benign manner that was so
characteristic of the man, I cannot say that I understood a
great deal of what he was saying, but I had the impression
that I was listening to philosophical discourse in the manner
in which Plato had carried it on with the students in his
academy. Here was a genuine quest for truth that shunned
intellectual pyrotechnics in patient submission to the ultimate
mystery that lies behind all questions and all answers. Where
one professor had closed his course on a note of intellectual
triumph after demolishing every philosophical system attempted by man, Professor Whitehead left us not with a
sense of futility but with a sense of awe.

It was also towards the end of my college career that I
first came to appreciate the contribution which the Middle
Ages had made to Western political theory and institutions.

I was concentrating then on the study of government, and through lectures and contacts with Professors Elliott, Holcombe, and McIlwain I was brought to a new appreciation of the importance of the Middle Ages for the development of Western political institutions. Under their guidance I developed a strong intellectual interest in the relationship between ethics and politics, an interest I have pursued ever since. But I was a long way from Christianity and organized religion. I knew something about the political philosophy of St. Augustine and St. Thomas Aquinas but I knew little or nothing about their theology and cared less.

Like many of my contemporaries and some of my professors I had reached the conclusion that Christianity was a childish myth and that no intellectually respectable adult could possibly subscribe to its doctrines. Except for the writings of Swedenborg, however, I had never read any Christian theology, although I was familiar with the writings of many critics of Christianity. I knew nothing about orthodox Christianity except a few Bible stories I had learned in Sunday School, and these had no relevance to anything that I had studied in college or to the studies I wanted to pursue afterwards.

Four years of graduate study in the field of political science left me little time or inclination to think about religion. I was busy preparing for a professional career as a college teacher and all my intellectual energies were absorbed in technical studies. But the existence of Fascism in Italy and of National Socialism in Germany did trouble the liberal conscience with which I had emerged from college. For, like most of my contemporaries in the 1930's, I was a liberal ready to crusade for every liberal cause and impatient to bring about the social utopia that would right the wrongs that temporarily plagued the world. But tyranny, once only a word encountered in history books, was rapidly becoming a reality in Russia, Germany, and Italy.

What could explain the decline of liberalism and the rise of totalitarian dictatorships? Why was liberalism everywhere on the defensive? It was easy to say that Russia, Germany, and Italy never had any liberalism to decline or that the rise of tyranny in these countries was simply a reflection of the peculiar national characteristics of the people or of their history, but these answers did not satisfy me. I had spent a year in Germany and the people did not seem to me to be essentially more brutal than Americans. Indeed, many of them seemed to be as much victims of the Nazi system as propagators of it. I discovered, too, that Germany had had a liberal tradition which if less vigorous and politically successful than the liberal tradition in Great Britain and the United States was still in the same orbit. How was it possible for prominent German professors, judges, lawyers, and civil servants, who before 1933 were professed liberals, to accept, and in some cases even to acclaim, a despotism that repudiated everything for which liberalism stood? In an effort to answer that question I decided to write my doctoral dissertation on the decline of liberalism in Germany. I reached the conclusion that the forces which produced the Nazi dictatorship in Germany were not peculiar to Germany but that the same forces, in varying degrees, were present in every other nation of the Western world. The intellectual and spiritual crisis, I concluded, out of which totalitarianism emerged was a crisis peculiar not alone to Germany but to Western civilization.[1]

[1] *The Decline of Liberalism as an Ideology: With Particular Reference to German Politico-Legal Thought* (Berkeley: University of California Press, 1943).

While I was writing the dissertation I "happened" one Sunday to attend a church service in the Princeton University Chapel. The speaker was Reinhold Niebuhr. I had not been to a church service for years and I had come out of curiosity to hear the man who some of my friends said was an unusual preacher. He was, indeed. He discussed with great profundity and intellectual clarity problems that I had encountered in writing about the decline of liberalism. Indeed, he seemed to have a greater grasp of the reasons for the decline of liberalism than I had. If these insights were the product of his Christianity, then Christianity was certainly relevant to what I was attempting to do. I cannot say that I immediately appropriated them as my own, but I did begin to think about Christianity in a serious way.

In the course of the next few years I began for the first time in my adulthood to read what Christians had to say about the meaning and relevance of Christianity. Somehow it had never occurred to me before to consult those persons who presumably know better what Christianity is than its critics. I had erroneously assumed that they would gloss over the difficulties of faith and dispense the same kind of saccharine-sweet piety that had characterized much of the "religious" reading I had encountered in my youth. That Christianity embraced a robust faith with a formidable intellectual heritage came to me, I must confess, as a surprise. That one can remain so ignorant of such a heritage must be attributed in part to an educational system that had relegated theology many decades ago to the confines of "divinity" schools. But whatever the reason, I have had to discover theology for myself and it has proven to be the most fruitful of all my studies. It would be difficult to list here all the books that I read during this period, but among contemporary writers those who have exerted the strongest influence upon my thinking have been C. S. Lewis, A. E. Taylor, Reinhold Niebuhr, Etienne Gilson, Emil Brunner, Jacques Maritain, and William Temple. From my reading of them I have been encouraged to turn back to the Christian classics themselves, to the writings of St. Augustine, St. Clement of Alexandria, St. Thomas Aquinas, Luther, Calvin, Richard Hooker, and others. From them I have gone back to reading the Bible with a new interest and a new understanding. Much that I read was confusing and upsetting (and still is) but more and more I was convinced that Christianity, despite the paradoxes one encountered and despite the lack of agreement among the authorities, revealed the truth about life as I had encountered it nowhere else.

The lack of agreement among the authorities was disturbing, but it seemed to be more a lack of agreement as to the precise intellectual formulae in which the Christian doctrines could be expressed than a lack of agreement as to the Christian story itself. Either the Christian story as told in the Bible was a gigantic deception or it was the truth, either Christ was what He said He was and what His followers believed Him to be or He was a liar. His disciples were either incredibly naïve or dishonest, and the evidence did not suggest that they were either. On the contrary, they were frequently skeptical, and when Christ lay in agony upon the Cross they deserted Him. This was not the kind of behavior one expected to find among men who were attempting to create a myth. Nor did their acts of martyrdom afterwards, acts which were to be repeated by countless disciples century after century, suggest the actions of deluded men. The weight of probable evidence seemed more and more to be on the side of the truth of Christianity. I cannot say at what precise time faith in Christ as the Son of God and Redeemer of man was given me, but I do know that it was a long maturing conviction. It is not yet a conviction that cannot be assailed by doubts nor is it a faith without intellectual difficulties, but it is a faith that illumines my mind and sustains my spirit as no other faith has ever done.

I was first attracted to Christianity once I was shown that it was intellectually relevant to the problems with which I was professionally concerned. The relevance which Christianity has for the understanding of politics I have tried to explain in other places. Suffice it to say here that the Christian understanding of man, particularly the Christian understanding of man's fallen state, enables us to avoid both the unrealistic expectations of idealism and the despair of cynicism. It explains the political crisis of our times better than either liberalism or Marxism since it understands better than either the dimensions of evil and the true nature of man's self-estrangement. It illumines the crisis in which we find ourselves by focusing our attention on the ever-present judgment of God, and gives a meaning to suffering that otherwise would be intolerable. Either history is, as Christianity claims, a drama of salvation or it is a very unfunny joke. I prefer to think that it is the former.

It was not long before I came to recognize that the faith which served so well to widen and deepen my understanding of the times in which I lived had also something significant to say to me personally. The Christian doctrine of original sin, which served so much better than the liberal's equation of evil with ignorance or the Marxist's equation of evil with surplus value to explain why society was constantly threatened with disintegration, also served to explain many of my own inner conflicts. I had only to examine myself honestly to find proof for the doctrine I had once dismissed as absurd and morbid. The psychological vocabulary which I had acquired in college, though not totally worthless, had proven to be more a vocabulary than a description of reality. It was useful for labeling purposes, but the labels never quite described the reality and too often served only to obscure the root of the trouble. And in any case the feeling of frustration was not to be eased by labeling even when the label was appropriate. Feelings of anger, envy, hatred, and jealousy were constantly frustrating my better intentions and I was at war with myself. Indeed the root of the trouble was, as St. Paul once said, that I was doing the evil I would not and not doing the good that I would. For such trouble I needed the kind of help that was beyond my own power, indeed, beyond the power of any man to provide.

These considerations in addition to the responsibilities of marriage and children did much to mature my faith and to suggest that I should affiliate myself with a Church. The necessity for a definite decision came when I was forced to decide what I wanted for my children. And that inevitably involved deciding what I wanted for myself. I took my problems to the local rector of our Episcopal Church and after attending at his suggestion church services for a year both my wife and I asked to be confirmed by the Bishop.

But why the Episcopal Church? Having become convinced of the truth of Christianity I wanted to affiliate myself with a Church that preserved the orthodox teachings of Christianity, a Church where I could worship God with sincerity and where I could find the help that I needed. I could not return to the Church of my childhood since its teachings still seemed to me to be eccentric, where the "revelations" of Swedenborg seemed to obscure the revelation of Christ, and its sectarian exclusiveness cut it off from the main stem of the Christian tradition.

Of the theological reading I had done I was least attracted by the writings of Luther. They reflect an anti-intellectual bias that seems to me to do less than justice to the wisdom that has been acquired outside the Christian community. Ever since I first encountered the writings of Plato I have been impressed by the wisdom which they contain and I was delighted when I discovered that Christianity confirmed and supplemented many of his insights. But the appreciation of that wisdom which one finds among many, if not all, of the early Church fathers is not only lacking in Luther's writings but is replaced by outright hostility. A man who could write that "reason is directly opposed to faith" and that "in believers it should be killed and buried" did not speak a language that I could understand. I found Calvin's *Institutes* more impressive intellectually but doctrinally defective, particularly in the notion that man's nature is so depraved that it cannot be healed even by the grace of God.

The classical Protestant doctrine of justification by faith *alone* seems to me to be a one-sided emphasis. The idea that God merely imputes to us the righteousness of the Son, that man is utterly vile and can do nothing whatsoever to merit eternal life, does not seem to me to embrace the whole Christian message. The idea that the grace of God saves a man without transforming him seems to me to make nonsense of the idea of salvation. For what is salvation if it does not issue in a new life? With Hoxie Neale Fairchild "I prefer the more rational and inspiring view that Christian belief and Christian living, inseparably concomitant, actually remake man into a being acceptable to God."[2] While I recognize that the image of God in man has been defaced by sin, I cannot subscribe to that particular form of Christian belief

[2] Hoxie N. Fairchild, *Toward Belief* (New York: The Macmillan Co., 1935), p. 120.

that regards man as totally depraved. For if man were totally depraved he would have no means of recognizing God's will when he encountered it, nor would he have the capacity for good that is just as evident as is his propensity to do evil. Recognition of the sinfulness of human nature was never intended, it seems to me, to paralyze man's capacity for intelligent thought and moral action but rather to liberate that capacity in the service of God rather than of self.

At the same time I recognize that many of the criticisms which Luther and Calvin leveled at the medieval Church were justified. I am uncomfortable with them doctrinally but I recognize the legitimacy of their demands for the reformation of the Church. Because I recognize the legitimacy of those demands I could not affiliate myself with the Roman Catholic Church. Although sympathetically disposed to the doctrinal position of the Latin Church, particularly as it found expression in the writings of the early Church fathers, I cannot accept many of the modern doctrinal accretions and practices. The doctrine of Papal infallibility is one of these and the present tendency to elevate Mary to the position of co-redemptrix is another. In some countries the Roman Catholic Church does not seem to me to try as hard as it might to eliminate superstitious practices among its communicants but, indeed, seems to encourage them. Its close association with reactionary political forces in many parts of the world—its reluctance, for example, to condemn Fascism in Italy—also casts some doubt on the sincerity or at least the efficacy of its social pronouncements. Liturgically the Roman Church seems to me to be defective to the degree that its services are conducted in a language not readily understood by the people and to the degree that the Mass is presented as a spectacle from which the people are prevented from taking an active and vocal part. The emphasis which the Roman Church places upon indulgences impresses me as presumptuous and excessively mechanical.

Where could I find a Church that preserved the Catholic tradition without the defects of Roman Catholicism? My attention was first directed to the Episcopal Church by my reading of Hoxie Neale Fairchild's *Toward Belief.* I do not remember how the book came into my hands but I am grateful that it did. His argument persuaded me that this was the Church for which I had been seeking, and experience has since confirmed it. For it seems to me that I have found in the doctrines and practices of the Anglican Communion the Catholic Church reformed.

Based upon the Bible, reason, and tradition, the doctrinal position of the Anglican Church avoids both the intellectual obscurantism of "fundamentalism" and the doctrinal laxity of "liberalism." Although it insists upon no official doctrinal interpretation it clearly affirms the Christian Faith as expressed in the Apostles' and Nicene Creeds. It does not, like some Churches, hedge or equivocate on its doctrinal position, but neither does it insist that its communicants accept any particular philosophical formulation of its beliefs as official. Unlike that form of Protestantism which regards the Bible as the sole source of truth and unlike Roman Catholicism which makes the authority of the Church and ultimately that of the Pope supreme, the Anglican Church accepts three sources of authority—reason, Scripture, and tradition—which, in the words of Richard Hooker, all alike emanate from God, "each in certain matters bearing a special . . . sanction from Him, all in certain matters blending and co-operating." The Anglican Church grants to all believers the free use of critical thought and speech. Because it believes that Christ is the living embodiment of the Truth, that He is the Word of

God made flesh, it welcomes and seeks the truth from whatever source derived and wherever it may be found. It does not look upon reason as an enemy of faith but as an ally. It does not look upon secular learning with suspicion but welcomes whatever contribution such learning can make to a genuine knowledge of reality. If it opposes the presumption of Papal and Churchly infallibility it also opposes the gnostic pretensions of that kind of Puritanism which claimed precise knowledge of God's purposes and had no difficulty in singling out God's elect on earth.[3] It regards the Church not as a home for saints but as a haven for sinners.

The Anglican Church makes no claim to infallibility, but in a spirit of humility freely acknowledges its liability to error. That spirit is reflected in a collect which is found in the Book of Common Prayer and one which is frequently used in its services:

O Gracious Father, we humbly beseech thee for thy holy Catholic Church; that thou wouldest be pleased to fill it with all truth, in all peace. Where it is corrupt, purify it; where it is in error, direct it; where in any thing it is amiss, reform it. Where it is right, establish it; where it is in want, provide for it; where it is divided, reunite it. . . .

Although it rejects any claim to infallibility the Anglican Church does claim to be a legitimate branch of the Holy

[3] It is unavailing, Richard Hooker has said, to present Scriptural truth to unbelievers without showing them any reason why they should accept it and "even to ourselves it needeth caution and explication how the testimony of the Spirit may be discerned, by what means it may be known; lest men think that the Spirit of God doth testify those things which the spirit of error suggesteth . . . Wherefore albeit the Spirit lead us into all truth and direct us in all goodness, yet because these workings of the Spirit in us are so privy and secret; we therefore stand on a plainer ground, when we gather by reason from the quality of things believed or done, that the Spirit of God hath directed us in both, than if we settle ourselves to believe or to do any particular thing, as being moved thereto by the Spirit."

Catholic and Apostolic Church and, though subject to human error, to be a divinely instituted channel of grace. It claims historical continuity with the primitive Church. It has maintained the apostolic succession and ordained its priesthood by the laying on of hands, upholding the historic threefold ministry of bishops, priests, and deacons. It believes that God's grace is mediated to man principally through the sacraments of Baptism and Holy Communion, and it regards participation in Holy Communion as the distinctively Christian mode of worship. Although it rejects the Roman Catholic doctrine of transubstantiation, it believes that God is actually present in the sacraments and that through the sacramental life of the Church the communicant may be infused with a power that is not his own to help him to become a new creature worthy of participation in God's eternal kingdom. The sacramental nature of the Anglican Church is what distinguishes it from many Protestant denominations and this, in my experience, is its most attractive characteristic. At the risk of sounding smug, which is far from my intention, I cannot adequately explain what the Episcopal Church has meant to me without saying that through its sacraments and its liturgy I have been brought closer to the reality of God than through any other religious experience of my life.

In part I attribute this to the sacramental nature of the Church and in part to the liturgy preserved in the Book of Common Prayer. Critics of the Anglican Church sometimes refer disparagingly to its liturgy on the grounds that it is a kind of aestheticism. That beauty should be allied with truth and goodness does not seem strange to me for, indeed, it is part of the ancient wisdom that these three should be found together. That material things should be used to testify to the glory of God, that the senses of man and his body should pay homage no less than his soul to the greatness of God, seems only to testify to the unity of body and soul and to the sacramental nature of the universe. Familiarity with the prayers and services of the Church may conceivably result in a mechanical kind of worship, but in my experience such familiarity has only served to make the liturgy more meaningful. The Book of Common Prayer is truly "an anthology of the piety of ages and nations" and one feels as he uses it that he is participating in a form of worship that knows neither national boundaries, sectarian differences, nor barriers of time. Here already, it seems to me, are to be found the essential ingredients of that ecumenical Church for which many of my Protestant friends are still seeking. It does not remove the tensions that are to be found throughout the Christian Church, for the Anglican Church includes among its communicants every shade of orthodox theological opinion and, within the framework of the Book of Common Prayer, different liturgical emphases; but by virtue of the limitations imposed by the Book of Common Prayer and by virtue of its episcopal authority it does preserve unity among diversity.

I have returned to Christianity because it is the only thing that makes sense out of life, because if life is not a drama of salvation it is nothing. The evidence that the world is in need of salvation of some kind is abundant, and I have had only to examine myself to find evidence there for the kind of evil from which men must be redeemed if the world is to find the salvation which it needs. I have come to worship God at the altar of the Episcopal Church because I believe that it represents Christianity in its most rational, most Catholic, and most beautiful form.

2

W. H. AUDEN

One of the most distinguished poets in the English-speaking world, Mr. W. H. Auden, born in 1907, was educated at Gresham's School, Holt, and at Christ Church, Oxford. Several collections of his poems have been published, one of the best known being For the Time Being. *He received the Bollingen Prize in Poetry in 1953, and the National Book Award for Poetry in 1956 for* The Shield of Achilles. *He was the editor of the* Oxford Book of Light Verse *and of* Selections from Tennyson, *and was co-editor of* Poet's Tongue. *He has summarized his essay with the sentence, "The way in is sometimes the way 'round."*

W. H. AUDEN

THE CHRISTIAN doctrine of a personal God implies that the relation of every human being to Him is unique and historical, so that any individual who discusses the Faith is compelled to begin with autobiography.

So far as my own family is concerned, my generation is the first, I believe, in which no member wears a clerical collar: both my grandfathers and four of my uncles were Anglican priests. When I was born, the Church was still regarded as one of those professions, like the Army, the Navy, law, and medicine, which it was respectable for the middle-class to practise. One of my uncles, for example, would have preferred to go into the Army but there was not enough money to get him into a good regiment, so he was ordained instead.

The many clergy I met in my youth were, with very few exceptions, hard-working, decent-living men, trying to do their duty by their parishioners and educate their children on inadequate stipends, but one could not say that they gave an impression of following a unique vocation. Their virtues, which were many, were those of their class; so were their defects. This is not intended as a sneer or to suggest that a celibate priesthood is necessarily superior. So long as the vast majority of people thought of themselves as Christians and attended church regularly, the decision to take Orders could not seem so drastic as it seems today. Further, before the spread of general education and the development of transport and mass media of entertainment, the country clergy had many functions to fulfill besides their cure of souls, and the notion of having a "gentleman" in every parish was by no means contemptible. And today, when the worldly inducements to enter the priesthood are so small, who will assert that the spiritual level of candidates for ordination has greatly risen?

The atmosphere of my home was, I should say, unusually devout, though not in the least repressive or gloomy. My parents were Anglo-Catholics, so that my first religious memories are of exciting magical rites (at six I was a boat-boy) rather than of listening to sermons. For this I am very grateful, as it implanted in me what I believe to be the correct notion of worship, namely, that it is first and foremost a community in action, a thing done together, and only secondarily a matter of individual feeling or thinking.

It so happened that the bishop of our diocese was an extreme modernist who refused to visit the church we attended; consequently I was accustomed from my earliest years to doctrinal and liturgical controversy. Dissenters and Low Churchmen were known as "Prots" and accused of squatting instead of kneeling; on the other hand, a firm line was drawn between "Devotions," which were all right, and "Benediction," which was definitely over the Roman border. I grew up, therefore, with a conception of the Church which is, I suppose, uniquely Anglican, as a community in which wide divergences of doctrine and rite can and do exist without leading necessarily to schism or excommunication.

At thirteen I was confirmed. To say that shortly afterwards I lost my faith would be melodramatic and false. I simply lost interest. Cases may occur in which a dramatic decision is taken and a person says to himself, "Yesterday I believed the Creed; today I do not," but I am sure they are rare. In describing what usually happens in this age, so far as I can judge from my experience, I am not trying to excuse it. Essentially the reason why any person in any age who has been brought up a Christian loses his faith is that he wants to go his own way and enjoy the pleasures of the world and the flesh.

There are, however, certain aspects of the present age which have made the victory of the prince of this world easier than he has any right to expect. As he reaches adolescence, every boy or girl today begins to notice two phenomena, official religion and religiosity. Official religion is not the same as conventional religion. A conventional Christian is someone who does not distinguish between his faith and his culture; he believes in the Nicene Creed as unquestionably and in the same way as he believes that no gentleman wears a celluloid collar.

An official Christian, on the other hand, is someone who, for various reasons like setting an example to the young or doing business in his community, attends the rites and recites the formulas while knowing perfectly well that he, personally, does not believe in them. In the boarding schools I attended, chapel was compulsory for the masters as well as the boys, and one very soon realized that many of the former were definitely not Christians but that attending chapel was a condition of their employment. One could not call them hypocrites because this was an open secret which they made no serious effort to conceal.

At the same time, the adolescent begins to notice that, of those who take religion most ardently, a number are unfortunate in one way or another, suffer from physical or mental ill-health, or are unhappily married or too unattractive to get married. He may, as I did, go through a pseudo-devout phase himself and then realize that behind it lay a quite straightforward and unredeemed eroticism. He is apt, then, to draw the conclusion that people only love God when no one else will love them, a tendency, incidentally, which "Crisis" theology sometimes encourages, I think.

A more formidable difficulty for the Church today than either officialdom or religiosity is the gulf between the language and imagery of her liturgies and devotions and those of contemporary culture. Whatever drawbacks it may have, a liturgy in a dead language, like Latin, which the average worshipper does not understand or to which, at least, he has no personal relation, has one great advantage over a vernacular liturgy: it cannot strike him as comic.

Agnus Dei has the attraction, at least, of a magical and musical spell; *Lamb of God,* in a culture, mainly urban, to which the notion of animal sacrifice is totally strange, is liable to evoke ridiculous images.

In ages typified by personal rule and social hierarchies, it was natural to express awe and admiration by honorific titles like *King of Kings,* and to think of performing such extraordinary acts as that proposed in the hymn "Crown him with many crowns," but in an age when rulers are constitutional officials and the real power belongs to the lifeless machine, even the title *Lord* is excessive; in fact, the more we revere and admire someone today, the more we value our relation to him, the less likely we are to use any ceremonial forms of address; those we reserve for our business correspondence. Even the term *Our Father* as a metaphor for God's relationship to us has become awkward since the decline in spiritual authority of the male and of old age.

The clergy, I believe, underestimate the seriousness of this problem, since, for them, liturgical and devotional language is "shop talk," technical like the discourse of doctors among themselves. An adult layman with some imagination and some knowledge of cultural history can learn to use it with understanding as he can learn to understand Homer, but the adolescent is in a different situation.

Having just reached the age when personal belief becomes possible—hitherto it was not really he who believed but his parents and godparents who believed for him—when his relationship to God has to become contemporary, he finds that the terms in which the Church expects him to think about God (as distinct, of course, from *what* she expects him to think) are terms in which neither he nor any of his contemporaries, Christian or not, can think, sincerely or accurately, of anything. At the same time—I am thinking now of England in the twenties but, though the climate has changed a bit, it has not changed that much—he finds, whatever his interests may be, that most of the people who talk or write in terms which he does understand and which excite him are not Christians and are often actively hostile to the Christian Faith.

Writers did and do exist who, if not always, perhaps, completely orthodox, are effective Christian apologists, capable of showing the meaning and relevance of Christian dogmas to secular thought and action, but I never heard of them. I sometimes wonder, for example, what would have happened if, when I was at school or the university, a godparent or a friend had given me the works of Kierkegaard or Rudolf Kassner, both of whom were, later in my life, destined to play a great part. The only theological writer I knew of at that time whom I found readable and disturbing to my complacency was Pascal.

Today I find a certain element of fake in his writings, a kind of romantic indulgence in unhappiness not so far removed from *The Sorrows of the Young Werther,* which may well have been what attracted me at that time; but at least he did not talk like a parson and he prevented me from banishing the thought of God from my mind when I should very much have preferred to do so.

Two other pieces of good fortune exerted a similar saving influence on me as a boy and a young man. I was lucky enough to be born in a period when every educated person was expected to know the Bible thoroughly and no undergraduate could take a degree without passing a Divinity examination. In consequence, whatever attitude one might take towards the Bible, that it was great literature, an interesting anthropological document, or what have you, the events and sayings upon which Christianity is founded were as familiar to one as Grimm's fairy tales. In the United States today, even among students who come from Christian homes, I rarely find one with even the most elementary knowledge of the Bible, and this must make the task of the Church appallingly difficult.

Secondly, I was lucky enough to have a voice and a musical sense adequate to the modest demands of school choirs to which, first as a boy and later as a master, I belonged. In consequence, however bored I might be at the thought of God, I enjoyed services in His worship very much, more, probably, than many who were more devout than I but who had no active role to play. I can say this with some certainty because now, when I profess myself a Christian but, owing to circumstances, cannot be a choir member, I am often bored and distracted in church in a way that I never was when I had a function irrespective of my feelings or beliefs. I wonder if parish priests or church choir masters have ever considered one little fact, that the treble line of a hymn, the tune, after all, is too high for the male members of their congregations to sing. I have no idea how this problem is to be solved satisfactorily, but for those of us who can read music it would be a great pleasure if there were a few hymn books about with all four parts in them. This may sound a frivolous request but it is tied up with a very serious problem indeed for the life of the Church. As the late Dom Gregory Dix has shown so clearly in his wonderful book *The Shape of the Liturgy,* Christian worship is corporate action and anything which tends towards division, whether it be a Roman Catholic Low Mass in which the priest and acolyte perform the rite between them while the congregation occupy themselves with their private devotions, or an Anglican Matins in which the choir sings and the minister preaches while the rest listen, obscures the true nature of the Church as the mystical body of Christ and is a threat to its spiritual health.

The various "kerygmas," of Blake, of Lawrence, of Freud, of Marx, to which, along with most middle-class intellectuals of my generation, I paid attention between twenty and thirty, had one thing in common. They were all Christian heresies; that is to say, one cannot imagine their coming into existence except in a civilization which claimed to be based, religiously, on belief that the Word was made flesh and dwelt among us, and that, in consequence, matter, the natural order, is real and redeemable, not a shadowy appearance or the cause of evil, and historical time is real and significant, not meaningless or an endless series of cycles.

They arose, as I suspect most heresies do, as a doctrinal protest against what one might call a heresy of behavior exhibited by the orthodox of their day. By a heretic in behavior, I mean not simply someone whose conduct or thinking on secular matters is inconsistent with his faith, but someone who is quite honestly unaware that there is any inconsistency and defends his actions as Christian.

One is entitled to say of him, therefore, as one is not of a simple sinner, that, however orthodox he may imagine himself to be, in fact he holds some heretical doctrine of God, that in some way or another he is "dividing the Substance" and "confounding the Persons," for if this were not so, he would recognize the inconsistency and, though he might continue to act as before, he would know his actions to be sinful.

The doctrinal heretic perceives, usually more or less correctly, what doctrine is implied by the particular actions of which he more or less justly disapproves, and in protest propounds a doctrine equally one-sided in the opposite direction.

My own experience convinces me of the folly of trying to protect people from heresy by censorship or repression. In all the figures I have mentioned, I have come to realize that what is true in what they say is implicit in the Christian doctrine of the nature of man, and that what is not Christian is not true; but each of them brought to some particular aspect of life that intensity of attention which is characteristic of one-sided geniuses (needless to say, they all contradicted each other), and such comprehension of Christian wisdom as I have, little though it be, would be very much less without them.

What was one looking for at the time? Nothing is more difficult to recall than past assumptions, but I think the state of mind among most of my contemporaries was somewhat as follows. We assumed that there was only one outlook on life conceivable among civilized people, the liberal humanism in which all of us had been brought up, whether we came from Christian or agnostic homes (English liberalism had never been anti-clerical like its Continental brother).

To this the theological question seemed irrelevant since such values as freedom of the person, equal justice for all, respect for the rights of others, etc., were self-evident truths. However, the liberal humanism of the past had failed to produce the universal peace and prosperity it promised, failed even to prevent a World War. What had it overlooked? The subconscious, said Freud; the means of production, said Marx. Liberalism was not to be superseded; it was to be made effective instead of self-defeating.

Then the Nazis came to power in Germany. The Communists had said that one must hate and destroy some of one's neighbors now in order to create a world in which nobody would be able to help loving his neighbor tomorrow. They had attacked Christianity and all religions on the ground that, so long as people are taught to love a non-existent God, they will ignore the material obstacles to human brotherhood. The novelty and shock of the Nazis was that they made no pretense of believing in justice and liberty for all, and attacked Christianity on the grounds that to love one's neighbor as oneself was a command fit only for effeminate weaklings, not for the "healthy blood of the master race." Moreover, this utter denial of everything liberalism had ever stood for was arousing wild enthusiasm, not in some remote barbaric land outside the pale, but in one of the most highly educated countries in Europe, a country one knew well and where one had many friends. Confronted by such a phenomenon, it was impossible any longer to believe that the values of liberal humanism were self-evident. Unless one was prepared to take a relativist view that all values are a matter of personal taste, one could hardly avoid asking the question: "If, as I am convinced, the Nazis are wrong and we are right, what is it that validates our values and invalidates theirs?"

With this and similar questions whispering at the back of my mind, I visited Spain during the Civil War. On arriving in Barcelona, I found as I walked through the city that all the churches were closed and there was not a priest to be seen. To my astonishment, this discovery left me profoundly shocked and disturbed. The feeling was far too intense to be the result of a mere liberal dislike of intolerance, the notion that it is wrong to stop people from doing what they like, even if it is something silly like going to church. I could not escape acknowledging that, however I had consciously ignored and rejected the Church for sixteen years, the existence of churches and what went on in them had all the time been very important to me. If that was the case, what then?

Shortly afterwards, in a publisher's office, I met an Anglican layman, and for the first time in my life felt myself in the presence of personal sanctity. I had met many good people before who made me feel ashamed of my own shortcomings, but in the presence of this man—we never discussed anything but literary business—I did not feel ashamed. I felt transformed into a person who was incapable of doing or thinking anything base or unloving. (I later discovered that he had had a similar effect on many other people.)

So, presently, I started to read some theological works, Kierkegaard in particular, and began going, in a tentative and experimental sort of way, to church. And then, providentially—for the occupational disease of poets is frivolity— I was forced to know in person what it is like to feel oneself the prey of demonic powers, in both the Greek and the Christian sense, stripped of self-control and self-respect, behaving like a ham actor in a Strindberg play.

Much as I owe to Kierkegaard—among many other virtues, he has the talent, invaluable in a preacher to the

Greeks, of making Christianity sound bohemian—I cannot let this occasion pass without commenting upon what seems to be his great limitation, a limitation which characterizes Protestantism generally. A planetary visitor might read through the whole of his voluminous works without discovering that human beings are not ghosts but have bodies of flesh and blood. (It is interesting to notice that while Kierkegaard shows great love of and insight into literature and music, he shows no interest in the visual arts whatsoever.)

As a spirit, a conscious person endowed with free will, every man has, through faith and grace, a unique "existential" relation to God, and few since St. Augustine have described this relation more profoundly than Kierkegaard. But every man has a second relation to God which is neither unique nor existential: as a creature composed of matter, as a biological organism, every man, in common with everything else in the universe, is related by necessity to the God who created that universe and saw that it was good, for the laws of nature to which, whether he likes it or not, he must conform are of divine origin.

And it is with this body, with faith or without it, that all good works are done. All Catholic doctrines, such as the unity of the Two Natures, the special veneration due to the *Theotokos,* the Real Presence of Christ in the Mass, and Catholic practice, such as the liturgical use of the sensible— vestments, lights, incense—and the emphasis upon auricular confession, stress the physical reality of the flesh into which the Word was made. Admittedly this can and at times has led to an obscuring of the Word behind the splendors of the flesh, reduction of the spiritual life to a mechanical and automatic routine of physical acts against which the Reformers were fully justified in protesting, but their consequent denial of the value of anything visible and objective

made the Christian Faith into something even more difficult
than it is. It is easy to forget, particularly if I do not wish
to remember, what I thought or felt yesterday, but it is
difficult to forget what I did. Even mere routine has its
value, as a reminder. A man may go to confession in a
frivolous state of mind, rattle off some sins without feeling
any real contrition, and go away to commit them again,
but as long as he keeps up the habit he cannot forget that
there are certain actions which the Church calls sinful, and
that he has committed them; similarly, a man who likes
Dover sole better than beefsteak may be a greater glutton
on Friday than he was on Thursday, but as long as he
observes the habit of ordering fish on Fridays, he cannot
forget that Friday has a special significance.

Into the question of why I should have returned to
Canterbury instead of proceeding to Rome, I have no wish
to go in print. The scandal of Christian disunity is too
serious. As Charles Williams has written:

> The separations in Christendom remain, nor will they be
> soon or easily ended. But the vocal disputes are a little sus-
> pended, and courtesies between the clamant bodies are easier. . . .
> It might be possible now to praise the confessors of other
> obediences without supposing that we compromised our own.
> It might be possible to "exchange" our ignorance, even if our
> decisions and certitudes must remain absolute. Those definitions
> apart, what is there anywhere but ignorance, grace, and moral
> effort? Of our moral effort the less said the better; grace is
> always itself alone, and demands only our adoration; and there-
> fore it is between our ignorances that our courteous Lord might
> cause exchange to lie, till the exchange itself became an invoca-
> tion of the adorable Spirit who has so often deigned to instruct
> and correct the Church by voices without as well as within the
> Church.[1]

[1] *The Descent of the Dove* (New York: Farrar, Straus and Cudahy, 1950),
p. 232.

3

ANTONIO D. MARQUEZ

*Until recently a member of the Jesuit Order, Mr. Antonio
D. Marquez served on the staff of the Cathedral of St. John
the Divine as a guide and acolyte while undertaking studies
for the degree of Doctor of Philosophy in the field of
philosophy of religion at Columbia University. He was born
in Spain in 1923, entered the novitiate in 1942, and graduated from the Jesuit College of the University of Madrid in
1951 with the degree of Master of Arts in Philosophy. Thereafter for two years he served as Professor of Contemporary
History and Director of the Dormitories at San Gabriel
College, Quito, Ecuador. In 1952 he served as President of
the National Committee on History, broadcasting frequently
in Ecuador on the history of that country.*

Mr. Marquez is author of Nuevos Cuestionarios de
Historia, *published in Quito in 1953. He was received by
Bishop Donegan into the Episcopal Church at the Cathedral
last year. He has returned to Spain to identify himself with
the life of the peasants of his country, and to write.*

ANTONIO D. MARQUEZ

WHEN I left the Jesuit Order and the Roman Catholic Church less than two years ago, I was something like an agnostic or a skeptic. Actually it was something more complicated than that, for my despair about finding truth had already permeated at that time all the realms of my intimate as well as my practical life. If we were allowed to transfer the word *agnosticism* from the levels of theoretical functions to the area of will, I would say that I was both theoretically and emotionally an agnostic. The whole of my personality was in chaos and my destiny surrendered to Fate.

Needless to say, that situation was some kind of Hell, if not Hell itself, for I understand Hell today as a state of being in which our spirit—our most inner being, the deepest region of meanings and values—is separated, cut off, from the stream of life. Furthermore, such a situation was not a sophistication *a la mode,* a bourgeois feeling of being lost right after reading a novel of Kafka or attending a performance of Sartre's plays. My agnosticism carried away not only my membership in the Order and the Church, but also the possibility of returning to my country, my family life, my best friends, and my social as well as my economic position. As these essays will be read mainly by American people, I consider it indispensable to state here with some anticipation that in the Spain of today changing from Roman Catholicism to non-Roman Christianity is as disreputable as for an American soldier to decide to stay in Red China. It is worse, of course, if you are a clergyman, and especially difficult if you have been a Jesuit. The latter was my case.

I cannot speak of Heaven yet. The process of salvation, as well as that of condemnation and much more, is not a matter of an easy trick. It is my conviction from the experiences of many and from my own that there is nothing like "instant" salvation. I feel terrified listening to some American preachers speaking of rapid ways to success and happiness. They are responsible for cutting off the depth of millions; for making the American culture chronically rachitic. They do bring comfort to many. No doubt about it. Narcotics do, too.

I can write only of *a process of redemption* through the Episcopal Church in the United States. It is a matter strictly reserved to God whether any process of redemption will end in salvation or condemnation. Moreover, I consider it a very grave mistake to identify any church with God's Heaven or even with the Kingdom of God. The only thing within our scope is to look for and associate with the redeeming power wherever it becomes manifested. To me it has been offered in a Church and more concretely through an agency of that Church, the Cathedral of St. John the Divine in New York City. I will narrate afterwards how it happened.

FROM ROMAN CATHOLICISM

I was born a Roman Catholic. In Spain, or wherever Roman Catholicism is the religion of the State, we have no choice to be something else, or, to speak with the technical vocabulary up to date, we have the individual but not the social right to choose a non-Roman Catholic faith. This is a tragic irony of which very few people in America are aware. When one has an individual right, but this right is not socially guaranteed, can we call that a full right? That is the case of religious freedom in Spain. Not to be a Roman Catholic in Spain today is not only a social risk; if you take your faith seriously, it is also a moral impossibility. According to the Spanish Charter of Rights—a document whose origin is completely unknown to the great majority of Spaniards—Roman Catholicism is the "official" religion of the State and no other religion whether Christian or not is allowed to be propagated in any way. In such a "pure" religious atmosphere, we all followed the same pattern. Could it be otherwise? When the time for self-determination came —the years in the University for instance—we were so involved in Roman Catholic environment and interests and had such a great lack of information about other religions that we were not actually free to choose anything. Then, if some especially gifted minds ran into crisis, the common solution (a solution that some prominent Spaniards have recommended to me) was to take religion as a social affair, being inside whatever you want to be. Although I do not share that solution with them, I cannot honestly blame them for doing so, for it seems to me very logical and human to take things as they are given to you. If religion is given to, practically imposed on, you as the official religion, why not take it just "officially"? This is not indeed the reasoning of a hero. But who can say that it is an immoral reasoning from the point of view of the people? The immorality would be rather in the institution that put the people in the situation of behaving thus.

It is unnecessary after that analysis to go into details about my religious education. If somebody asks me—many have done so already—why I was a Roman Catholic before I was an Episcopalian, my answer will be, following the dialectic often used by Jesus, this other question: What else could I be? About being an Episcopalian I will write shortly. But let us state and stress here that I did not come directly from Roman Catholicism to Anglicanism. I went from Roman

Catholicism straight down to nothingness and despair, and from it up to the new life. The ascension is not yet completed.

THROUGH DESPAIR

When I was about eighteen I joined the Society of Jesus, or, as it is popularly known, the Jesuit Order. I saw the Jesuits passing through my village just as I had imagined them from my textbook on the history of Spain; the half fascist, half Roman Catholic hero devoted mainly to scholarly leadership in Europe and in missions abroad—the monk and the soldier proclaimed as the ideal for our youth by the founder of the Spanish Fascist Party.

I joined the Order with the strong devotion of a convert, and with the same devotion followed the regular steps toward the priesthood for some twelve years.[1] It was only when I was sent to Madrid for a three-year course in Scholastic Philosophy that the crisis began.

My case was not unique at all. Moreover, it was quite common among us to speak with some naïve terror and conventual secrecy about the dangers of losing the Faith at the end of the first year in logic and metaphysics. In a more official and serious way we were lectured on how to face that danger, shortly before we were sent from the School of Humanities to the School of Philosophy. I was personally advised by two of my Superiors on how to prevent my own crisis. They foresaw a lack of humility in me as a gate to ruin. They were right.

[1] Denis Meadows has candidly described his career as a Jesuit in a book entitled *Obedient Men*, published by Appleton-Century-Crofts in 1953. I would not hesitate to recommend the book to those who want to know only the ordinary routines among the Jesuits. But the very inside—I do not speak of course of "secrets" of any kind—is completely missed. The book has the *imprimatur*.

Textbooks and manuals were carefully selected. Practically all of them were written by Jesuits. (The Constitution of the Jesuits especially forbids any doctrinal differences within the Order, even in matters that are disputable within the Roman Church.) This inquisitorial selection was extended to professors, visitors, and contacts with the outside world, especially with Madrid cultural circles. Our building was quite close to Madrid University City. Nevertheless, I do not recall anybody who was allowed to attend a lecture or any other school event during the three years. Even to pass through the campus we were obliged to ask special permission. The instances could be multiplied indefinitely.

With so many defenses around our only truth, few of us were suspicious about it. I did not yet know—I learned it from Gandhi much later—that the paths to truth do not need to be guarded, but opened wide. Nevertheless I conceived a strong dislike for the method. Thus my crisis began.

In spite of all warnings, in studying Dialectics we had to face the classical problem concerning the objectivity of knowledge. It was for most of the Jesuit students the only moment in which they were allowed (but not without being carefully *guided*) to examine the roots of the Roman Catholic system: the foundations of dogmatism. (I understand by *dogmatism* here—and I am sure the Jesuits will share my opinion—the belief in absolute truth held as a whole in deposit by a particular institution, the Roman Church, whose right and mission are to impose that truth even upon people who think otherwise.) It was also the moment for a general crisis about faith. We took it as a vaccination. But in some colleges the problem has been at times so broadly spread and deeply rooted that they were near to being dissolved. The climax was usually reached at the beginning of the third year in the discussion of the reality of God and His nature.

Whether Augustinian or Thomistic proofs were brought into discussion, some students did not honestly see their validity.

After the first year of Philosophy I was quite confused, but sure enough that there was no such thing as an absolute truth valid for everyone. That was my final conclusion about Logic. About Metaphysics my confusion was greater. I could not see any light in the doctrine of the analogy of being (the most radical of all metaphysical problems to me), but I was afraid to deny it because one of our professors was an expert in the matter. Only much later I came to the conclusion that the truth was relative and the problem of being a mystery.

Why did I come to that conclusion while many others did not? This is a question so dear to Roman Catholic apologists and to modern psychotherapists that it must be briefly answered here before we proceed further. My very definite answer, on the other hand, is extremely simple: the ground of my mind was not favorable to that Logic and that Metaphysics. An analysis of it is completely outside the scope of this essay. But an elementary honesty with both Roman Catholic dissenters and psychoanalysts demands the acceptance most openly that every intellectual crisis is rooted in the realm of our total life and that no pure argument is enough explanation of it. I agreed with my Superiors on this point. Any particular formula of truth requires a proper ground in order to be accepted; and my ground was not the proper one for that formula. On the other hand, this reason, instead of solving my problem, convinced me more deeply that the truth was relative. It means exactly that any truth is related to something that is behind our minds, namely, the whole of our lives as parts of a universal given environment. As far as Roman Catholicism is concerned, the proper ground is of course docility. For a humble mind there are no serious problems in Logic and Metaphysics. I was not endowed with that gift.

Courses in Cosmology and Psychology were not so disturbing. But neither the existence of the soul nor a solution to the problem of *continuum* was clear to me, and they were of great importance to the understanding of the formulae of many Roman Catholic dogmas.

I looked forward to the third year with some kind of desperate hope. The main courses were in Natural Theology and Ethics. Contrary to my hope, it was the year of the principal losses: a sense of the reality of God and the metaphysical foundation of ethics. As far as the theory was concerned, the demolishing task was completed.

At that time a discussion between Father Copleston and Bertrand Russell on the BBC of London was published in Spanish. I read it in the Jesuit quarterly *Pensamiento* and it impressed me very much. The core of the discussion was the reality of God and the ethical problem. But what impressed me more was Russell's intellectual dignity in conducting the discussion. To me it was a revelation, for I was always very definitely against our two sources for public speech: Latin Rhetoric and Classical Dialectic. While Copleston was most of the time speaking as a logician, an orator, Russell spoke from the depth of personal convictions and experiences, never passing from one level to another by ambiguities. My conclusion then was very drastic: neither do we have the whole truth nor are we honest about the portion of truth we should live by.

When the courses were over and, in spite of all my troubles, an M.A. in Philosophy was given to me, I was in the darkness.[2] I was not able to decide about anything, but as I had to be ordained, I asked a young professor for help. After several talks with him the best I could do was to name my darkness "mystery" and my conviction about the irrelevancy of the Scholastic Philosophy to my life "a temporary crisis." That I did and went to teach in a Jesuit College in Ecuador.

My Superiors and some of my friends sincerely assumed that my crisis was due to a little too much of philosophy and that the contact with "the living Church," teaching and counseling youngsters, would rebuild my faith. But the truth was just the opposite. At the end of my second year I was not only an agnostic, but a cynic about religion and morals. It was impossible to go farther. I decided with the Superiors of Ecuador to submit my case directly (*soli*) to the Father General in Rome and wait for his decision in Fordham University, New York.

After a few months in the United States I received a friendly and official acceptance of my resignation. When I signed the document I was very much aware of two things: first, that my resignation was not only from the Order and the Church, but also from my country, my family, my best friends; secondly, that I could not help myself from doing so. Then I felt for the first time the tragedy of being completely free. It meant to me being completely alone. Here ended the crisis.

To The Episcopal Church

The end of a crisis is either death or the beginning of a new life. There is its danger and its value. Being totally

[2] Three years later the records from the College, required for admission by Columbia University, were denied to me only on the ground that I had not taken the oath of the profession of faith. This is not true. I took the oath before I got the diploma, though I did it with a very tormented but very sincere conscience. Happily, under the circumstances the University nevertheless recognized my degree.

alone—New York is quite a good place for a case like mine to be so—was for me a painful but priceless experience. I suddenly realized that if I wished not to be completely swallowed by my own situation I had to associate myself with something. With what and how?

Hyde Park on Hudson. As I was entirely unable to make any important decision, I chose at random to take a rest for a while in the country. New York—my favorite city in the world today—was then a little too congenial to my chaos. Because of a short stay in Saint Andrew-on-Hudson, the novitiate of the Jesuits for the New York Province, the only place I knew out of the city was Hyde Park. So I went there.

Since then, the community of Hyde Park has always been to me one of the greatest means for salvation: a favorable emotional environment. When one goes down to skepticism by rational means, it is, I think, most unwise to try to get out of it by the same means. Any attempt to do so makes the situation worse.

My contact with the Episcopal Church there was accidental; some may call it providential. I want only to stress here that it was not on purpose. When I asked Mr. and Mrs. St. George (the owners and managers of the Dutch Patroon Motel, where I first stayed) for an interview with "a Protestant minister," they drove me to the rectory of St. James. They could have driven me to any other church, for neither were they Episcopalians nor did I suggest any particular denomination. My intention in approaching a non-Roman Catholic clergyman was merely of a practical character. I wanted to rent a room with some family and I thought that my case was strange enough in a small community to arouse suspicion if I went to do it without any recommendation. Who could understand my case but a clergyman? And as it was impossible to go to a Roman Catholic priest (the Jesuits denied me any help), I asked for a Protestant.

From the day I knocked on his door to the present, the Rev. Gordon L. Kidd, the rector of St. James, and his wife have been the most impartial helpers. Through them I met my first friends in Hyde Park, got my first job, and saw, without having to go into religious discussions, the possibility of rethinking my religious situation. A favorable emotional climate made me unconsciously take the first step toward salvation: my skepticism, I thought, is but a reaction against an extreme dogmatism; why not try another way? I fought for months with this question. But finally I decided to take the risk of a new attempt.

Columbia University. My prejudice against churches—a prejudice that is still very much alive—drove me to the conclusion that if I had to study religion again, it would never be in a religious institution. I thought first of Harvard—I had a remote but powerful attraction toward William James; I tried Bard College and then came to Columbia.

While I was seeking the possibility of getting into some non-religious institution, Father Kidd introduced me to the Dean of New York. Father Kidd believed that the Dean, having been himself a Roman Catholic—Jesuit trained— and formerly the Chaplain and still a professor at Columbia, was specially qualified to help me. He wisely suggested the Department of Religion at Columbia University as the best place to continue my studies. A few months later I was registered there.

A close contact with Tillich's thought and personality as well as with some of my schoolmates during two semesters convinced me that religion was something more than just

what I was against and that my skepticism could be overcome somehow. In spite of that, I was very far from the idea
of joining any church. I saw a triple obstacle to doing so:
the rebuilding of a philosophy, the acceptance of a creed,
and the obedience to an ecclesiastical discipline. It was the
Dean's strategy that accelerated the process. (The reader
probably will perceive the strategy—I did not. So I got
caught.)

The Cathedral of St. John the Divine. Columbia University
is not far from the Cathedral of St. John the Divine (some
of the Cathedral clergy are at the same time members of the
faculty at the University), and the Cathedral engages in an
extensive program with students.

To me the contact with the Cathedral clergy was something more than a mere accident. But it happened very acci-
dentally during one of my visits to the Dean that I proposed
to him some of my difficulties not only in joining any church,
but even in liking one. I felt myself a hero for having the
courage to tell the Dean my drastic objections after he had
helped me. But he was rather pleased with them. And instead
of attacking my position, he considered it a good preamble to
faith. On the contrary, I had always understood that the
classical *preambula* were connected with one or another
kind of rational philosophy or natural theology.

I recall the substance of our conversation. When I said to
him that I could not go anywhere by pure reason, he very
happily agreed. Trying to clarify myself, I explained to him
that I could not accept any particular philosophical system.
He assured me that no particular philosophy was required
to join the Church. And finally, when I added that it would
imply a "leap of faith," he agreed also. It was very hard for
me to understand that this position was not antirational or

arbitrary. I was working yet on Roman Catholic presuppositions. Today I am ashamed of pure reason and absolute logic. To a great extent today, I see faith as depending mainly on decision.

The other two objections were not so difficult to refute. The core of my crisis about religion was always related to the impossibility of accepting, as faith, a philosophical system. I was expecting, after the former explanation, that the creed should be interpreted as it was written: as a historical formulation of a symbolic character. Of course no special theological *system* was required. From Tillich down to Hooker, and farther, any theological explanation was good insofar as it did not deny realities of the Creed. An Episcopal scholar, for instance, could follow St. Thomas, Karl Barth, or nobody. And as for the discipline of the Church, the Church itself was conceived in the Anglican tradition as a community of life (love and action) rather than as an institution of power. The intolerable burden of a legalistic ethic and the control of the conscience by the priest were discarded. Ecclesiastical discipline was much more a matter of order than of anything else.

With those explanations my difficulties were notably reduced. Nevertheless, it took me a few months more to assimilate them. The pride factor was then involved in my acceptance. If I had spent five years in demolishing my faith, who could be the magician to rebuild it in a few hours?

It was not only a question of pride. I have to stress here for those few who have not seen it yet that my objections were not solved but discarded. Moreover, they were used as a sound introduction to faith. (Was it the strategy?)

I was received into the Episcopal Church with the idea that no philosophical or theological systems will ever be imposed upon my mind; that the Creed could have different symbolical explanations; and that the discipline of the Church was a matter of order with no interference with my conscience.

After a short period within the Church I do not feel defeated. Many of the old difficulties are still very much alive, for as I said from the very beginning, there is no "instant" salvation. But the difference is immense. While before I was first submitted to dogmatism and later to fate, today I am working with a Redeeming Power for the free determination of the very self.

On that basis I see the Anglican Communion as the means to salvation for many spirits tortured by the extremes of dogmatism and anarchy. This is my testimony.

4

DONALD SLESINGER

A distinguished analytic psychologist, Mr. Donald Slesinger was born in 1897, served in the First World War, graduated from Columbia University, and did graduate study at Harvard and Columbian (now George Washington) Universities. After several years as a psychologist with various institutions, he served as a Sterling Fellow at the Law School of Yale University and joined the faculty of that school in the field of psychology of law, serving also as executive secretary of Yale's Institute of Human Relations. He then went to the University of Chicago as Professor of Law, serving five years as Associate Dean of the Division of Social Sciences of the University.

Mr. Slesinger has served as educational consultant to the Tennessee Valley Authority, the War Department, and the Federal Security Agency, and was chief of the Visual Training Section of the U.S. Office of Civilian Defense. Since 1947 he has been a practicing analytic psychologist in New York City, being President of the Association of Psychoanalytic Psychologists. Last year he was admitted as a postulant for Holy Orders by the Bishop of New York. He has been a frequent contributor to legal, psychological, and sociological periodicals and has written for Harper's, Scribner's *and* The Nation. *He is married and has two children.*

DONALD SLESINGER

NOT LONG ago I was lost on unfamiliar streets in Alexandria. I knew where I wanted to go—to see my friend Mollegen at the Virginia Theological Seminary—but once I left the well-marked highway I was on my own with only a poor road sense to guide me. First I kept to a broad avenue; then, thinking it might be a short cut, I followed a truck down a side street to another avenue. A street name stirred a faint recollection and I drove along it to what seemed like a throughway, but I did not know which way to turn. There was a filling station a block to the left and I went there for directions. You're on the right road, the attendant told me, but going the wrong way. Turn back, and at the seventh light you will see the Seminary wall.

If Canterbury, like the Seminary, were a place and one knew it to be his destination, maps and friendly attendants would always be available to point the way. But it is at once nowhere and everywhere and no one looks for it till he has found it. Then he knows he has always been there. For Canterbury is where time meets eternity and there are no roads to it, yet any road pursued long and diligently enough leads the traveler there, although he may find that the natives call it by another name. The names do not matter; they serve only, like the street name in Alexandria, to stir a recollection, to bring some portion of the past to the present. The traveler knows where he is when he finds the present taking a new dimension, the past a new meaning, the future a new direction. All time is enriched, for this is a way from and to eternity; eternity becomes almost understandable because the way has entered time. Sorrow is there and pain, hunger and injustice along with the yellow daffodils and the soaring lark. And love, temporal and eternal, and the faith it inspires, the hope it brings.

We sat, a group of fourteen-year-old boys and girls in our Saturday best, between the pulpit and the golden gate which guarded the sacred scrolls. A few minutes before the gate had been raised and we had gone, two by two, boy and girl, to complete the ritual of confirmation by kissing the Torah and receiving the blessing of the rabbi. Now we were to learn the meaning of the ceremony as the rabbi entered the pulpit to deliver the Shevuouth sermon. We had proclaimed in a hymn that we were God's suppliant children trembling before His throne to confirm the vows of Horeb to serve the Lord alone. What had we promised? What would God do if we kept, or failed to keep, it?

If I was vague about what we were doing and undergoing it was because I had been a half-hearted Sunday scholar, attending chiefly to humor my grandparents. They had drifted from the orthodox synagogue to the reformed temple and my parents, with conviction, had left the temple to become members of the Ethical Culture Society. As the rabbi started to talk my mind wandered first to the gold watch that was the traditional confirmation gift in our family, then to an oration I had composed but was not asked to deliver. It told of a wise and ancient man with two daughters, both kind and loving, one almost as ancient as he, the other young and beautiful. The old man was God, his daughters Judaism and Christianity. The oration was a plea not to forget the glory of the elder in beholding the glamor of the younger, for they were sisters, both children of the one Father.

I was startled out of my daydream by a sudden anger in the rabbi's voice. I could see his upraised fist and learned later that when he thrust his arm forward his shaking finger pointed directly at my mother. He was declaiming against those weak assimilated souls who deserted the faith of their fathers for Godless humanitarian societies. "What good will it do?" he shouted hoarsely. "Will it make you an accepted member of the Gentile community? A thousand times no. For remember this, you're a Jew, a Jew, you're always a Jew."

In spite of my undelivered oration I did not know what he meant, for I was not really aware of any basic hostility between Christians and Jews, nor of any reason to be one or the other except that you were born that way. My friends were Jewish, but since they were also my neighbors I must have assumed the latter to have been the reason. Our maids were mostly Irish so I was familiar with crosses and beads without knowing their significance. I can remember my grandfather winking at my parents as he told me that Teddy Roosevelt's real name was Rosenfeld, and I more than half believed him. Lincoln was obviously Jewish—his first name and face proved that, and I had the feeling that Washington probably was too. The only difference I knew was the curious Christian belief in Christ the Man-God who died and came to life again. As a child of the nineteenth century who knew that the story of Adam and Eve was a myth, I wondered why the Christians could not see that Christ was just the hero of another tall tale.

The one vicarious experience of anti-Semitism I had as a boy was lost because of the amazing bit of information I acquired through it. In the fifth grade, presided over by a fiery Irish Roman Catholic teacher with a genuine love for people, one of my classmates called another a "dirty Jew." Our teacher promptly sent the Jewish lad out of the room on some pretext, and then lit into the rest of us as though we were all in some way responsible for the crime. "Don't ever let me hear one of you say that to another;"—her eyeglasses shook as she bobbed her head up and down in fury—"don't you know our Lord Jesus Christ was a Jew?" Christ a Jew? Surely there was a colossal bit of irony in that. The world was made up of Christians and Jews and now it turned out we were really all Jews. That would have been a funny one to try out on the maids. But between three o'clock and dinner there was a ball game in the vacant lot next to our apartment house, and by the time I went home the incident was forgotten.

When in college I ran into atheism—pre-World War I variety—I was too much the pragmatist to be concerned about it. Why embrace antireligion when it involved accepting an idea as rationally untenable as a belief in a personal God? If you couldn't prove He existed neither could you prove He didn't. If He did exist and had created the universe, He wouldn't be a petty tyrant who made salvation depend on the solution of a conundrum; and if He didn't, well, that was that. In either case it didn't matter, the world had its own problems and goals and the thing was to get at them and let Heaven take care of itself. Socialism was a goal, and before long a lot of Russian boys and girls would be giving up everything to bring it into being. Pacifism was a method and you didn't have to be a Quaker or any other kind of Christian or Jew to see that it made sense politically and socially as well as morally. You could learn all about both and many other values from Bertrand Russell and John Dewey, and they learned about them by being human and reasonable.

Since religion did not matter any more than the moons of Jupiter you needn't fight it, and you could get married in church as well as in City Hall, if a church would have you.

Dorothy had been baptized in one in Exeter, Maine, where she was born, and confirmed in another, Trinity Chapel in Portland. She was a devoted little Episcopalian for a while, singing in the choir, playing the organ, leading her father back to worship. But by the time we met, at the end of her junior year at Wellesley, she stood about where I did. The higher criticism and philosophy had watered down her faith in a personal God and made her skeptical of all miracles including the Resurrection. So because her parents cared and mine didn't, and neither did we—and the vicar was willing—we were married in Trinity Chapel.

Looking back I must in all honesty say that while I was deeply moved by our wedding, it was not because I was aware that a holy sacrament was being administered. What moved me was that I was being married to the girl I loved, that she was very beautiful, and, I am afraid I must add, that her rejected suitors all sat together in one of the front pews.

Once again during the service I discovered as I had in the fifth grade that we were all Jewish under the skin. The vicar, using an old Prayer Book (we were married in 1921), read that the ceremony by which Dorothy and I were being united had come down to us from Isaac and Rebecca. She squeezed my hand as I wondered if he were really reading that out of the book or had tactfully inserted it to please my parents and me. In either case the idea was as surprising as the fact that Christ was a Jew. But I let it go at that and was not to concern myself about it again for almost twenty-five years.

An open-minded psychoanalyst learns very quickly from his patients that the religious hunger is as strong and universal as that for sexual union. And, like the hunger of boy for girl, when it lacks cultural sanction it is repressed and erupts in perverse or sublimated behavior. The natural object of religious hunger is God. Objects of perversion include the gang, the political party, the right or wrong nation. The object of sublimation—and I am aware of the paradox in considering that the sublime can be sublimated—is good works, the devotion to such humanitarian causes as peace, justice, and mercy, with no reference to God.

My hunger was sublimated in part as a result of learning from John Dewey that means and ends could not be separated. My first vote was straight Socialist, but I could not follow some of my friends into the Communist Party with my strong conviction that terroristic means could only lead to terrible ends. And I gave up pacifism as a method and enlisted in the army when an older friend convinced me that pacifism would contribute to a German victory which would destroy the freedom of democratic Europe. I was aware of an inconsistency, but I allowed myself to see a difference between the horrors of a defensive war and the violent excesses of a revolution.

By the time I was graduated from college in 1920 I had adopted a sublimated religion. The world had to be saved, no doubt about that; and wars and revolutions would surely destroy it. What it needed was constructive leadership, and where could leaders be more effective than in the field of Education, definitely spelled with a capital "E"? First we were attracted to the Progressive Education movement, and Dorothy and I made a contribution by establishing a summer camp for young children to supplement in a living experience the work done in progressive schools during the winter. I believe what we did was good, but I soon became restless with the vanity I now understand to be characteristic of religious sublimation. I needed new fields to conquer; I also needed a greater prestige than I thought belonged to a camp director.

By chance (Providence?) I met a dedicated young educator, Bob Hutchins, and was invited to join him at the Yale Law School. We blocked out for ourselves the scholarly task of making a psychological analysis of the rules of Evidence, particularly of the exceptions to the hearsay rule. And before I realized it, I caught his enthusiasm for saving the world, this time through legal education. First we were going to marry the law to the social sciences; then, by rigorously educating a selected group of young men and women in the new co-operative discipline, we would develop future Justices of the Supreme Court and the higher state courts. Thus the ideas hammered out in the dusty office of Hendrie Hall, the old Law School building, would be implemented by becoming the law of the land. Symbolic of my high destiny was the fact that the office (with a reinforced floor) I occupied had once been that of William Howard Taft. An ex-President and future Chief Justice shared with me an ancient roll-top desk.

Again vanity cut across effective work. When Hutchins became president of the University of Chicago I was willing and eager to give up legal reform to follow him there, and at his inauguration I was certain I had found not only a creed, but an institution to further it. I went down with the Yale contingent—I had not yet taken up my post at the Universiy of Chicago—and with it was given an honored place in the academic procession that marched in cap and gown down the Midway from the Library to the Chapel. The inaugural address delivered by the handsome young president gave dramatic form to ideas that had taken shape more or less opportunistically in New Haven in administrative decisions and annual budget requests. I can no longer remember the creed but I can still feel the emotion, the excitement of my response. There I was in the church of my community listening to the high priest I loved and admired, offering myself, soul and body, a fitting and reasonable sacrifice to a cause that needed no God to direct and sanctify, for it came from the mind and heart of Man who was the measure of all things. One does not kneel at an academic ceremony but the impulse was surely there as I dedicated myself anew to the holy and creative work of educational leadership. I was not offering myself as a humble laborer. I was offering myself as a leader, and such an offering can only end in failure.

This is the story of my religious life, not my career, but up to that day in the university chapel the two were one. I can see now what I could not then, why a Godless religion crowned with apparent successes had to end in failure. When a natural hunger is repressed and sublimated it can never be satisfied; and like every insatiable neurotic I was climbing furiously up a treadmill ladder, each step of which left me where I started. Time and again I offered myself generously as top man on some totem pole; the world was to be saved by a summer camp that would serve as a model, a school that would train future Chief Justices, a university that would lead the blind to new heights. Always there was a corrosive vanity eating away at the foundations. There were to be "good works" all right, but *I* was to do them; *I* with the aid of a carefully chosen few.

I was still in Chicago when I began to feel the need of a more genuine religion. The neo-Thomism of Adler and Hutchins touched me just enough to start a train of thought. I had never seriously doubted the existence of a God, but since, in false humility, I doubted His concern for a minute particle like me, I could not concern myself about Him. I was willing to grant that He had created the universe; not, on the evidence, that He was interested in how it came out. There was enough determinism in my psychological orientation to make me see that a just God would have to operate on an absolute principle that would make Him equally loving or indifferent to Jesus and Hitler, since each lived as he had to live. There was a small comfort in that, as I thought about my own shortcomings, for it made me one with all mankind. I could not think of Hitler's or my shortcomings as sins, nor of Jesus' love as a virtue, for each of us was acting according to his nature as influenced by his culture.

The small comfort gave me no feeling that living was meaningful. All it did was to indicate that we were all in the same boat, and that the boat had neither rudder nor helmsman. The good, the true, the beautiful were satisfactions, not goals, not too different from a charcoal-broiled steak or a glorious evening with the woman one loves. They were demands of our human nature not related to anything beyond ourselves. Even one's love for wife, children, friends was only a natural way of behaving, frequently corrupted by society or culture. I did not raise the question of how natural human goodness which carried its own reward in immediate satisfaction could create a corrupt society. It was enough to see the harm done by possessive parents and to assume that they were victims of parents who had been over-possessive with them. The sins of the fathers were visited upon the children who transmitted them to their children until one of them was lucky enough and rich enough to hire a psychoanalyst to reverse the trend. All that was acceptable to a God who was a First Mover and did not care a whit about what He had set in motion.

When we returned to the East and lived in the northern Westchester hills, where there was beautiful country to walk about in solitude, thinking about religion became a major preoccupation. I tried to fit whatever I was doing into a meaningful frame of reference and soon found I needed a God-concept to round out the pattern. I began to wonder about God and the more I wondered the more I believed, but what I believed was always carefully constructed to solve problems without creating new obligations. I wanted a God who would help me, not one I would be required to help. I wanted Him to fill my emptiness just by being. Above all I wanted a philosophic, not an historic one.

So I communed with myself and with nature and did not bother to read the Bible or consult the authorities. The Bible was the record of only one religion; the theologians would all be apologists for their own creeds. God, if He existed, could talk to me directly and did not need to be mediated by book, priest, or theologian. I sought a universal God, a universal religion, not a sectarian one that depended on the insights of a people who were prisoners of their culture without knowing it. Knowing the relation between culture and personality-development I believed I would not be similarly imprisoned.

Then four things occurred. Dorothy returned to the Church. I again took up the career I started with and gave full time to the practice of psychoanalysis. As a result of both I started reading, and my reading led me to talk to the very people I had considered locked in tradition.

What influenced me most was the way Dorothy returned to the Church. There was no vision on the road to Damascus to resolve the doubts she had learned at college. Quietly responding to an inner need, without fanfare or announcement, she went, with her doubts, to St. Augustine's Church in Croton. Much later she told me that one day, after she had returned, she started down the hill to ask Gerardus Beekman, then the rector, if she had the right to take her doubts to the altar. She walked up and down before the church but could not bring herself to go in. The rector was easy enough to talk to, but what she wanted was deeper than human counsel; she needed, though she did not formulate it then, the prompting of the Holy Spirit. Even without the talk she felt free to go to church, to take Communion, to wait and see. Wisely she never asked me to accompany her; patiently she tolerated the affectionate kidding of our son and daughter. She went Sunday after Sunday and she made friends of Beekman and his wife and helped make them my friends also. When we moved to New York I started going with her to St. James', first only at Christmas and Easter, then more frequently. Again she made friends with a priest, this time William Chase, and again she helped make him my friend as well.

When I went back to working with individuals instead of trying to save the world by wholesale measures it meant a partial abandonment of my dreams of glory. I was now content to be of what use I could to one person at a time. I expected to earn a living at it. I did not expect that it would revolutionize my religious thinking. Little by little, as I worked patiently with troubled men and women, I came to see that their basic problems were religious—although they seldom saw them that way for they, like me, were children of pragmatism. Together we explored relationships to parents, brothers and sisters, spouses, children, friends, bosses. Often we were able, by correcting distortions, to free them from bondage to the past, to set them on the road to living and loving productively. Yet the end of each analysis left me with the sense of something not accomplished. A physician may help a patient heal a broken leg and thus be able to walk again, without trying to find out if the patient knows where to walk, but a psychoanalyst cannot be satisfied with healing alone. For then, as one patient put it to me, the result of the process may be that a once troubled person will find himself "all dressed up but with no place to go." As I thought through that problem I realized that the solution was not giving the patient a fixed goal—a Cross, a Star of David, or a hammer and sickle. It would be enough if I could help him to come to see that there was a goal beyond community, beyond history perhaps; that his life would be enriched by seeking even if he never found it; and that in seeking he would never be alone. How better could I help these people than by diligently seeking answers myself?

I began intensive reading the way you would expect a professor to, by turning to the theologians instead of the Bible. I read Niebuhr, Buber, Tillich. When I turned to the Bible the academic tradition led me to the letters of Paul instead of to the history he was writing about. And of course I found myself in disagreement with him more often than with the theologians. I had read *The Apostle* by Sholem Asch and knew what a bigoted young fanatic Paul had been, and since I did not believe in miracles I assumed that he had just moved from one fanaticism to another. I was particularly outraged by what appeared to be his attitude toward sex, for I knew the harm it did to my patients.

When I started reading the Old Testament and the Gospels I was looking for insight, not history. The myth, like the dream, I knew was a mixture of wisdom and wish-fulfillment expressed symbolically, and I tried to separate one from the other as I read. The only history I sought was a history of the human soul's quest for the meaning of life. I had looked for it before in the philosophy of John Dewey; I was now looking in the myths of ancient history.

Somewhere along the line I began to lose my smug sense of superiority to the people of the Book. And that led to the need for talk. For once I deserted the academic tradition, and instead of talking to many and gathering all sorts of opposing views, I chose only the priests I had met through Dorothy and the friends I made through them, chiefly Albert Mollegen and James Pike. There is no point in separating the contribution each made to my thinking, for the impact of the whole was more important than the parts. And I hope none of them will take offense at my saying that I learned as much from their doubts as from their certitudes. If the worst in me hoped I would find a closed system, the best responded happily to the fact that none of my friends offered it. Like me they were often in doubt, troubled by the results of new research and by their own new thoughts. And like me they were sinners stirred sometimes by vain dreams like mine. Best of all, the Church they presented to me was not *the* Church, but *a* Church, sinful as are all human institutions, filled with the dynamic tension of dissent essential to growth and to fulfilling its function of mediating God's love to man. It did not claim arrogantly to represent directly God in His talk to men, but, in humility, to represent men in their attempt to open their hearts to the grace of God.

Reading, listening, thinking, I found myself cautiously approaching faith. The God I had never denied was becoming a living reality to me as He had been to my ancestors in the fertile crescent, and I was no longer bothered by not being able to prove His existence by a set of coherent propositions. Something in me was responding to the Prophets and the Gospels as another—or the same—something had responded to a sonnet, a play, pink and white May flowers under green arbutus leaves, or Dorothy coming down the stairs the first time we met. The heart has reasons, the soul has reasons;

the mind reasons from theirs, putting into words what the heart and soul grasp by faith.

My mind needed the words, for I was still the teacher wanting to share what he knows with his students. And the words came, as I was walking in the park or over the hackberry-covered hills back of our Pamet home. I experienced God—I can put it in no other way—as a purposeful, fatherly Creator whose purpose was being revealed gradually, whose fatherliness was sometimes obscured because He wanted His children to discover, accept, and further His purpose in freedom. The gift of sin implied in freedom was balanced by the divine gift of reconciliation. All this was clearly set forth in the Bible. Abraham, the man of faith, showed his absolute trust in his Creator by his willingness, against all human goodness, to sacrifice his son because God asked it. There was no force, no pressure; the almighty God with power to compel merely asked, and Abraham, with freedom to refuse, chose to obey. And, in the fullness of time, God responded to the perfect trust by revealing His infinite love in sacrificing his Son for man's salvation. The love was always there—"Before Abraham was I am"—but because we learn in time it was revealed in time and the Biblical tradition was completed.

The worship of God is man's need, not God's, and it became mine. It was there in the park and the Pamet valley, but I now felt a great urge to express it with others, to be part of a community, to perfect my worship by choosing to be part of a tradition that was mine from the beginning of time. I still could not shake myself free from my intellectual habits and insisted that while the Bible expressed the ultimate truth, it did it as poetry, not history; the great Miracle was symbol, not record. Yet I believed, and when I presented my beliefs and doubts to Chase and Mollegen one evening at dinner, they felt my belief secure and my mind open enough to warrant the Church's receiving me. And on Dorothy's next birthday, with her and her sister Helen as witnesses, I was baptized by Mr. Chase at St. James'.

As I expected, becoming a member of the Episcopal Church brought me no new peace of mind, no power of positive thinking. If anything, the tension between doubt and faith was stronger than before. But through the tension, as well as through faith when it triumphed over doubt, I found a new depth, a new dimension in all my relationships. As a social scientist I know that I am part of the trend back to religion, a trend related to the hostility of nations and the threat of disaster. As a psychoanalyst I know how the world situation insinuates itself into every individual life and how easy it is to repress the sense of tragic insecurity by a flight into a projected wish-fulfillment. But as a Jewish Christian, which includes and transcends both roles, I know that in some way I am free; that God and man work together; that I can freely and without shame be part of a trend and accept in myself the reality of a providential universal hunger.

When some forty years ago our rabbi shook his finger at my mother and shouted, "You're always a Jew," he was wrong. I was never a Jew until I was baptized; until I chose to belong to the people I belonged to whether I chose them or not. As a boy I knew little of my people. As a young man it was enough to be an American, and I acted as though the culture I inherited sprang into full being when the Pilgrims landed on the shores of Cape Cod. Today I feel securely rooted in the race that first, in our culture, understood that God was in history as well as in eternity, that He worked and works with man. Whether my ancestors were chosen or, in the long dialogue between God and the Prophets, chose themselves to fulfill His purpose matters little. In either case their mission and their tragedy would have been the same. For myself I know that having been born into the Old Israel and choosing to be part of the New Israel as well breaks no tradition. Christ was not more rejected by the Jews than were many of the Prophets—or than Copernicus and Galileo were rejected by the Christians. The Prophets and Christ were rejected by some Jews, the scientists by some Christians; in both instances by Jews and Christians with vested interests to protect, interests that had to do with status, not truth. In both there was acceptance by some Jews, some Christians. So, in becoming a member of the community of the New Israel I feel myself grasped by the Judaism that was latent during my long indifference. For the first time, especially in saying the Creed and kneeling at the Communion Rail, I know and feel in all my being that I am a Jew, that from now on I shall always be a Jew.

One night after trying to understand the Canterbury I had discovered to be my end and my beginning I dreamed a dream. I had been reading a book about miracles by C. S. Lewis and was reflecting on it as I drifted off to sleep.

In my dream I was in the hospital where my father had died, and it was the moment after his death. Four of us were in a reception room off the corridor: my cousin, the doctor, who had just pronounced my father dead, my older brother, my sister who at the time of my father's death had already been dead a year, and myself. While we were discussing funeral arrangements my sister slipped away to my father's room. She returned and said quietly, he's alive, I saw the rise and fall of his chest as he breathed. Nonsense, the doctor said; I examined him. He's dead. Science knows he's dead. That rise and fall of the chest is a frequent post-mortem phenomenon. My sister asked me to go to the room with her. No doubt about it. He was breathing; he was alive. Back in the reception room I insisted that we stop all funeral arrangements and that the doctor examine him again. It is not necessary, he said. Once is enough. Dead is dead. Let's go on and bury him. Tess and I went to the sick room once more and saw our father standing, his pajama top characteristically unbuttoned, chewing the usual unlighted, half-unrolled cigar. His face had the deathly pallor I remembered seeing on Lazarus' face in the O'Neill play. We reported the new development and again the doctor said nonsense, the dead don't rise. I became very angry and since I could not even get a candid examination of the facts from Science I decided to appeal to the Law. The lawyer I tried to reach was not my present one, but a very old friend, the first of our contemporaries to experience death, when his young wife whose name was the same as my sister's was killed in an automobile accident. While I was dialling his number I awoke.

Awake, I remembered another dream of some years before. I was alone in a synagogue mourning my dead. A rabbi holding an old overcoat on his arm and looking very much like my father walked before the pulpit. When he saw me he stopped and said quietly: Mourn not your dead, nay mourn instead your unborn generations, for them have ye betrayed.

A dream, like a myth, sometimes portrays the fulfillment of a repressed wish; sometimes it portrays a repressed truth; sometimes the truth may come from the Holy Spirit.

5

D. R. DAVIES

The Rev. D. R. Davies first became known in this country through his Down Peacock's Feathers, *a popular commentary on the General Confession. He is author also of* The Art of Dodging Repentance, On to Orthodoxy, Reinhold Niebuhr: Prophet from America, The Sin of Our Age, *and* Thirty Minutes to Raise the Dead. *Born in 1890 in Wales, he spent almost a decade as a coal miner, and then studied at Edinburgh University and prepared for the Congregational ministry at United College in Bradford. Ordained in 1918, he served Congregational churches in Yorkshire, Lancashire, and Wales. Ordained to the Anglican ministry in 1941, he served successively at Hull, Dulwich, and Brighton, and is now rector of the Church of St. Mary Magdalen in St. Leonard's-on-Sea in the diocese of Chichester. He is married and has three children.*

D. R. DAVIES

I WAS BORN sixty-five years ago in a Welsh mining town of parents who were intensely Welsh, and passionately, profoundly Nonconformist. This fact symbolizes the paradox, and indeed the contradiction, of my religious pilgrimage. Since the more significant aspect of my entry into the Church of England lies in the disclosure of the character of that Church by my experience, it is necessary for me to enlarge a little the fact of my birth.

In the closing years of the nineteenth century, before the Church of England had been disestablished in Wales,[1] Nonconformity was still a dynamic, national force, especially in the industrial areas. One of the elements of Welsh Nonconformity was conscious hostility to the Church of England, which was regarded as an alien Church. It was the Church *of England,* buttressed by economic and social privilege. Without any propaganda, we children of Nonconformist homes drank in hostility to the Church with our mothers' milk. To me, therefore, a child of "the chapel," the Church was an "outsider." Its worship, belief, and organization were a completely unknown and foreign territory. This attitude of mine towards the Church persisted, in all essentials, until almost the eve of my Confirmation, which took place in 1941. How did it come about that a Church which seemed to be an embodiment of all to which I was most opposed proved to be, in the end, the answer to my deepest need and spiritual hunger? This is the question I shall try to answer. It is an answer which will, I trust, reveal the relevance of Anglicanism to the universal needs of the modern man—

[1] Disestablishment of the Church in Wales took place in 1914.

not only to the modern Englishman, American, Canadian, Australian, or missionary convert, but to the modern *man*.

After eight years spent as a working miner in South Wales, I went to Edinburgh University, where I studied Greek, philosophy, and economics. From Edinburgh, I went to Bradford (Yorkshire), to United College, a Congregational theological seminary, to prepare for ordination in the Congregational ministry. This part of my story I have told at some length in my book *On To Orthodoxy*. In due course, I was ordained in 1918 in Ravensthorpe, a textile town in the West Riding of Yorkshire, where I spent five years, and then left for Southport (Lancashire), where I ministered for another six years.

Almost unconsciously, my understanding of the Christian Gospel, which I had been ordained to preach, gravitated into what is now known as the "social gospel," that the primary purpose of Christianity was the abolition of social injustice and inequality, and the ultimate establishment of an ideal, classless social system in this world. As I look back upon it, I can see that socialization of the Gospel in my early ministry was, to some extent, the reflection of my mining environment. The first decade of the twentieth century witnessed the rise of the Independent Labor Party in South Wales, which, under the leadership of Keir Hardie, preached an idealistic Socialism. In those romantic pioneer days, Socialism was not merely a bread-and-butter agitation, but a crusade of idealism which aimed at the translation of Christianity into a social reality. It was an illusion, of course, but a wonderful and magnanimous illusion while it lasted. It gave significance and zest to my daily toil and life. In agitating for Socialism, I was, in fact, crusading for the Kingdom of God upon earth. It was in terms of this visionary Socialism

that I was interpreting the Gospels, and it was this interpretation that I carried with me into the Christian ministry.

This equation of the Gospel with Socialism was, of course,
altogether an unconscious reaction to a class struggle. While
it was conditioned by that struggle, it was stimulated and
shaped by social and theological studies, particularly those
of three American writers—Francis Peabody, Shailer Mat-
thews, and Walter Rauschenbusch, whose *Christianization of
the Social Order* came to me as a revelation.[2] It swept my
mind along as in a torrent.

It was almost inevitable that my vision of Socialism as
applied Christianity should at length force me out of the
ministry. A succession of events, which finally proved to be
personally catastrophic for me, drove me out of the Christian
ministry into politics and secular journalism, in which I
struggled for ten years, to be engulfed at the end in utter
abysmal despair.

The beginning of the end of my work as a Congregational
minister was the great lock-out of the miners in 1926, coincid-
ing with the General Strike in May of that year. I can, alas!
look back upon a lifetime of follies and errors. But my passionate championship of the miners in 1926 was not one of
them. I was nearer to selflessness in that activity than I had
ever been. I supported the great struggle of the miners in
defense of their miserably low standard of living by a plat-
form campaign throughout the whole country, as well as by
my preaching in my own Church, which I split in consequence. With the fatal sequence of a Greek drama, one
thing led to another. My activity on behalf of the miners

[2] It is interesting to note my great debt to American theologians. It was
chiefly these three writers who provided me with the "social gospel," which was
the only gospel I preached in my Congregational ministry. It was another American theologian, my friend Reinhold Niebuhr, who, also under the impact of
experience, revealed to me the New Testament Gospel.

led to an invitation to stand as Labor candidate in municipal
politics, and for three years I was a Socialist Town-Councilor.
For one of those three years I was the only Socialist in a
Council of sixty Liberals and Tories. I had a high old time. I
painted the town of Southport red with my propaganda
speeches in the Council chamber. These speeches, in due
course, brought me an invitation to contest a by-election for
Parliament at Lancaster in 1929, where a great majority of
the electors enthusiastically rejected me. This brought matters
to a head, and I resigned soon after from the ministry.

Thus, at the age of forty, I found myself, so to speak, on
the street, faced with the necessity of starting a new career,
which proved to be a grim business. England, like America,
was slipping steeply into the depth of the "great depression,"
with an unemployment roll of 3,000,000. Not a good time
for an unemployed parson to start a secular career! Under the
merciless pressure of that situation, my "social gospel" began
to subside, down at the foundations. It took another eight or
nine years for my whole philosophy of life to collapse. One
of my first discoveries was that the confident platitudes in
which I had indulged in my preaching, and to which parsons
are so prone—it is one of the vices of the clerical calling—
didn't stand the strain. Things which were abstractly true did
not prove to be, in my case, concretely true. So I learned that
a platitude is a truth unverified in the personal experience of
the platitudinizer.

Another discovery I made had deep-going consequences,
namely, that the "social gospel" rarely reflected itself in personal relationships. So I began to wonder what was the difference between a conventional gospel which promised "pie
in the sky when you die," and a modern, up-to-date social
gospel which promised chicken and champagne in the class-

less society. This prompted a further train of reflection, in which, timidly at first, I began to question a few more of the confident assumptions of my social gospel. I struggled with the mystery of the process of realizing Socialism. At what point in the process were personal relationships going to be changed? I never found the answer to that one, nor have I to this day.

The solution of my personal economic problem—how to make a living—lessened for a time the intensity of the disintegrating process. Indeed, for a brief time it was arrested by a conversion to Marxism, which was effected by a very thorough, concentrated study of Marx's *Das Kapital,* followed by Plekhanov, Lenin, and most of the standard Marxist writers. But, as events turned out, my Marxist phase proved to be no more than the tubercular flush preceding death. It died a convulsive death on August 22, 1939, the day of the announcement of Stalin's pact with Hitler. But by that time other influences had also been at work. My Marxism, in fact, was a desperate device, though all unconscious, to sidetrack a growing personal sickness of soul which was, by divine providence, "a sickness unto death." My Marxism was but a pill administered to a soul dying in agony. Karl Marx turned out to be a quack.

It was in Spain, in the throes of a civil war, that the realization began to dawn that the game was up—this futile game of trying to resolve man's desperate personal situation by hectic extroversion. I knew at last that Socialism, Marxism, and all the other "-isms" that stem from belief in human omnicompetence were mere rationalizations of a need beyond man's power to fulfill. This knowledge, which had for me a dynamic immediacy, was not the fruit of unhurried reflection, of leisurely logic, but of a bitter and devastating experience. I can still recall the overwhelming shock I felt when at that time, quite by accident, I read the seventh chapter of St. Paul's *Epistle to the Romans*. "Oh wretched man that I am! Who shall deliver me from the body of this death?" Exactly! I didn't need a commentary to explain those words. *I was myself that man.*

This fact and reality of experience, of an experience irrefragable and undeniable, was the decisive feature in my situation. I had grasped, by experience, the essential, fundamental theology of the New Testament. This is what I want to stress and make clear to the reader. Subsequent theological study merely assembled and classified an experience concretely endured and appropriated. I was in the position of a man who was familiar with the topography of a district without knowing its name. Theological study gave me the name. The details of the landscape I had already come to know by direct exploration. The dogma of original sin—it categorized my desperate sense of impotence through the years of suffering, calamity, and failure. Justification by Faith—it identified for me the inner peace and security which had miraculously possessed me. "The wind bloweth where it listeth, and thou hearest the sound thereof, but canst not tell whence it cometh, and whither it goeth: so is every one that is born of the Spirit." That was it. *I had been born again.*

Through the experience thus briefly described, I felt the urge to return to the Christian ministry, which was greatly facilitated by the publication of my book *On to Orthodoxy*. I was inducted into the charge of Richmond Road Congregational Church, Cardiff, in October, 1939. I had barely begun my ministry there before I knew, in my bones, that I could not remain a Congregational minister. For this certainty I could give no reason. I wasn't restless, and certainly not unhappy. On the contrary, I felt a deep serenity and satisfaction. I had been given the warmest welcome by the leading men of Congregationalism, particularly by Dr. Sidney Berry, Secretary of the Congregational Union, Dr. John Whale, Principal of Cheshunt College, Cambridge, Dr. Micklem, Principal of Mansfield College, Oxford, and Mr. Bernard Manning of Jesus College, Cambridge. Nevertheless, I knew I was only a sojourner in the Church of my fathers. But I had no plans. I vagrantly thought of the Methodist Church and the Presbyterian Church of England as possible future spheres of work. But none of these ever crystallized into definite purpose. The one Church I did *not* think of at that time was the Church of England.

While, as I have said, I was unaware of any conscious reason for my feeling about my future, I began to sense an insufficiency in Congregational worship. I felt more and more, as the days passed, the bareness of our worship. I found myself increasingly longing for a liturgy, especially in the celebration of Holy Communion. More and more also I was conscious of the utter inadequacy of the unvaried order of extempore prayers in public worship. I was experiencing a sense of strain, what Dr. Forsyth once said in reply to a question about belief in "free prayer." "Yes," he said, *"if you can keep it up."* I was feeling that an uninterrupted course of "free prayers" was degenerating into mere words.

Early in June, 1940, I happened to spend a few days in St. Deiniol's Library, Hawarden, North Wales, at the invitation of the Rev. Alec Vidler, its Warden.[3] I attended Matins and Compline in the little chapel, which was both simple and beautiful. In a way I cannot hope to describe, I suddenly

[3] St. Deiniol's Library is a unique institution. It is a residential Library of over 80,000 volumes, endowed by the Gladstone family, where students of all denominations can stay and pursue their own studies. It is a Church of England foundation, where the Offices are said daily, beginning with Matins and ending with Compline. Dr. Vidler, its Warden at that time, is now Canon of St. George's, Windsor.

felt that I had come home. I was uplifted in heart and mind. It was like a revelation of the Divine Presence.

These services in St. Deiniol's were the first Anglican services I had ever attended. I was fifty years old! To that worship I brought a lifetime of suffering. I wasn't a raw youth to be impressed by a mere aestheticism. This was a case of "deep calling unto deep." "I was in the spirit." Late that first night of my stay in St. Deiniol's, I sat up reading, *for the first time in my life,* The Book of Common Prayer. "How is it," I asked myself, "that I never read this before?" But I am glad that I hadn't read it until then, that the heart and mind which I brought to the Prayer Book had emerged from the depth. I found the Prayer Book to be more exciting at that first reading than any novel. I experienced that night a sense of ecstasy. I knew then that I had found my spiritual place of abiding, that my buffeted, storm-tossed bark had reached its haven. And today, fifteen years later, I am more certain of that than ever before.

It would, possibly, seem more impressive, more imposing, if, like Newman, I could report a process of severe wrestling with doctrinal doubts, theological distinctions, and ecclesiastical claims before finally deciding to seek admittance into the Church of England. But it wouldn't be true. I had no struggle whatsoever about leaving Congregationalism and entering the Church. My struggle had been for a fundamental, New Testament theology, which had already been fought and concluded. Indeed, when I got down to the Thirty-nine Articles, I felt I was being pulled into the Church.

For example, Articles IX and XI. "Original sin standeth not in the following of Adam . . . but it is the fault and corruption of the Nature of every man. . . ." And "We are accounted righteous before God, only for the merit of our Lord and Saviour Jesus Christ by Faith, and not for our own work or deservings." Why! This was exactly what the doctor ordered! In a letter to Archbishop Temple just before my ordination, Canon Vidler wrote that he didn't think that the Archbishop had ever had a candidate who believed more whole-heartedly in the Thirty-nine Articles than myself.

Thus I discovered that the Church of England met my need in worship and defined my fundamental theological conviction—that conviction for which I had paid so great a price in suffering and striving. Here for me was the pearl of great price. The two great obstacles to the Nonconformist conscience, re-ordination and State Establishment, I vaulted in my stride. I wasn't going to reject a most desirable residence because the drawing room carpet wasn't to my liking. This means that I don't look upon these questions as fundamental. Of course I don't. What is fundamental is the fact of man's moral impotence, and that salvation is in Christ alone by faith only in Him. It was these fundamentals on which the Church was crystal clear.

I spent six months in St. Deiniol's Library, from October, 1940, to March, 1941, during which time I was confirmed. It was a blessed time for me, in which I was given the opportunity to absorb the tradition and ethos of the Church of England. I kept many a tryst in the chapel with the Lord. I had entered into a great inheritance. I took nothing for granted. It was all so new and wonderful. Every day, almost, I was finding new treasures. I can recall the sense of thrilling wonder with which I heard the Collect on Advent Sunday in the parish church of Hawarden. And every day I was seeing deeper and deeper into the Daily Offices of Matins and Evensong. The General Confession so excited and stirred me that I wrote a book about it during my stay in St. Deiniol's, which was later published under the title *Down Peacock's Feathers*. It was Canon Vidler who found the title for me in one of the

Homilies. And they were a discovery, too. There was no end to it and there isn't now, even after fifteen years in the Church.

So at long last, in Lent, 1941, I was ordained deacon by the late William Temple, then Archbishop of York, in York Minster. What a wonderful place in which to be ordained. I could hardly contain the ecstasy that surged within me. The following Trinity, also in York Minster, I was given my priest's orders. "Right was the pathway leading to this." My history since could be summed up in the Victorian cliché, "he lived happily ever after." The truth is that I found my way into the Church of England because God led me there.

In this essay I have tried to do what I was asked, namely, to tell the story of my pilgrimage into the Church of England. But I cannot conclude without one or two reflections on my subsequent experience.

The term *Free* as a description of the Nonconformist Churches, if it is meant as a contrast to the Anglican Church, is a complete misnomer. I was a Congregational minister for ten years. I have been an Anglican minister for fifteen years. On the evidence of experience, there can be no doubt whatever in my mind about that particular issue. Never have I enjoyed such freedom as that which I have experienced in the Church of England, especially in the essentials of the ministry, and above all, the preaching of the Word. No Church affords such freedom for the exercise of a prophetic ministry as the Church of England. Surprising? Maybe, but it is a fact, nevertheless. In this matter, the time is overdue for a thoroughgoing, disinfectant revision of prejudices.

"I am not ashamed of the Gospel of Christ." Neither am I ashamed of the Church of England which is a part of the

Catholic, Apostolic Church of Christ. I have been to Rome, and witnessed the outer power and splendor of the Roman Church. But give me Canterbury every time. Rome is a great Church and also a part of the Catholic Apostolic Church of Christ. But I have not the slightest sense of inferiority feeling as an Anglican, whether in Rome or anywhere else. The *Ecclesia Anglicana* is a great Church, a wonderful Church, to which all Christendom owes an imperishable debt. I cannot conceive a greater privilege than to serve the Kingdom of God as a humble parish priest in the Church of England.

> I love this Church, O God,
> Wherein Thy Presence dwells.

6

THEODORE O. WEDEL

One who may be called the first Presbyter of the Church not only because of his presidency of the House of Deputies of the General Convention but because he probably has had more influence upon the theological thinking and preaching habits of the clergy than any other single man, the Rev. Dr. Theodore O. Wedel is a Canon of Washington Cathedral and Warden of its famous College of Preachers. Dr. Wedel was born in Halstead, Kansas, in 1892. After graduating from Oberlin College in 1914, he continued his studies at Harvard, where he received his Master of Arts in the field of the classics, and at Yale, from which he holds the degree of Doctor of Philosophy in English Literature. He later spent a year in theological studies at Marburg, Germany.

From 1918 to 1934, Dr. Wedel was engaged in university and college teaching—at Yale University, the University of Texas, and Carleton College, Minnesota. The turning point in his career came when he was appointed organist in an Episcopal church. Becoming interested in the Church, he studied at Seabury-Western Seminary, and at the age of nearly forty was ordained to the ministry of the Protestant Episcopal Church. Soon afterwards, he joined the staff of the National Council of the Episcopal Church, being appointed Secretary for College Work in 1934. He was made a Canon of Washington Cathedral in 1939, and became Warden of the College of Preachers in 1942. In 1940, Sea-

bury-Western Theological Seminary honored him with the degree of Doctor of Sacred Theology. Canon Wedel has *written several books*: The Mediaeval Attitude Towards Astrology, The Coming Great Church, *and* The Christianity of Main Street. *He has two children. Mrs. Wedel has also given leadership to the Church, having served as President of the Woman's Auxiliary and to National Council and having recently been elected President of the United Church Women.*

THEODORE O. WEDEL

APILGRIMAGE to Canterbury from the shores of the Black Sea." If such a title for a travelogue had appeared as a news item in the days of Chaucer, it might not have caused great surprise. Pilgrimages were international in medieval times. The same title for a biographical sketch in this series, however, is probably not so self-explanatory. Yet it may serve as a point of departure for my story, though it must obviously be transformed from a symbol of travel across geographical boundaries to one of wanderings in the realms of faith and church allegiance.

My grandparents on both sides, along with their children (my father twelve years old), arrived as immigrants on our American shores in the early 1870's from the Ukraine, settling on the then wild and still unbroken prairie lands of Kansas. They were German-speaking Mennonites, members of one of the Reformation communions or sects whose history constitutes a saga in itself. I shall be tempted to dwell on this sect history for a space, since it deserves to be better known, and since it can throw some light upon the vocation of Anglicanism as, on the ecumenical scene, it may increasingly be called upon to enter into sympathetic understanding of the multiform "Sect-Christianity" of the post-Reformation era, and to woo it, in turn, to an acceptance of Catholic church order.

Most Americans know the term "Mennonites" only as descriptive of the "plain people" or Amish whom travelers through Lancaster and adjacent counties of Pennsylvania meet as the bearded men and the black-bonneted women drive their antiquated horse-drawn buggies through whirling automobile traffic. Pamphlets and even novels have exploited

this isolated fossil-culture and labelled it quaint, acknowledging at the same time that it deserves high praise as an
agricultural model. Yet any competent history of the Mennonites would inform the reader that this island of antiquar-
ian culture is only a relatively small offshoot, isolated since
its immigration era in the seventeenth and eighteenth centuries, of a communion spread through many lands, whose
main stem and branches have not been thus fossilized. The
main branches of the Mennonite Church are, culturally
speaking, quite modern, though the phrase "plain people"
can still be retained to describe their communal life.

The sect takes its name from Menno Simon, a Dutch
reformer contemporary with Luther. Amidst the chaos of the
reform movements of his time, there were numerous Anabaptist sects. Anabaptism signified the belief that only adult
baptism was Biblical, even when this meant a second or
ana-baptism of those christened as children. The more radical
and militant of these Anabaptist sects fell into great disre-
pute. Menno Simon, although also of Anabaptist conviction,
gathered about himself a group who took pacifist vows and
dedicated themselves (as did the Quakers later in England)
to a literal obedience to the precepts of the Sermon on the
Mount. In their homeland of Holland they paid heavily for
their attempt at sect-independence, suffering literally thou-
sandfold martyrdom at the hands of both Roman Catholics
and State Church Protestants. More than one informed
Church historian is prepared to admit that—in proportion
to their numbers—no group of Christians anywhere in history has been called upon to yield a larger harvest of martyrs.
A *Mirror of Martyrs,* a huge volume with realistic stories
and even pictures of martyr-agonies, lay on the hall table
in my home and in that of most of our Mennonite neighbors.

To be a Mennonite and to suffer persecution were still considered well-nigh synonymous. During the First World War, when pacifists had not yet won charitable recognition, such persecutions, as a matter of fact, became grim reality for my own generation. The prison cells of Leavenworth, with torture not unknown, harbored many of my former co-religionists and several members of my own immediate family.

The immediate Mennonite community from which I made my Canterbury pilgrimage traces back to the persecution era in Holland. Pilgrimage, in fact, became symbolic of its corporate life. A sizable group of Dutch Mennonites, famous even as early as Reformation days for extraordinary competence in agriculture, were offered asylum as a colony, with the privilege of retaining their pacifist convictions, in an uncultivated marshland of eastern Prussia. From the sixteenth to the eighteenth centuries they remained in this isolated area, preserving intact their Dutch language and customs, yielding only gradually to Germanization. As marshland became transformed into flourishing farms, however, the envy of neighbors inspired renewed persecution—pacifism, of course, furnishing the main pretext. A new asylum, fortunately, loomed. Catherine the Great of Russia invited the colony to migrate to the Ukraine, offering privileges of colonial self-government and perpetual freedom from military service (a promise honored, by the way, by the Czarist government until its own liquidation). For a hundred years this second migration prospered. But after the Crimean War the handwriting on the wall once more prophesied a "time of troubles." A third migration, this time to the new Canaan of America, followed. I spare the reader an account of the colony's pioneering on the western plains—a somewhat scattered group now in Kansas, Nebraska, and Minnesota, planting, as time went on, daughter communities in Canada and other western states.

Their subsequent history resembles, in part at least, that of scores of other immigrant church groups—Lutheran communities from Germany or the Scandinavian lands, Moravian, Evangelical, Reformed, Polish Catholic, and a variety of Orthodox—whose gradual incorporation into our American community life is one of the as yet only partially recorded sagas of our nation's history. Seen from within, the story is one of loss as well as gain. The democracy of Coca-Cola and of economic free enterprise, or even that of our public schools, is scarcely a fully worthy substitute for the corporate witness to the Gospel which marked many of these immigrant groups in their pioneering era. My ancestral Mennonite community is today "Americanized," surviving the agony of a change of language in their worship life. But, probably more than most of such once foreign entrants into the American social scene, it has preserved a measure of corporate independence. The pacifist witness of the Mennonites is still intact, as the records of the Second World War can validate. So also is their quite outstanding record of social witness to the Gospel. Their work camps and distributing centers for relief of war sufferers parallel those of the Quakers and the Brethren. As conscientious objectors during the last war, many Mennonite draftees were assigned as internes to mental hospitals. This experience is inspiring the various Mennonite groups (ultra-plain groups as well as those modernized), under a unifying Central Committee, to establish mental hospitals of their own, their young people volunteering to serve without salary as a nursing corps.

To come now, however, to my personal story. What did a "pilgrimage to Canterbury" from such a tightly knit community involve? It meant breaking ties with a church family deeply anchored in loyalty to a tradition nurtured by four hundred years of heroic sect-independence, which had witnessed to a corporate community life of Christian brotherliness seldom, I believe, equalled anywhere. I experienced this in a very vivid way in my childhood and youth. One of the earliest acts of my Mennonite group was the establishment of a college on the Kansas plains. My father, having secured a college and seminary education, was its first president and I grew up in its pious and sheltered atmosphere. It was in my last year in this home environment, before leaving for eastern college and university scenes, that my introduction to the Episcopal Church came by way of mere chance. I had, while pursuing my academic work, achieved amateur standing as a musician. The little Episcopal church in our Kansas town needed an organist. I volunteered as a candidate and was accepted. A kindly choir-mother gave me a week's training in "responses, canticles, and chants." Then came the first Sunday's initiation into the Book of Common Prayer.

I shall describe that Sunday's experience in some detail, and for two reasons. My long preamble of ancestral Mennonite history would be inexcusable robbery of a reader's time unless it has meaning as the backdrop for a climactic event in this little epic. And, secondly, my story as such deserves attention only if it can be seen as typical of what, though with variations in detail, a "pilgrimage to Canterbury" must cost by way of a revolutionary religious experience for any or all non-Anglicans who know Christianity in no other than its pietistic "sect" manifestation—and this number, we may well recall, includes the majority of our fellow American citizens.

My first "Prayer Book Sunday," then. Bewilderment, of course. Kneeling and standing in place of the monotonous sitting posture. Read prayers. A *book* of prayers, no less, in the worshippers' own hands. No worrying on the part of the man in the pew as to whether the minister would receive inspiration for *his* prayer, or whether it would ever end (the *book* had terminal facilities). The shock of what externally looked like Romanist sacerdotalism—a priest (a very bad word to a Mennonite brought up on the *Mirror of Martyrs*) in the sanctuary, with strange popish vestments.

But—and this was a catastrophic but—there arrived also a sudden illumination that I was experiencing something rich and strange, something which satisfied a long felt, though never consciously realized, hunger and need. I was participating in "common" prayer! The "sacerdotalism" of the sanctuary was, in a way, an illusion. The priest was servant of the worshipping congregation, not its master. He was voicing petitions and thanksgivings singly, yes, but the *book* from which he read was a common possession. And then came the corporately spoken General Thanksgiving. Except for the Lord's Prayer, this was the first prayer uttered in chorus by a congregation (the General Confession an earlier analogue to be sure) that I had ever heard.[1]

A further insight soon followed—this time into the nature of the Church itself. "Church," in the form of a fellowship of the baptized, living a new kind of life as members one of

---

[1] Those familar with Anglican worship forms will have noted that the service described here was that of Matins or Morning Prayer, and not the Lord's Supper. A first introduction to the latter can have for the stranger great meaning also. In due time it will be seen as the climax of the Church's worship life. But as a "mission" service, one which bridges the chasm between free and liturgical worship forms and which gives meaning to "common" prayer, the traditional "low" service of Matins or Evensong still has incomparable value. The congregation participates more freely, more "communally," by way of the recital of psalms and canticles, by common prayer, and by the larger place usually given to the ministry of the Word. And is it going too far to suggest that even others in a congregation besides strangers may need preparatory disciplines? The Lord's Supper is the marriage feast of Bridegroom and Bride. The Bride ought to come to the feast "adorned," so that the Lord "might present it to himself a glorious church, not having spot, or wrinkle, or any such thing; but that it should be holy and without blemish" (Ephesians 5:27).

another, was, of course, not a novelty in my experience. In fact, as I later came to appreciate my ancestral inheritance, this mark of the New-Covenant people of God has found expression among the Mennonites and Quakers and Moravians and many another of our contemporary Christian sect-groups as it has simply *not* become a manifestation of church life in our larger so-called "historic" churches. A clue to the peculiar nature of sect-Christianity (*das Sektenwesen*, to use a German term coined by one of the best historians of this strain in Christian history, Ernst Troeltsch) is to see in it, on Protestant soil, an analogue to the monastic orders in Catholicism. The latter, too, are separatist Christian fellowships, under disciplines which set them apart from the world, yet which permit them frequently to dedicate themselves to an outgoing service to the needy and the sick beyond their walls. But in Catholicism monastic orders constitute a part of a larger whole—a "Catholic" Church. The Church of England, mother of the Anglicanism of today, was in origin a national Church, by definition the opposite of a sect. Sects arose within national state churches as protests in behalf of dissenting freedoms.

My cataclysmic Sunday, accordingly, gave me another "first" experience: that of the Church as more than a sect. It was not easy for me at first to understand and to appreciate the difference, since the little flock of Episcopalians in our Kansas town was, of course, far from being the local habitation of a national, let alone a state, Church. Sociologically considered, the Episcopalians of Kansas constituted a smaller "sect" than that of the Mennonites. Yet worship according to the Book of Common Prayer simply *was* "Church" in a new and horizon-widening form. It was— and this can be the liberating appeal of Anglicanism's Catholic heritage to all fellow Christians who are still confined within sectarian walls of separation—the Church in time as well as in space or merely in the form of a contemporary gathering of believers. It was the latter too, of course. But the worshipping membership was, somehow, not limited to that gathered flock. Here was the Communion of Saints of the ages at prayer. The prayers were themselves the "common" prayer of uncounted Christians of the past, now mysteriously joining with us in worship, though removed from our sight to the Church Triumphant. The little Episcopal chapel, with its struggling flock and underpaid minister, did not count very significantly in the community. It was vastly overshadowed by the rival church structures and congregations next door. But—and this is once more the paradox of the Catholic heritage—I had the strangely moving conviction that a majority was nevertheless in our humble sanctuary.

With the above perhaps over-dramatized story of my first Anglican Sunday (yet memory has laid tenacious hold upon it) this tale of a pilgrimage might well end. I was virtually a son of Canterbury from that day, though Confirmation, out of respect for family sensibilities, was delayed until two years later. Nor, alas, did loyalty to my newly-embraced Church allegiance remain untarnished. University sophistication brought in its train a decade of lukewarm churchmanship. An intellectual pilgrimage through the forest of modern skepticisms had to follow upon the earlier voyage from sect to Church. But this second pilgrimage would demand another essay. It parallels that of many of my contemporaries and will have been told better than I could here attempt it by other writers in this series.

I venture to employ these closing paragraphs instead for a generalized comment. It concerns the vocation of Anglicanism on the ecumenical frontier. If my pilgrimage has more than purely personal significance, it underscores the fact that

Anglicanism has gifts to bring to Christians of other names which, once truly experienced, are received with unbounded gratitude. Let no one despise the humble Bible-centered sect-Christian. When he has not yielded to self-righteous legalism, but is witnessing to the Gospel by the brotherliness of his community life, or, even more, by ministering Christ to the hungry and the lame and the blind, he voices judgment upon the self-centered institutionalism of the larger church families from which he once revolted. Shall Quakers and Mennonites and Brethren be the only Christians of the land remembered by name as angels of mercy ministering to the needy in war-torn lands or to the mentally ill in our own? What, indeed, would the Catholicism of Rome be without the ministry of her monastic orders—her brethren of the poor and her sisters of charity? But even Rome is wiser than to ask all her children to take on separatist and puritan monastic vows.

The Great Church—state church tyranny no longer with us—can, as indicated in an earlier paragraph, bring liberation to those for whom the sect, in its turn, has become a confinement, and whom it has isolated from the world. One of the unsolved problems of Anglicanism, surely, is how it can find a place in its larger corporate life for the separatist puritan group or for other forms of "lay monasticism"—in a word, for the sect. The Methodist exodus is vivid in memory. But Anglicanism's correlative vocation is already clear. It can open for those imprisoned within walls of isolation doors into the universal fellowship of the baptized—the One, Holy, Catholic, and Apostolic Church.

7

W. G. PECK

A widely-read author, especially in the field of Christian ethics, the Rev. Dr. W. G. Peck studied at the Methodist Theological College in Victoria Park and the University of Manchester. After his ordination in the Methodist ministry, he served a number of north-country circuits. In 1925, he was received by the late Dr. William Temple (then Bishop of Manchester) as a postulant and was ordained priest the following Easter. He then served for four years at Whalley Range and for seven years at Hulme. For fifteen years he was Lecturer in Christian Social Doctrine for the Industrial Christian Fellowship, and is now retired.

Dr. Peck is author of fourteen books, including The Social Implications of the Oxford Movement, The Return of Holiness, An Outline of Christian Sociology, *and* A Christian Economy. *Seabury-Western Seminary honored him in 1934 with the degree of Doctor of Sacred Theology. A widower, he has a son who is in Holy Orders and a daughter who is married to a priest.*

W. G. PECK

LOSE upon twenty years after he had left the Church of England, John Henry Newman defended that action in the book, *Apologia Pro Vita Sua,* which became an English classic and a gift to the Christian culture of mankind. But the last of his acts as an Anglican priest was to preach the unforgotten sermon *On the Parting of Friends.* My own passing from Methodism to the English Church could rightly be described as a parting of friends. No Methodist minister, leaving a Methodist denomination for the Church of England, his intention of identifying himself with the Anglo-Catholic element in that Church well known, could have received a *vale* carrying more of deep interest and true charity. On the other hand, although my course had for several years involved me in some controversy, I had been withheld by the grace of God from attacking the denomination in which I had received that Christian teaching which I had absorbed, and which had bestowed upon me its commission to preach the Gospel.

It is almost certain that any man passing from the ministry of one church to that of another, in our divided state, will involve himself in some serious consideration of the essential nature of the Church. In my own history this was indeed so. But I did not at first know what I wanted. I shall speak presently of the course of my inward debate, and of the nature of the outward contacts which necessarily followed. It was not, however, until I read Dr. Karl Adam's *The Spirit of Catholicism* that I discovered the enunciation of the simple and profound truth, which included all the spiritual, social, and aesthetic ends which I was dimly and vaguely trying to associate with a conception of the Church of Christ.

"The Church," says Dr. Karl Adam, "is a supra-personal thing, which does not pre-suppose Christian personalities, but itself creates and produces them. . . . The Church, as a community, as an organic unity, is a divine creation. In the last resort she is nothing less than the unity of a fallen humanity accomplished by the Sacred Humanity of Jesus, the Kosmos of men, mankind as a whole, the many as one." It was this conception with all its theological and sociological implications for which I had been groping for several years. It has remained with me as the substratum of my thinking. But it seemed to me not to mean that the Church is no more than an ideal yet to be realized, but also to imply the necessity for every Christian denomination to examine itself in the light of this conception. I could not then, nor can I now, suppose, as no doubt Dr. Adam did, that the Roman Catholic Church is actually the only realization of this conception. At the same time I was led, even before I met Adam's book, to test the claim of the United Methodist Church (as it was known after 1907) in which I was now a minister, to be regarded as *a* church, and therefore entitled to stand for me as *the* Church. I was led to apply to that denomination tests of philosophical theology, of history, and of man's whole life, social, economic and aesthetic. Before long, it seemed to fall short in several ways; and therefore, without leaving it, I was attracted, about 1915, to the Free Catholic Movement, which was to prove my bridge to the Anglican Communion, as it proved to Dr. Orchard and others the way to Rome. I was not alone, by any means, in passing from Free Catholicism to Anglicanism. With me travelled by that same road, but from a Scottish Presbyterian body, the present Provost of Oban Cathedral, the Very Rev. D. A. G. Muir. In this brief essay, I cannot provide historical accounts of the forces which have influenced me. But there is no doubt that at this time I was discovering within myself a deep sympathy with concepts of the Christian Faith which were basically Catholic.

It is here, perhaps, that I should go back, to speak of my origins, and of the Christian environment into which I had been born. For these things largely shaped me, and even though I have left the Methodism in which I was taught, there was much of it that I could never leave, and have carried, and still bear, in my heart. There abides in my soul a love of those things that stirred the Wesleys and which I desire to hold in the Catholic Church, its forms and its theology: for to hear as a Communion hymn, Charles Wesley's lovely

> O Thou who camest from above
> The fire celestial to impart,

after the glorious singing of an Anglican Mass setting is an experience which leaves me weeping with joy. I cannot forget the gratitude I owe to God for the fact that I was born into a home where religion was a living reality and set upon me a mark which I pray may never pass.

My father was a man of great physical strength, decided opinions, and tremendous vigor in religion. He had been converted by a conversation with a local Methodist preacher, on a Sunday morning when he was a shepherd-boy keeping his flock in a field in Cambridgeshire. My mother was a gentle lady, daughter of a Suffolk miller who was certainly a character. As a young girl she had attended the village church. Having both of them left their villages while young, they at length met in London and were worshipping at a small Methodist chapel, where they were married. There my father was Sunday School Superintendent, and afterwards occupied in turn nearly all the leading lay offices.

At home I grew up in an atmosphere of family prayer, Bible reading, and grief; for at the age of five I was to have a brother, as well as the sister I already possessed: the brother was born an invalid and lived in pain for more than forty years, and the sister died of diphtheria when she was just eleven years old. Somehow my parents endured these blows, and their religion seems, in my memory, to have been intensified. And they recovered an interest in life. My father, who had a typical Nonconformist concern with liberal politics, developed a great passion for social reform, without ever becoming a Socialist. It seems strange to me now that in spite of his ardent Methodist convictions he sent me to be educated at the Anglican day school of the parish, and later at an Anglican secondary school in the City of London.

Eventually I found my way to the staff of Bishopsgate Institute, a great City library. There I discovered a passion for reading and an interest in philosophical and theological books. I felt a nascent attraction toward a liberal vein in religion. This involved a negative attitude toward the miraculous element in the Gospel, and many warm debates with my father, though I never ceased to believe the doctrine of the Incarnation. And he evidently did not despair of me; for when he was leader of the "open-air meetings" which were a feature of the life of our Methodist chapel, the day came when he asked me to speak at a service to be held on a main road, on a Sunday night, after chapel service. That was my first attempt at public utterance, and I was in a condition of terror. The result, two or three years later, was that I entered the Methodist Theological College in Victoria Park, Manchester, and duly became a Methodist minister. I had, I suppose, a successful college career, which led me into Manchester University. Thence I passed to the ministry in a succession of north-country circuits, for several years increasingly liberal in theology, suspected by many of the older ministers, but regarded as their leader by a group of younger men.

Through this period I had been constantly reading the theology and criticism of the liberals of Germany as well as of England. Yet, somehow, I had never come to deny the essentials of the Christian Faith, though, so far, I had never had any deep and fervent personal Christian experience. But about the year 1915 I was becoming critical of Methodism as a church. I began to see that the liberalism I supposed to be a satisfying answer to the rather vague evangelicalism in which I had been brought up was itself a vague and doubtful thing. I read Schweitzer's great book and saw that liberalism shattered. I could not become uncritically Evangelical, with all the pietism and individualism this implied. Eventually I realized that what I was actually seeking, though scarcely yet consciously, was Catholicism. I wanted the Church, as the historic structure, always claiming Christian allegiance. I wanted beauty in worship, and a sacramental philosophy of life.

It was at this time that I came to the Free Catholic Movement of which I have already spoken. I could do this, without ceasing to be a Methodist minister, probably incurring some amount of Nonconformist criticism which did not frighten me; but I was thus able to defer making a final decision. I think most of the Nonconformist ministers in the Free Catholic Movement were in that position, though we had a real philosophy of Reunion. We argued that all Nonconformist bodies had their deepest roots in the historic Church of the West. We desired to recall them to their Catholic origins, not necessarily casting away the whole treasury of thought and devotion which they had gathered in their

Nonconformist experience. We looked for a Church, Catholic in the historic sense, but free, not from credal profession, but chiefly in the sense of self-government and freedom from State control, with the acceptance of corporate responsibility within the Church's own life.

This movement had for some years a considerable influence, but I discovered that the integrity of one's spiritual life needs a church in harmony with it. Dr. Orchard found his way to Rome, but I was increasingly considering the Anglican Communion. Orchard had never loved the Church of England and had never belonged to it, but he said of me that I was a typical Anglican, seeming to judge by the shape of my face. My friend, Maurice Reckitt, said of me in later years, that I was an *"anima naturaliter Catholica."* And indeed I had not concealed my Catholicism in the books I had written while still in the Methodist ministry. While some Methodists regarded my position as indefensible, and even appealed to Methodist authority to put an end to it, that authority declined to do anything of the sort, and assured me that I should not be attacked. One of the high officials, telling me that I had nothing to fear, asked me what I should say in the extremely improbable situation of my being called upon to defend my position as a Methodist minister. I said to him, "You know, as well as I do, that quite a considerable proportion of our ministers do not even pretend to believe the ten required doctrinal tenets. But I hear of no proposed attack upon them. I believe all those tenets most sincerely. But I believe some others, which I do not regard as destructive of those I accept. Why pick on me?" He laughed loudly and again assured me that no attack upon me would be allowed.

This was the official Methodist attitude, even to my sacramental philosophy and my acceptance of the metaphysical doctrine of transubstantiation. I have never complained of

Methodism's treatment of me; and when at length I handed in my resignation, I was treated with love and honor.

By this time I had explored most carefully the Anglican faith and practice. I believed the Church of England to be the Catholic Church in this country. I had been approached by notable Roman Catholics, but when they told me why I ought to join their Church, I found that their reasons simply did not touch my mind. I felt that I could provide better reasons for joining the Roman Church, but discovered that my reasons simply did not touch their minds. I am still convinced that my transition to the English Church was a wiser and happier movement than any other could have been. Before I took the necessary steps, I studied the day-to-day parochial life of the English Church. I knew its variety. I learned of the ordinary relation of a parish priest to the Thirty-nine Articles, and at least they presented me with much less difficulty than I should have found in Indulgences had I been contemplating Rome as my goal.

At length I had an interview with the Bishop of Manchester, who was then Dr. William Temple. It was largely his presence there as Bishop that led me to that diocese, from Leeds where was my last Methodist circuit. Dr. Temple received me with the utmost cordiality, and approved the reasons I gave him for my proposed change. This happened in March, 1925, and at the next Michaelmas I was made deacon. At the following Easter I was ordained priest. It is one thing to look forward to such a change in life, from the basis of theory and conviction; but another and more searching experience to enter upon its new disciplines, new duties, new contacts, in fact. Especially was this so with me for I was then aged 42, with the responsibilities which a man with even a most sympathetic wife and family must carry.

I must, however, say that all the problems and perplexities melted without delay.

I found that my previous writings were quite well known in the Church. The Bishop had already shown his acquaintance with them; but I found now what I had not anticipated: an open-hearted reception by the rank and file clergy of Manchester, and the beginning of a ceaseless stream of invitations to lecture and preach for Anglican parishes all over England. It has not ceased, even now.

Quite early, soon after I had become rector of St. John's Church, Hulme, I went to the Bishop with what I felt to be a real difficulty. I told him that I was contented to be a parish priest, but that I was being constantly asked to serve all over the country. He asked if I had made any rule about this. I replied that some of my friends had made it possible for me to engage a curate; that I was declining all invitations for Sundays, and accepting no more than one engagement each week that would cause me to spend a night away from my parish. He replied, "I think nobody can object to that. You have no cause for worry. When I ordained you, I did not suppose that I was ordaining you for one parish alone. I believed I was ordaining you for the whole Church of England. I am happy to know that the Church of England agrees with me." Not knowing what was happening, I was actually receiving a commission for a task which I do not believe could have come to me in any other but the Anglican Communion.

I was quickly called to service by the Anglo-Catholic Congress Movement, which was then concerned to effect the conversion of England to the Catholic Faith as that was presented in the English Church, and to this cause I gave a deal of service. But very early in my Anglican days I was called to the field of social and economic witness, chiefly as expounded by the Church Union Summer School held each year at Oxford. It was here that I was most influenced, most usefully taught, and where I did most of my subsequent work. That is a long story, which I cannot tell here even in outline; but I think that my doings in connection with our Anglo-Catholic sociology brought me into some large enterprises. In the year 1932, when I had been six years ordained, and by which time I had written some more books, I received from Dr. Frederick M. Grant, dean of what was then Western Seminary, an invitation to deliver in the following year the Hale lectures upon the subject *The Social Implications of the Oxford Movement*.

By that time, Dr. Temple had become Archbishop of York. I went to Dr. Guy Warman, his successor at Manchester, to ask his permission. He said, to my surprise, "I am proud that one of my clergy is to be thus honored. Kneel down and let me bless you, for this task." I came to the United States in 1933, travelled through many cities and wide lands, performing many tasks besides that of delivering the Hale lectures at Evanston. It was, for me, an enthralling experience, and I shall never forget it; but in my mind the greatest moments were those when I preached in the glorious Cathedral of St. John the Divine in New York City.

At home again in England, I soon received an invitation to address an Anglo-Russian conference in Paris; and a little later another invitation to the United States, to deliver a course of lectures at a September School of the Episcopal Church, at Adeleynrood. I then spent a virtually unbroken year in my own parish in Manchester, accepting only some English engagements. But in the following year I received from Prebendary P. T. R. Kirk the offer of a new post which was then being created by the Industrial Christian Fellowship, the lectureship on Christian Social Doctrine to Anglican clergy and theological students. I took counsel upon this issue. Archbishop Temple, several bishops, and my friends in the Christendom Group all wished me to accept it, with the result that for the following fourteen years I was travelling all over England and Wales, and in Scotland and Ireland, lecturing to clergy and students, preaching in cathedrals and parish churches, and addressing a great number of public meetings. These were the most physically and mentally exhausting years of my life, and the coming of a great domestic grief brought me, thus overworked, into a series of illnesses which made any continuation of such labors impossible.

I have covered in this essay much more than the story of my actual passing from Methodism into the Anglican Communion. But upon reflection the reader will see that what I have done in the English Church has been the fulfillment of the hope which Dr. Temple had when he ordained me. And now I am in quiet waters doing a little service in the life of a parish, in that Church of England wherein, please God, in His good time, and by His grace, I shall die.

8

JOSEPH WITTKOFSKI

A Maryknoll Father who served on the faculty of the order's seminary, the Rev. Joseph Wittkofski was received into the priesthood of the Episcopal Church in 1944. He was born in 1912, received his early education in parochial schools, and his higher education at St. Joseph's College, Collegeville, Indiana, St. Gregory's Seminary in Cincinnati, and the Maryknoll Seminary in New York. After his ordination he did graduate work at the University of Illinois and Fordham University, where he received a Master of Science degree. Since he began his service in the Episcopal Diocese of Pittsburgh, his church in Charleroi, Pennsylvania (St. Mary's), has grown from a small mission of 140 communicants into a parish of nearly 600. For several years he was editor of the Pittsburgh diocesan magazine and is co-author of the Pittsburgh Plan *of religious education. He is author of* The Secret Way *and* Little Book of Contemplation, *and co-author of* Unity in Faith. *He frequently conducts retreats and missions in various parts of the country. He is married and has three children.*

JOSEPH WITTKOFSKI

JOE, IT IS a very bitter thing to become an old man and to realize that you have given your life for something which you now see to be a fraud. What can I do now? Where can I go? Who would have me?"

The above words of a great Roman Catholic theologian and a widely respected priest mark a turning point in my life. He had been a devoted teacher of mine and he had become a close friend. In the light of my experiences, at that time of my life, the implicit advice of his unhappy words forced me to examine my own intellectual position and my convictions and they eventually carried me from the Roman into the Anglican Communion.

I hesitate to write about this journey of mine because I constantly fear that I may bring harm to innocent and deeply sincere people. I cannot have any feelings of bitterness toward Roman Catholic people. Often I have found myself torn asunder between truth and the love which I owe to all people. I would never wish to be associated with any wave of blind prejudice that might be raised against convinced and devout members of the Latin Church. I must not betray the wholesome friendship of my many Roman Catholic friends. I have often experienced their loyalty to me. Recently, in spite of some Roman Catholic clerical opposition, many of my good Roman Catholic friends stood firm and they succeeded in having me elected Department Chaplain for the American Legion in Pennsylvania. Moreover, in the Teen Club of my present parish, I have nearly one hundred Roman Catholic young people. As a Christian, I can have nothing but love for members of the Roman Church. I would never wish to take from them what they have unless I was sure that I could help them find something better.

Yet, in spite of the demands of Christian charity, I am convinced that many of the activities of the Roman Catholic hierarchy threaten the very foundations of the Kingdom of God and of His Christ. Of almost equal importance is the fact that the Roman Church openly seeks to overthrow the historic freedoms of citizens of the United States. I know that the overwhelming majority of Roman Catholic people are out of sympathy with some of the activities of their Church. They must not be blamed. But God, in His merciful kindness, has given me the grace to see through the clouds of darkness and I dare not pretend that I have not been given this help of a loving Providence.

I am grateful to God for my many years as a Roman Catholic. I must be honest and admit that there were many happy aspects of the Roman Church which I can never hope to discover in the Anglican Church. For example, the sincere Roman priest wins a love from his flock which is usually far removed from the type of affection which the Episcopal clergyman gains in his parish. In the Roman parish, the devoted priest is given a blind allegiance while the Episcopal priest enjoys hardly more than a constantly questioning affection. I cannot say, in consideration of the welfare of souls, which is best; but I am sure that the position of the Roman clergyman is more enjoyable.

If the Roman Church could wipe away a thousand years of history and remember that Christ's Kingdom is not of this world, it would become a tremendous force to bring mankind to God. That the Pope should be a prince of this present world and have his Secretary of State indicates the distance the Roman Church has departed from the teachings of Him who reigned from a tree. How great are the ills that are created when the Kingdom of God is confused with that of this world! Well did Dante write of the later Papacy:

> Ah Constantine, to how great ill gave birth
> Not thy conversion, but that plenteous dower
> Which the first wealthy pope received of thee!

In the early days of my Roman Catholic ministry, I was brought face to face with some of the political activities of the Roman Church. I saw how little some of the authorities of the Roman Church at that time valued the internal security of the United States. These men clearly placed the interests of the Roman Church above those of any nation. I could not fit myself into this picture. I began to realize that Latin Christianity had not changed its aims since medieval times. In one of my private indoctrination sessions, I was told, "Joe, we must forget patriotic slogans. The basic concepts of democracy are nonsense. We must work to establish in this country a government which will concentrate authority and divide responsibility."

As I began to realize the implications of my firsthand experience, I was confused and very much bewildered. I owed loyalty to my country and to my Church. I lost the power to reconcile the two loyalties. My position was very much like that of a young child whose parents are divorced. When I complained to a highly-placed Roman Catholic ecclesiastic that I felt that I was being called upon to commit some treasonable acts against the United States, I was answered, "Joe, why do you worry about treason to your country? After all, your country will last two or three hundred years but the Church will last forever. Why should there be any worry about treason in your mind?"

The answer above did not provide me with any peace of mind. I felt myself in the hands of a driving force to escape the net of the years and eventually planned to take the information I gained to the Federal Bureau of Investigation. In the bitter early days after America had entered the Second World War, I was sure that the safety of the nation was being tampered with. But first I had to retrace my steps and seek out the reasons for the position in which I found myself. I well realized that Roman Catholic theology created the important sanctions for the various activities of that Church. If I could not find substantial error in theological thought, I must admit to myself that what I had seen was completely justified. My graduate studies, after seminary training, had been in the fields of the sciences. This provided me with an advantage which I did not have as an undergraduate seminarian. I knew nothing about the concept of objective thinking until my studies at the University of Illinois. This became of great value to me as I reviewed my theological thinking.

My personal study first took me to the most obvious place for a priest—before the altar. Here I found evidence which threatened to vitiate my priesthood completely.

Few will dispute that our Saviour's most precious gift to His Church is the Sacrament of His Body and Blood. In the words of Jesus, without the benefits of this Sacrament, properly received, the Christian can hardly hope to gain eternal life. Following the divine command, the Christian Church is expected to consecrate bread and wine to become the Body and Blood of Jesus. As Christian people both eat and drink of this Sacrament, they vitally unite themselves with our Saviour so that they become one with Him. Surely, to receive this Sacrament properly, they must partake of both the consecrated bread and wine. Our Lord commanded, "All of you eat . . . and all of you drink of this."

As a priest of the Roman Church, I could not give the consecrated cup to Roman Catholic people and I found myself in the way, blocking the fulfillment of our Lord's command. Any Roman priest knows that, if he dares to press the chalice to the lips of the faithful, in the law of his Church he commits sacrilege. Surely, to make obedience to the command of Jesus into sacrilege approaches very near to blasphemy.

Before the great divisions of Christendom, the Church realized that it could not do away with any direct command of Jesus. When He instituted the Blessed Sacrament, our Saviour clearly directed His followers to partake of the hallowed bread and of the consecrated wine. A long line of Roman bishops supports the practice required by Christ. In the fifth century St. Leo, Bishop of Rome, thus condemned some early temperance people who refused to drink of the consecrated wine: "They [taking the bread alone] receive Christ's Body unworthily and entirely refuse to quaff the blood of our redemption; therefore, we give notice to you, holy brethren, that people of this sort . . . are to be expelled from the fellowship of the saints."

Many later Bishops of Rome followed in the way of Leo's teaching. Gelasius I, referring to people who abstained from the chalice, wrote, "Let such persons either receive the sacrament in its entirety, or be repelled from the same sacrament, because the division of the one and same mystery cannot take place without great sacrilege." In A.D. 1095, Urban II wrote that "no one shall communicate at the altar without he receive the Body and the Blood separately and alike." Finally, in A.D. 1118, Paschal II wrote, "Therefore, in receiving the Lord's Body and Blood, let the Lord's tradition be observed; nor let any departure be made, through a human and novel institution, from what Christ the Master ordained and did." In the mind of Pope Gelasius and of many of his successors, nearly every Roman mass today must be seen as a "great sacrilege."

My study of the mass naturally carried me into a consideration of the central doctrine of the Papacy. From Holy Scripture, it is clear that Jesus gave His Apostolic college a commission which contained the essential authority with which He had been endowed by His Father. The determination of the repository of divine authority is a matter of greatest importance. Whereas the Roman Communion vigorously holds that the full authority of our Lord is first reposed in the Bishop of Rome, another important historic theory holds that all bishops jointly and equally share the commission which Jesus gave to the Apostles. Hence all episcopal authority has been derived from a common episcopacy that is jointly inherited by all bishops.

How did Catholic antiquity regard the first source of Apostolic authority? Today, the Roman Church holds that papal supremacy results from the alleged inherited primacy of St. Peter. St. Paul, however, seemed to know nothing of any such Petrine supremacy since, on several occasions, he showed outright disrespect for Cephas. The Apostle of the Gentiles rebuked Peter (Gal. 2:14) and he made fun of the Corinthians who claimed to be of Peter (I Cor. 1:12).

St. Cyprian, an early bishop in Africa, was one of the first to outline the doctrine of episcopal authority. In opposition to what is the modern Roman Catholic view, St. Cyprian wrote:

> The episcopate is one, of which each bishop jointly holds a part. . . . Each bishop has in the administration of the Church

freedom of decision according to his own will and is here-after to give account of his conduct to the Lord. . . . No one of us sets himself up as a bishop of bishops, or by tyrannical terror forces his colleagues to a necessity of obeying inasmuch as every bishop, in the free use of his liberty and power, has the right of forming his own judgement, and can no more be judged by another than he himself can judge another.

St. Augustine, great doctor of the Western Church, knew nothing of the present concepts of papal infallibility and supremacy. Once the great Bishop of Hippo wrote:

Supposing those bishops who judged at Rome were not good judges, there remained still a plenary council of the Universal Church where the cause could be sifted with the judges them-selves, so that if they were convicted of having judged wrongly, their sentence could be annulled.

One of the most saintly of Roman Bishops, St. Gregory the Great, nearly fourteen hundred years ago rejected the current Roman Catholic theory of the Papacy. Gregory prayed that no bishop of the Church

. . . would ever admit this name [Universal Pastor], ever agree to it, ever write it, ever receive a writing wherein it is contained, or add his subscription; but, as behooves the minis-ters of Almighty God, keep himself clear from such poisonous infection, and give no place within himself to the crafty strata-gem; since this is done to the injury and disruption of the whole Church, and, as we have said, in contempt of you all. For if one, as assumed, be Universal Bishop, it follows that you are not bishops.

Thus we can see that the Catholic Faith of the ancient Church held no doctrine like the present-day theory of the Papacy.

I have met many unfortunate former Roman Catholic priests who, in their intense disaffection with papal institutions, have seen fit to give up their Catholic Faith. Through God's kindly grace, my lasting interest in the great mystical theologians did much, I believe, to strengthen my own hold upon the essential elements of the historic Catholic religion. In Roman Catholic thinking the doctrine of the Papacy is so identified with the Catholic Faith that it is generally thought impossible to reject the dogmas of the Papacy and yet keep Catholic convictions.

In my own case, above the inner confusion which I came to experience, beyond the forces pulling now one way and then another, the life-giving truths more clearly imprinted themselves upon my consciousness. "God was in Christ reconciling the world unto Himself." Redemption had to come from man but, left to myself, I could not establish it. As a result of an unmeasurable love, God Himself became man through the Incarnation of our Blessed Lord. In His life of perfect offering, sealed by His death upon the Cross, Jesus surmounted the mighty obstacle of my own human selfishness. To the extent that I am vitally united with the life of Christ, I find myself relieved of my spiritual disabilities. Purification, through the Blood of Christ and by the operation of the Holy Spirit, creates a real, vital union with God. The unified society of the redeemed constitutes the Mystical Body of Jesus. The Church, in its proper structure and function, is the operating agent of God's love for mankind. Thus every concept of law, except the rule of love, is largely secondary in the life of the Church.

During my college years I had developed an academic interest in Anglicanism. For my bachelor's degree, I wrote my thesis on the reunion of Rome, Constantinople, and Canterbury. As I looked at the totality of Christian theology, I was forced to admit to myself that my own grasp of the truth was much nearer to the Anglican position than to the Roman.

My actual journey from Rome to Canterbury requires much more space than is allotted to me for this writing. Since there is much that involves American security, I cannot go into these matters until the United States government has first lifted the veil.

I have never been so conscious of the guiding hand of the Holy Spirit as I was at that time. As I look back, I can see that every move that I then made was the right one. For a reason which I do not yet know, I made my way to Buffalo, New York. I began to attend services at St. Paul's Cathedral in that city. Within a few months, I was brought into the Episcopal Church by Bishop Cameron Davis and he placed me on the staff of St. Paul's Cathedral to spend my required canonical year under the direction of Austin Pardue, then Dean.

At the time of my interviews with the Federal Bureau of Investigation in Buffalo, I was warned to be extremely careful. A high-placed Roman Catholic Churchman came to Buffalo and warned me that if I did not return to the Roman Communion, I would be sent into the U. S. Army as an enlisted man. In spite of my newly established relation with the Episcopal Church, this eventually came to pass. I sought to block this development by enlisting as a chaplain but, since I was without any parochial experience, I could not qualify.

I was placed under the direction of Dean Pardue in May, 1943. In the summer of that year, my draft board, in spite of the objection of Bishop Davis, changed my classification from 4D to 1A. I was ordered to report for induction at Wilkes-Barre, Pennsylvania, in mid-September. After my physical examination there, the Army reclassified me 1AL for limited service and sent me back to Buffalo, since I was not needed at that time. A few days after my return, my draft board again changed my classification, from IAL to 4F. Although this hurt my pride, Dean Pardue advised me to forget about it, as it was likely the draft board's way of dismissing the case. But within another couple of weeks, my draft status was again changed, from 4F to 1A, and I was once more ordered up for immediate induction.

Since it was clearly evident that someone was tampering with my draft status, the case was taken into Federal Court. Of course, I kept the Federal Bureau of Investigation aware of the situation. When I eventually came to the Camp Upton induction station, the Federal Court had already issued a writ of habeas corpus against my commanding officer. I presented an unusual picture when I arrived at Camp Upton, for Dean Pardue had advised me to wear clericals. No one quite knew the protocol for that situation. On my first day in camp, I was obliged to spend several hours with Army Intelligence. My military career, as a private in the U. S. Army, was spent in the New York City area. During this period, I was given much moral support by Canon Edward N. West of the Cathedral of St. John the Divine.

After my honorable discharge at the beginning of June in 1944, I immediately went back to work as a priest. My past twelve years in the ministry of the Episcopal Church have been wonderful years. In contrast to the Roman scheme of life, which tends violently to destroy the natural life of man to make room for the supernatural, the Anglican idea seems to be a gradual elevation of human nature to a supernatural mode of action. With the great emphasis upon the Love of God instead of upon the Canon Law of the Church, the Episcopal priest can create some deeply satisfying relationships with people which are almost completely unknown to the average Roman Catholic clergyman. With reference to the polity of the Episcopal Church, I can agree with the remark of one of my many beloved converts from Rome: "This is what I always thought the Church should be."

I am aware of the serious shortcomings of the Episcopal Church, but I am also convinced that God does not expect us to have the perfection of Heaven while we are here on earth.

As anyone would expect, I have been bitterly attacked by the clergy and the news organs of the Roman Church. These do not provoke me to unkind feelings because I realize that if the situation were reversed I would likely have been tempted to do as has been done to me. Although some of the attempts to blacken my character have been a bit nasty, most of them have been on the farcical side. I have a photostatic copy of a letter, written by the managing editor of a Roman Catholic publication, which typically contains nearly a dozen misstatements of fact about me. For example, according to this editor, I entered the Episcopal Church because I had a great need of funds and the Anglicans gave me one of their larger parishes in Detroit. Actually, I have not been in Detroit since I was a small boy and, during the twelve years of my Anglican ministry, I have lived on a salary that has been little more than subsistent. I could have earned much more as a geneticist in the Civil Service. From time to time, Roman Catholic newspapers have taken advantage of some loopholes in the libel laws in their efforts to discredit me but I believe that intelligent people usually see through this type of apologetics.

Somewhat more painful have been the attacks made on me by some fellow members of the Episcopal Church. I have been told that there is no room for the likes of me in the Episcopal Church. When I have sought to do a little to stem the tide of an engulfing Roman apologetic, I have found myself assailed in the Church press. Others have let it be known that they resent me because I may become a gate through which people of a different social class than theirs may come into the Episcopal Church. But people who react in such fashion constitute a very tiny minority of our Church.

In contrast, the kindnesses of bishops, priests, and laity across the nation have been far above any power of mine to describe. A great part of any success that I may have had in the ministry is largely due to the wonderful friendships with which God has blessed me in the Church. I suspect, however, that the hundreds of converts who have come into the Episcopal Church through God's use of my ministry are my greatest joy and consolation.

In retrospect, I can truthfully say that God has filled my heart with so much abiding happiness that there should be no room left for bitterness toward the past years. I can now look upon what has gone before as the sure working of God's grace on my behalf. In spite of past crisis after crisis and confusing years, I can plainly make out the pattern of God's wonderful love toward me. Truly, I cannot hope to repay Him but I must accept the task of bringing as many of His children as possible into this loving relationship with Himself. In spite of my own unworthiness—and I am even more without merit than the attacks in the Roman Catholic press would indicate—I believe that I have been shown the gracious path to life. With a constant eye upon my human weaknesses, I pray that I may not be allowed to fail in the labor which God has thrust upon me.

9

SAMUEL J. WYLIE

One who has devoted most of his ministry to college students and faculty, the Rev. Samuel J. Wylie is at present so ministering at Brown University and other Providence academic institutions in the name of the Diocese of Rhode Island. Born in 1918, he graduated from Wheaton College and the Biblical Seminary, and received the degree of Master of Sacred Theology from Union Theological Seminary. Ordained to the Presbyterian ministry in 1943, he first served as a chaplain with the Navy in the South Pacific, then as pastor of the John Hall Memorial Church in New York City, and in 1949 was appointed Counselor to Protestant Students at Columbia University. After his ordination to the Episcopal ministry in 1951 he was appointed Chaplain to Episcopal Students at the University of Virginia, where he served until going to Providence. Recently he was elected a Canon of St. John's Cathedral, Providence. He is married and has three children.

SAMUEL J. WYLIE

PILGRIMS to Canterbury from other Christian traditions may journey far, but they find on arrival a surprising familiarity about the place. In one sense they never left home. Many truths that nurtured them in their former fellowships are equally honored here. No man is asked to surrender vital past experience. Anglicanism involves its converts in affirming much that they formerly may have denied. It requires denial only of the exclusiveness that limits truth to the insights of one century, one world view, or one social tradition.

When I was ordained deacon and priest at New York Cathedral, friends were present who had shared my pietist Fundamentalist early life, and my later conservative Presbyterianism. Their fellowship in faith and prayer remains dear to me. I wondered how much of this important hour in my life could be shared with them; how much of it might seem like a repudiation of former convictions. For the most part I need not have worried.

The long service was unfamiliar and perplexing to the relatives and friends used to the informality of a prayer meeting. But the message of the sermon was not unfamiliar. The text was: "For we have this treasure in earthen vessels." The "treasure" was the Gospel, and the preacher reminded the congregation that though interest that morning centered around the particular candidates for ordination, they and their vows, and the bishop and his action, were all caught up in the greater drama of the Eucharist itself. Our Lord's "one oblation of himself once offered," making "a full, perfect, and sufficient sacrifice, oblation, and satisfaction, for the sins of the whole world," and our offering of ourselves, souls and

128

bodies, in response to Him, remain the central witness and wonder of the Christian community whether we are gathered at an early weekday celebration of the Holy Communion or attending a coronation, funeral, wedding, or ordination. To this affirmation of the Gospel, Fundamentalist and Anglican responded alike. They parted company where Fundamentalist conviction denied the Holy Spirit's power working through Apostolic order, historic liturgy, and Catholic sacraments.

Presbyterians present responded to the message, to the liturgy, to the witness of continuity and order in the bishop's action, but were uneasy about kneeling, signs of the cross, the use of the senses in worship, because these elements of the Catholic tradition were repudiated by them (with some justification) four hundred years ago. They judged, or at least feared, like their forebears, that outward signs were idolatrous; a substitution of form for content.

It became apparent that tension with friends in the Reformed tradition arises not so much from any Anglican repudiation of precious Reformation convictions as from Anglican affirmation of Catholic convictions and practices denied at the Reformation. At any rate, only the Anglicans in that particular congregation were keeping faith with the positive insight and practice of the Reformers on the one hand, and the Fathers, Saints, and humble faithful of the preceding fifteen centuries on the other.

It is this reconciling mission in Anglicanism that strongly drew me to Canterbury. As a student of history, I was not content to draw a parenthesis around Church history from the second to the sixteenth centuries, as if nothing significant had happened in Christian thought between St. Paul and Martin Luther. I was tired of militant Fundamentalism's claiming an exclusive interest in the Gospel. I admired a

Communion which held the historic Faith as proclaimed by councils of the undivided Church, making concessions neither to Protestant liberalism nor divisive Protestant orthodoxy. I was responsive to a tradition of worship that does not seek to perpetuate regional Christianity, or frontier Christianity, worker or white-collar Christianity, but a liturgy of devotion which has grown out of twenty centuries of prayer, binding third-century Fathers, courageous Popes, medieval Saints, Renaissance scholars, Reformation theologians in one company with princes and peasants, factory workers, merchants, and magnates. I felt a reconciling power here for the brokenness of our day: the power not of a new technique, but the continuing power of the Holy Spirit where men seek, and humbly keep, a bond of unity.

Anglicans do not always see clearly the inclusive implications of the word *Catholic*. It is possible to talk as if the universal Church is a sectarian club—but not for long. The weight of the Anglican ethos is against it. That is why converts need not feel that they burn their bridges behind them when they make their way to Canterbury. We are not so much Episcopalians as Churchmen: the Gospel which we have known vitally in Reformation communions is the same Gospel, but it is freed from the partisan controversy and iconoclasm of the sixteenth century, and in this liberation gains breadth, power, and authority.

If I was attracted by the "wholeness" of the Faith, in its Anglican setting, I was equally attracted by its relevance to the whole man, indeed to the material world as well. Like most American pietists I was puzzled by man's relation to the rest of the world. I was afraid to affirm the goodness of the material world, or to acknowledge the glory of the intellectual and artistic achievements of man, lest in so doing I minimize the reality of sin and man's fallen condition. I knew I was a sinner. No pietist falls into the heresy of the perfectibility of man! I knew that man's redemption in Christ forever was the truly significant aspect of his existence. But I could not be content to write off great feats of engineering, masterpieces of music and literature, or heroic deeds of gallantry as worldly and hence unimportant or even sinful in their distracting influence. I was not much happier about conservative Calvinism's tendency to trust words in giving formal expression to truth, while making sacraments inferior to words, and viewing the arts as scarcely trustworthy at all.

For that matter, how does one distinguish between the sacred and the secular in art? To accept a picture because it tells a sacred story or points a wholesome moral, but to reject a work of greater craftsmanship because its theme is rooted in man's temporal existence, leads one to question his theological presuppositions. In public worship, why need we pray in great austerity at 11:00 A.M. if it is permissible in the same church to offer a Byrd Mass or a Britten *Te Deum* at a concert in the evening? My own experience led me to doubt that worshipping God in spirit and in truth necessarily meant in barrenness of form, or with music interposed as contrast, respite, or refreshment between more vital parts of the service. The "spirit" that brought medieval patrons and laborers, artists and clerics into one loving building enterprise at Chartres Cathedral can hardly be foreign to our Lord's use of the word.

The denial of the world, the flesh, and the devil in rigorous Protestantism has been a bracing reminder that contemporary Christians, like the Apostles, must leave all and follow Christ. But it is possible in one's zeal to abandon some of God's own handiwork to the devil. I found in Anglicanism the affirmation that while the creation is distorted, it is still God's creation; that while man has fallen, the image of God is not destroyed; that in Christ man is not just rescued out of the created world into the security of Heaven, but that God in Christ is reconciling bodies as well as souls, things as well as people, to Himself. He has not given up the creation as a bad job. He is restoring, reconciling, redeeming. This reserves a place in the direct service of God for the physician, the artist, the stone-mason, and the cabinet-maker, along with the theologian. A man need not be a craftsman merely to keep his body fed while he gets on with the much more important task of nurturing his soul. He serves God through his craft or through any productive labor, and he may bring evidence of it with him to the altar, offering in his Eucharist himself: ransomed soul, disciplined mind, skillful hands, together with the product he creates.

Anglicans have no monopoly on this insight, of course. But Anglicans have never denied the good things of the world as God's gifts worthy of enjoyment. They affirm the flesh as having part with the spirit in worship, and put the substantial body down on sometimes groaning knees before God when they pray. In the sacraments the Episcopal Church affirms that God always works through the temporal to reveal the eternal. The firmament shows God's handiwork. The glory of God was revealed in the face of the Man Jesus Christ. Bread and wine, the humble stuff of earthly fellowship, become the medium of the shared life of eternity. Small wonder then, that disillusioned humanists in our time, humbled by the discovery that man is finite and sinful, but loyal still to man's dreams and his achievements, turn in considerable numbers to a Church which, acknowledging the awfulness of sin, yet sees God's creative and redeeming hand in all things human, and becomes the repository and guardian of the noblest achievements of the ages.

"Guardian" is an important word here. Literary men, scientists, and philosophers in disturbing numbers are ready to give man up as a lost cause in these days: his reason the dupe of his emotions, and his freedom and moral responsibility an illusion. The revival of a true Christian humanism is essential in the remaking or preservation of our culture. The support Anglican and all Catholic theology gives to the dignity of man—his reason and his autonomy—is good news to all men of good will whether Christians or pagans. It is also a bond between the "secular" culture and the Christian community; a common starting point from which each can influence the other. As Powel M. Dawley says, "Possibly the uniquely distinctive feature of the Reformation experience of the English Church was the achievement of a synthesis between the Christian elements in the Renaissance awakening and the truth that was preserved and transmitted through the medieval order. In that invigorating synthesis Anglicanism finds its justification."

Anglican sacramental theology also bears a contemporary witness in the healing arts. The development of psychosomatic medicine reminds us that spirit and flesh cannot be isolated from each other. The physician can no longer confine his interest to tissues. The pastoral counselor may not forget the influence of endocrine glands on Christian personality. Anglicans find this position congenial to their own experience. A theology which treats man as a unity of body, mind, and spirit, created by God and honored by His having accepted a like body at Bethlehem, does not balk at the cure of souls by physical means, nor has it ever ceased to expect that the prayer of faith will heal sick bodies. It is no accident that in the conversations among physicians, psychiatrists, and clergymen on the healing ministry, Anglicans have taken a conspicuous part.

The canticle *Benedicite, omnia opera Domini* in the Service of Morning Prayer invites all created things to bless the Lord. It is long, and the singing sometimes drags, but it gives liturgical voice to the cosmic inclusiveness of our Lord's dominion. "O all ye Works of the Lord," it calls, "bless ye the Lord: praise him, and magnify him for ever." And it lists over forty categories of God's handiwork by name, inviting them to join in His praise. Thoughtful men seeking a world view concerned with all aspects of existence, human and material, will find one in the Biblical view of the Old and New Testaments expressed in the worship and theology of the Book of Common Prayer.

We have considered two kinds of Anglican inclusiveness: a theological synthesis of the Catholic Faith tempered and purified by the fires of the Reformation, and an at-home-ness in both the eternal and temporal worlds. The third might be called a "therapeutic" inclusiveness, since it bears on the sick places in contemporary life.

We describe man's state by words like *isolation, loneliness, estrangement, brokenness.* We are aware that his soul (and even his bodily health) requires that the isolation be overcome. Man must be reconciled to God, to his fellows, and to himself. But how? We cannot be reconciled to each other without having some sort of community structure to our relationship. Some sort of hierarchy develops, some kind of authority gives formal expression to the "mind of the Church." The question of authority as a theological and practical problem led me to Canterbury as much as any other single factor.

Like most conservative Protestants, I accepted the authority of the Scriptures as ultimate. (I still do, but in a different context.) However, conflict among Fundamentalist groups themselves, and between liberals and conservatives, came close to justifying in my own experience the Roman Catholic view that there are as many kinds of Protestantism as there are Protestants. "The clear Word of God" in one setting was a theological system taught by some popular evangelist. "All creeds and scriptures," said another friend at a student conference, "must be brought before the bar of truth." The bar of truth, for him, was the world view of his liberal New England seminary in the particular decade of his studies. The infallible book was replaced by an infallible professor (or, in many instances, one's infallible self!).

The alternative presented by the Roman Catholic Church made no great appeal. It is difficult for anyone who assents to the Reformation and Biblical concern for individual responsibility before God, and the democratic political belief in free enquiry and speech, to accept a system where obedience is almost a synonym for faith, where dogma can be enjoined as of a particular date in 1870 or 1960. Most Protestant Christians recovering the vision of New Testament and early Catholic unity are prepared to reject the extremes of Protestant subjectivism, to approach historic dogmas with a new humility, to suspect that where the individual differs from the historic Faith confirmed by twenty centuries of experience, the individual rather than the Faith is probably in error. But they are not prepared to ascribe infallibility to any part of God's creation, even the Body of Christ, insofar as it includes finite men as well as the Son of God. They admire Roman unanimity, but they feel sure that the price of it involves sin equal to the admitted sinfulness of broken Protestantism.

To them Anglicanism presents a strong appeal. Here is no sharp choice between Book, Self, and Church. Rather, here is an invitation to be adopted into God's family, where the divine revelation and the wisdom of the Fathers is transmitted through the life and liturgy of the Church, interpreted by its collective experience. The individual is wooed to conformity because he loves the brethren, rather than commanded to obedience.

It is no accident that the *Via Media* developed in England. The British constitution defines the quality of British life as clearly as the United States Constitution, but it is not a document. It is centuries of cumulative experience in which documents play a large part. It is also the continuing influence of great men. It is a community life as much as anything else. So, in Anglicanism, a remarkable world-wide unanimity exists in faith, practice, and liturgy maintained, not by law, but because those who live in the fellowship prize it above their personal or regional preference for some deviation. Deviations exist, of course, and sometimes embarrass the Church, in their gravity or in their inconsistency with her official teaching and life. They are the price of freedom and the consequence of human finitude and sin. But they are insignificant in the light of the vast area of common experience within the Church. The Anglican Congress at Minneapolis in 1954 surprised even the delegates by its witness to joyful unity in Christ across language, cultural, political, and economic boundaries. Anglicans believe this to be the kind of unity the undivided Church of the first centuries knew. Many wistful Protestants and disillusioned Roman Catholics are coming to believe that this community formed by the Bible and the Creeds, the sacraments and Apostolic order makes a witness to Christendom which calls for a response.

Sometimes the response involves Confirmation. Sometimes it is expressed in a rethinking of the doctrine of the Church, the ministry, and the sacraments among Protestant Christians. The revival of interest in the early Fathers of the

Church, neglected by most Protestants for four hundred years, the sacrament- and prayer-centered liturgical movements in the Reformed and Lutheran Churches, all indicate that the ethos of Anglicanism is not merely its own brand of provincialism. There is something here which meets a human need. Many of us can witness gratefully that we have not lost our freedom or our critical faculties but have found them heightened in our "submission" to the Episcopal Church.

Related to the problem of authority and Anglican gentleness toward the seeker and the skeptic, is the problem of personal counseling. Must the "permissive" counselor be a complete relativist in morals? Shall he say, "Good is whatever functions best for A, though it might be evil for B?" Or is the pastoral counselor a sort of spiritual baker, obliged to use the Faith like a cookie-cutter, molding all human beings to the same form and discarding the scraps created in the process? People in trouble need to be heard sympathetically and understood when they complain that they literally cannot conform to their highest inner standards or the community's goals. But they rightly suspect a clergyman of selling his religion short if he has no moral absolutes at all in his counseling.

I found contemporary Anglican thought on pastoral counseling to be true to the New Testament awareness that we were called to holiness or "wholeness" in Christ. At the same time it abounds in understanding to the moral rebel or casualty. Anglicans by and large do not moralize, but their Catholic heritage in the liturgy reminds them many times a year that they are "called to be saints." The priest in a pastoral role is not there primarily because he is a good man helping

others to be good, but because he is a recipient of the reconciling grace of God, and a witness and a vehicle in its
efficacious work to others.

This does not mean that Anglicans put a lower premium
on clerical good behavior than others. It means that
sanctity in the priest is no barrier in his relationship to his
people. Both confess their common failure and common sin
in every service. The priest's authority is not in his personal
superiority (moral or intellectual) to his people, but in his
privilege, though unworthy, to share the burdens of Christ's
flock in Christ's name, to assure them of the redeeming power
of God's grace, to absolve and to bless.

He has certain additional advantages in counseling. He
does not equate Puritanism with holiness, so he will not be
tempted to confuse mores with morals. Nor need he pattern
his ministry upon the psychiatrist. He has a unique function
neither subordinate to, nor in competition with, the therapist.
Perhaps this is why such fruitful conversation has been going
on between priests and psychiatrists at the New York and
Washington Cathedrals, and elsewhere. Best of all, the counseling ministry is set in the community life of the Church.
If "acceptance" is what human beings need, if isolation and
competition cause our difficulties, then a healing ministry
cannot be exercised adequately in an office call. The Anglican counselor who can accompany his counselee to the altar,
and in the community of forgiven sinners and groping
seekers remember still one more, is in a position to tap both
the human resources of fellowship and the divine life of the
Holy Spirit.

The answer to human "estrangement" is dramatically
though quietly acted out at an early Eucharist in many a
parish church. On their knees, men and women of all kinds
remember One who "broke down the middle wall of parti-

tion between us, making peace by the blood of His cross, having slain the enmity thereby." And, as they hold up before God the one eternal reconciling Sacrifice, they remember also "thy servant Frank" and all the Franks and Georges who are in any sort of trouble. They remember John and Mary whose marriage has been blessed and sustained for five, ten, twenty years. They pray for Helen who has lost her Tom, and for Tom, too, as he "enters the gates of larger life." There is nothing spectacular about all this. But there is warmth and healing. There is nothing exclusively Anglican about this kind of fellowship. But I have not often found it in other traditions.

These are one man's reasons for the pilgrimage to Canterbury. For the most part they are subjective. They are not based on the truth or falsity of other traditions. Some have found their home in Anglicanism because conscience drove them from a theological position they considered untenable to one which they hold to be true. Others have quite simply become Christians through their fellowship with Anglicans. They had only a nominal relationship to any tradition. Their conversion is to Christ in the communion of the Church in its Anglican form. I came, as others have done before me, to continue a Christian life already begun and to exercise a vocation already received. I was impelled by my admiration for the breath-taking scope and inclusiveness of Anglican orthodoxy. Life in the Anglican fellowship has convinced me that the *Via Media,* despite its dangers and weaknesses, is the branch of divided Christendom which most fully holds the faith of the Apostles, most sympathetically understands man in his world, and brings to him with most immediacy the means of grace.

10

KATHLEEN BLISS

Well known as a leader in the Ecumenical Movement, Dr. Kathleen Bliss now serves with the Talks Department of the British Broadcasting Corporation and is charged with responsibility for fostering discussion between Christians and non-Christians. Born in 1908, she took first class honors at Cambridge in theology and, later, Aberdeen University conferred upon her the degree of Doctor of Divinity for a Christian critique of social developments. After seven years in India, she joined Dr. J. H. Oldham on the staff of the Christian News-Letter *in 1940, and succeeded him as editor from 1945 to 1949.*

Dr. Bliss is Chairman of the Board of the Ecumenical Institute at Bossey, Switzerland, and a member of the Central Committee and the Executive Committee of the World Council of Churches. She is married and the mother of three daughters.

KATHLEEN BLISS

A SPIRITUAL pilgrimage always, I suppose, has two elements. There is a search for one knows not what, to which one is driven by some inner discontent, so that while the search is on it seems as though all possibilities are open and anything might turn out to be the goal. But once the search is over, the goal seems to have a certain inevitability about it, and one remembers inklings that it would come to this, if only one were prepared to accept, to pay the price. I have that feeling of inevitability strongly now. I should say at the start that I am not talking about the struggle to find a faith to live by: that for me has been another story. I am here setting down how the question "What *is* the Church?" pressed itself upon me.

I grew up in a Congregational church, neither large nor wealthy, and was surrounded from earliest childhood with the sense of belonging to a close-knit, varied, and responsible fellowship. Congregational principles of church order were faithfully practiced. Once in three months, the whole congregation met on a Wednesday evening and, after a short service, all the affairs of the congregation—spiritual, organizational, and financial—were discussed and decisions taken. The minister presided and the business was laid before the meeting by the church secretary, acting on behalf of the deacons. Those elected representatives of the congregation met weekly. My father and both my grandfathers were, or had been, deacons of the same congregation. Nobody ever had to teach me that the Church is the whole body of Christ's people: I was born to it not as an idea or an ideal but as the working principle of the life of the congregation, reflected in a devotion of time, talents, and goods to the church which I have never seen excelled, and certainly not in the Church of England.

The congregation reached out beyond itself mainly through the strong missionary interest which prevailed. But "the Church" meant "our congregation," and the Congregational Union was—in fact and in our feeling about it—not a Church but a piece of machinery whereby congregations helped each other or acted together publicly. Critics often said that this isolation of the congregation would breed heresy in doctrine, but it hardly ever did, for the reason that theological education was long, thorough, and greatly prized: people expected to be taught from the pulpit, not merely exhorted.

The prevailing theological atmosphere of our congregation, as of others, was liberal, and liberal too were the politics of most of the members. A great gulf separated Anglicans and Free Churchmen. On the one side was the Established Church, with its bishops in the House of Lords and all the trappings of the state connection, which was yet a home for many types of piety, theology, and ecclesiastical principle; a typically English institution based on comprehensiveness, if not on compromise. On the other side lay the Free Churches, very different from each other in origin and ethics and not at all at one in doctrine or discipline. The very comprehensiveness and tolerance of the Church of England made her attitude to those outside one of uncomprehending astonishment, degenerating at times into sharp impatience. The memories of past disabilities and penalties and the experience of continuing pressures prevented most Free Churchmen from seeing in the Church of England anything but a church of privilege, power, and possessions. Personal encounter, either of leaders or of rank and file, was rare.

The main continuing grievance of the Free Churches in the early years of this century was the question of the Church Schools. The Church of England owned two-thirds of the nation's schools, and since in many areas there was no other school, children of Free Church parents had to attend them. (My mother used to sit behind a curtain at school while the other children learned their Catechism.) An Education Act of 1902 reorganizing and improving public education set up a certain degree of control over Church Schools and in return gave grants to them out of public funds (the rates). The indignation of the Free Churches at the perpetuation by public money of a detested system flared up into a most bitter campaign, and many Free Churchmen, including an uncle of my father's, a Baptist minister, refused to pay rates, were prosecuted, and fined or imprisoned. The results of all this were very great. Relations between the Free Churches and the Establishment reached a new low ebb; the liberal party came into power in overwhelming strength and was largely sustained there by a phenomenon unique in English politics, the "nonconformist conscience," ardent against privilege and for social reform; but the bitterness of the controversy between churches did incalculable harm to the cause of religion in England.

I grew up in the shadow of these events. I heard individual Anglicans spoken of with admiration, even affection, but the Church of England was remote, unknown, suspect. Yet the questions which were to lead me in the end into the Church of England were already presenting themselves to me before I knew anything about Anglicanism. My parents had been brought up as Baptists and they held to the Baptist conviction that baptism can only rightly take place upon profession of faith by the person to be baptized, and not by others on his behalf. I was therefore told that when I knew myself to be a committed Christian, I should ask for baptism. This had a very undesirable effect; I was converted altogether more times than is good for any young person, yet always there was some lingering doubt. My baptism, when it came, far from being a religious highlight was an inglorious flop. Finding our way to the church (entirely strange to me), we got lost in a venomous London fog. The heating apparatus had failed, so that I was numb long before the waters of the baptistry closed over my head. I was deaf for three days, and was mildly teased at school. But my baptism was an important step on my journey—perhaps it was the beginning of it. At school I had begun to specialize in the study of history and it was for me a real passion. I inflicted on my classmates illustrated accounts of the wonderful buildings which, in my holidays, I bicycled miles to see. Many of these were churches, not only historical monuments but the homes of living worship. I began to ask questions: were the Baptists right about baptism and everybody else wrong? Was the historic picture I gained in my own church right either? For it seemed on that account that Christian history began with the early Church, broke off, and was renewed in the same form by the Congregationalists of the sixteenth century. My historical studies made the continuance of the Church through the ages and the oneness of the Christian tradition from the earliest times a matter of great interest and importance to me.

I began also in my late teens to think about the nature of a sacrament, and again it was the shock of my baptism and the anxiety I had felt as to whether I was in a state of grace which drove me to questioning. The emphasis in what I had been taught was so much on *our* action. Baptism, in our congregation, was the dedication of the child; the communion of the Last Supper was a memorial feast; the Baptist minister who prepared me for baptism spoke of it as an act of witness to what God had already done for me. But about this time my grandmother came to live with us. She had been brought up as an Anglican and it had been a great leap over the wall for her, at eighteen, to marry my grandfather. (On the eve of the marriage he received an anonymous note which read, "Be ye not unlawfully yoked together with unbelievers"— an indication of how feeling ran in the little country town.) In her old age, her mind went back to the church in which she was confirmed, and it was from her that I first heard the words of the Prayer of Humble Access. What if it should be that the sacrament was a gift from God, immediate, specific, and actual?

Four years of university life at Cambridge brought me for the first time into close contact with Anglicans, both teachers and contemporaries. I forsook history and turned to theology for my final degree. But the greatest influence on me came not from the classroom but from the Student Christian Movement. Here I was constantly discussing, studying, and praying with Anglicans, and beginning to understand Anglican worship. But the effect of life in the Movement was as much to strengthen my loyalty to my own church as to draw me to any other. One thing happened at a Student Movement summer conference which was a turning point in my life. As I knelt in the chapel at an Anglican Communion Service as a non-communicating worshipper and we sang a hymn about unity, I felt an overwhelming sense of horror and misery that this sacrament, which in all churches we held most dear, and which had been given by Christ to bind us all to Him, was the very point at which we were most obviously and deeply divided. I became utterly convinced that the disunity of the Church of Christ was in very truth the rending of His Body and was sinful, and I resolved then and there to devote my life in any way which God might show me for the healing of the wounds in His Body.

The fellowship of the Student Christian Movement could show one the fact of Christian divisions and open one's eyes to the very real unity of faith which, by God's grace, underlay them, but no change could be effected except through the churches themselves. So when I married an Anglican it seemed to both of us right to stay in the church to which we belonged and to try to work out in the personal sphere what the tensions were. It seemed that the place where we could make the contribution we wanted to make was South India, and it was to us a touching underwriting of our youthful idealism that the principal of an Anglican theological college should be willing to accept my husband for training on the understanding that his ordination should be deferred until the negotiations for church union in South India were complete.

We sailed in 1932 to work in education under the London Missionary Society which, although it drew its support from Congregationalists, had a considerable number of others on its staff. When we returned on leave in 1939, to be caught in England at the outbreak of the war, the union which had seemed so near in 1932 had received a series of checks and seemed to be almost indefinitely postponed. The church under which we had worked was a union of Congregationalists and Presbyterians. There were many fine people in it, both ministers and laymen, Indian and European. But when a church is set in a wholly non-Christian environment, questions of church discipline are of critical importance, and also of great difficulty. The great weakness of Congregationalism appeared when one saw a minister at the mercy of his own congregation and without any authority higher than himself to support him (or to correct him). I began gradually to see that the *pastor pastorum* with his spiritual authority exercised not only at crises but all the time was an essential part of what makes the Church the Church, and that any fuller unity must contain it. But this growing sense of church order strengthened my belief that Congregationalism, when practiced according to its original principles, preserves something in the responsible life of the congregation and in the understanding of the office of deacon which the Church of England lacks.

But in the end what brought me into the Church of England was not hard thinking but personal need. In the middle of the war, separated from husband and children, carrying heavy responsibilities and anxieties, I came to see my own need for the sacrament. I approached a wise priest and asked whether, as the wife of an Anglican, I could come to the altar. He answered, "Yes: but if you continue to accept the privileges, I shall ask you why you do not assume the duties." I was confirmed shortly afterwards into that Church to which in assent and affection I knew myself already to belong.

11

OWEN C. THOMAS

Trained as a scientist, and serving in this field for the Navy in the last war, the Rev. Dr. Owen C. Thomas is Assistant Professor of Theology at the Episcopal Theological School. He was born in 1922, graduated from Hamilton College, and was awarded the Elihu Root Fellowship for graduate work in science, which he undertook in the Physics Department of Cornell University, where he held a graduate assistantship. During the war he served as an officer in scientific work in the Office of Naval Research.

After the war Dr. Thomas served as a lay assistant at St. John's Church, Lafayette Square, in Washington, and then went to the Episcopal Theological Seminary at Cambridge. After his graduation he received a Kent Fellowship from the National Council on Religion in Higher Education, and studied for the Ph.D at Union Theological Seminary and Columbia University, where he was awarded a University Fellowship. He served as Chaplain for College Work for the Diocese of New York before his appointment to the faculty of the Episcopal Theological School. He is married and has recently become the father of twins.

OWEN C. THOMAS

ASIDE from an annual visitation under the auspices of my aunt and the rigors of a required college chapel, I never went to church until I was twenty-one and out of college. My grandparents were devout Christians and my grandfather was a Methodist minister, but, as was normal in the first quarter of this century, my parents had nothing to do with the Church after they were married. A devout nurse once taught me and my brother "Now I lay me down to sleep...," but when some of my friends told me they were going to "Sunday School," I didn't know what they were talking about. I remember looking over the family bookshelf soon after I learned to read and wondering what the "Holly Bibble" was, as I pronounced it. There was another book next to it entitled "The Children's Bibble," which added to my confusion. I remember being quite startled at the age of six when, on the night of the sinking of the British ship *Vestris* off Virginia on November 12, 1928, my mother, moved by her early Christian training, suggested that we should pray for those who had died.

Required chapel at Hamilton College meant nothing to me except that I enjoyed singing the hymns. I recently tasted the other end of this when, preaching at Hamilton, I was devastated by the impassive reception I met. Now I know what those preachers I didn't listen to were putting up with. I always used all my chapel cuts early in the term, and I remember my astonishment upon discovering that one of my fraternity brothers went to chapel even when he had cuts left. I thought I had beaten the game when I made the

Dean's List with the privilege of unlimited cuts, only to discover to my horror that I was to receive an even greater privilege, that of taking attendance in chapel!

At Hamilton I majored in physics, mathematics, chemistry, and scientific German. Apart from a few survey courses I managed to escape getting a liberal education. Only one course really made me think; it was a survey of English literature taught by Thomas Johnston. This opened up a whole new realm of experience to me and left me completely befuddled and in a daze for several weeks. I was haunted by Wordsworth's *Prelude*. Here was a whole new world I never consciously knew before, and yet it seemed strangely familiar. I now understand that when you start from scratch, as I did, you don't start with Christian religious experience but with pagan religious experience, and Wordsworth's nature mysticism and romantic pantheism were the medium of this for me.

The outbreak of World War II brought me out of my daze, and since I was good at mathematics and the natural sciences, a professor convinced me that I should study physics and help out in the war effort. I received the Elihu Root Fellowship from Hamilton for graduate study in science, and a graduate assistantship in the Physics Department at Cornell, where I started the long grind for the doctorate in physics. Those were exciting days in the physics world, with hush-hush projects going on in the next room and colleagues disappearing regularly to go "out West" on another secret project, which later turned out to be the Los Alamos atomic energy laboratory. I was fascinated with physics and mathematics, but it was a purely intellectual fascination similar to that which one has for bridge and double-crostics.

Before leaving Hamilton, however, and spurred on by encounter with the romantic poets, I had decided that I should look into this "religion" business on which so many people seemed to spend so much time and energy. This idea was furthered by my meeting a young lady at Wells College who had been brought up in the Church but who was having serious doubts. We discovered that we were covering the same ground but in opposite directions. Talking with her helped me to get a new perspective on my fascination with physics and math. I remember once announcing triumphantly to her that I had figured out an equation for the motion of a cart with a swinging pendulum on it which was rolling down an incline, a good exercise in theoretical mechanics. Her devastating reply was "So what?" This really set me to thinking. So what, indeed. So what if I could solve all problems in mechanics and in electromagnetic and nuclear theory too. Slowly I began to perceive that math and physics did not deal at all with the most serious and interesting questions, what I would now call the existential questions.

Finally, I went to the Presbyterian chaplain at Cornell, the Rev. Frederick Brink, and said, "I guess I've got to look into religion. I wasn't brought up in the Church, so I don't know the first thing about it. But a lot of people seem to get a lot out of it, and I'd like to find out what this is." The chaplain very wisely prescribed two measures: reading and joining some church group. So in 1943 at the age of twenty-one I began for the first time to read the New Testament. I also read some of those little books in the Hazen series, Walter Marshall Horton's *God* and Georgia Harkness' *Religious Living*. These whetted my appetite and I devoured everything I could get my hands on. I spent hours in the library of Barnes Hall, the old Cornell United Religious Work building, reading and browsing and wondering what all this meant for my physics.

I found myself in a group known as the Sage Chapel Associates, which was described by Dr. Mendenhall, then the director of the Cornell United Religious Work, as a discussion group for "reverent agnostics." We met on Sunday evenings with the Sage Chapel preacher of the morning. Here is where I met some of the great preachers on the college circuit and had a chance to ask them questions. My membership in the Presbyterian student group got me involved in the Student Christian Movement and I attended several conferences. The sense of Christian fellowship and devotion that I found here moved me deeply, and along in here somewhere I decided that there really was such a being as God, and I began to pray.

My friend at Wells College was an Episcopalian and through her I met the Episcopal chaplain at Cornell, the Rev. Gerald O'Grady. He was only a few years older than I and we became close friends. He was just out of seminary and had a deep and compelling sense of the Church and the liturgy, something new to me and something of a contrast to the sentimental approach to these things which I often found in the S.C.M. The chaplain wanted his students to attend Sage Chapel and participate in the S.C.M., but he knew this was not enough. One evening we had been discussing this, and he dropped a remark that made me think. He said, "That's fine, having all the circuit preachers at Sage Chapel, but that's not the Church. What I want to know is, what are all those kids going to do when they go back home to their parishes where the preaching may be poor? I want to make darn sure my kids learn to say their prayers." This emphasis on formal corporate and private worship with serious content and purpose was a note that sounded right to me and made a permanent impression. This was the beginning of my realization that the Episcopal Church took prayer and worship more seriously than other groups I had run into.

My roommate at Cornell was a devout Roman Catholic who had attended Mass daily all his life. One morning I went with him to the service in the big auditorium at Barnes Hall. It meant nothing to me because I didn't have the slightest idea of what was going on. Undaunted, however, I began attending the mid-week Episcopal Holy Communion Service. Being in English, this made a little more sense, but it was still mostly lost on me, because the center of the Christian Faith was still a mystery to me. The one thing that did impress me, however, was the seriousness, objectivity, and dignity of the service, which told me that something was really going on here.

Then suddenly in 1944 the V-12 program in which I had been teaching physics folded up and I was classified 1A. My colleagues and I had heard about Ph.D.'s in physics peeling potatoes in the Army and swabbing decks in the Navy, so we began to look for some place in the services where our training in physics could be of some use. I visited and was offered jobs at the Manhattan Project at Columbia and the Oak Ridge plant in Tennessee. I couldn't figure out what was going on at these places and they couldn't say, so I finally signed up with the Navy and was sent to the Naval Research Laboratory in Washington and put to work on radar research.

But just before leaving for Washington I went to the annual New York State S.C.M. conference at Silver Bay on Lake George, and toward the end of the conference I was baptized by Mr. O'Grady. Looking back on this, I realize that I didn't really know what I was doing, but I knew I wanted to be in the Christian Church and I knew this was the way in.

I arrived in Washington on a Saturday and moved into a little apartment in Congress Heights just above Bolling Field. The next day, feeling very conscientious as a brand new Episcopalian, I made a pilgrimage to Washington Cathedral. The next Sunday I sought out the nearest Episcopal church, the Church of the Holy Communion in Congress Heights, and in my zeal went to both services. This produced a call by the rector whom I came to know as a devoted Christian man. I joined his Confirmation Class and was confirmed in November by Bishop Dun, who, five years later, was to ordain me.

I moved into a larger apartment with a liberal Roman Catholic, a lapsed Lutheran, a devout Southern Presbyterian, and a cynical agnostic. There were many discussions of religion both in the apartment and in the lab. I took on all comers and had a workout that I shall never forget.

In a few months I found myself the chairman of the young adults' group at the Church of the Epiphany on G Street in Washington. One evening our speaker was Dr. Pike, a young lawyer who had been a lapsed Roman Catholic and had finally, after considerable wandering in a "far country," found his way into the Episcopal Church. He had recently been ordained and, still in the Navy, was a part-time assistant at St. John's Church, Lafayette Square. He spoke of how God through Christ could change people. Although this was a part of the Christian Faith that I still understood very little, it rang a bell with me. I sought him out, and about a week later we had dinner together at the Hay-Adams Hotel across from St. John's and exchanged stories as to how we had landed in the Episcopal Church.

From then on my church activities shifted to St. John's and I met regularly with a group of George Washington students at the Pikes'. This was the first really close-knit

Christian community I had ever known, and it was a wonderful thing. As I look back on it now, no doubt with considerable idealization, it seems like the golden age of my Christian life. At least it was my first taste of the Christian life in its fullness. Most of us helped out at St. John's in one way or another on Sundays, and then we all had dinner together. One of my clearest memories of those days was the easy way we were able to take into the group and draw out some pretty unattractive people. Our meetings on Thursday nights at the Pikes' were searching discussions of the Christain Faith and life, concluding with Evening Prayer. The discussions were usually led by Jim Pike and the Rev. Howard Johnson, another assistant at St. John's, but occasionally others were brought in, among them Canons Wedel and Smith, Professor A. T. Mollegen, and the Rev. Brooke Mosley. The Catholic Faith as the Episcopal Church had received it was communicated to us by some of the best Christian minds of our day.

Great things happened in that little group: people's lives were changed. One example will suffice. Anne Thaler, one of our most faithful members, was engaged to one Harry Dalzell, who was an Air Force gunner overseas. Her rediscovery of the Christian Faith in our group made her wonder about her relation to Harry, who was an agnostic. Everyone was concerned about this. ("If one member suffers, all suffer together.") It was with deep concern in our hearts and a prayer on our lips that we welcomed Harry to one of our meetings when he came home. The power of the Spirit moving in that group was irresistible, and at one of our evening services at St. John's a few months later I was a witness at Harry's Baptism. Soon thereafter I read the lesson at his Confirmation, and in the spring of 1946 I was best man at his marriage to Anne. In the meantime Anne had finished college, so now she went to work and Harry went through George Washington and then the Virginia Theological Seminary. Six members of that group are now clergymen in the Episcopal Church, and the rest are faithful laymen and laywomen.

In the fall of 1945 Messrs. Johnson and Pike started a new and creative Church School program at St. John's, and all of us were drawn into it. It was a combination of the Bible story, the Church Year, and a system of theology. Johnson was the master mind of it and he met weekly with those of us who were teachers and expounded the Bible and the Christian Faith to us.

About this time I got out of the Navy and decided that I would like to do some kind of church work for a while to see if it was for me. One evening as Howard Johnson and I were walking home from a party, I broached the idea to him. We walked in silence for a while, and then he said, "Owen, this is providential. In a month I am leaving St. John's, and Jim has to divide his time between St. John's and courses at the Virginia Seminary. We need you at St. John's."

In December I moved into the apartment on the third floor of the parish house of St. John's and began one of the most hectic jobs I ever hope to hold. I was in charge of the Church School with its new program, the young people's group, an acolytes' guild, and assisted in the college work program at George Washington with its weekly meetings and Sunday evening services. Moreover, I called at a nearby hospital, and in my spare time I worked for the rector, Dr. C. Leslie Glenn, now returned from the Navy in his capacity as president of the Church Society for College Work. I was now thinking of theological seminary, and Dr. Glenn said that if I lived through this without losing my mind or my faith, I was all set.

It was a wonderful year. For the first time in my life I lived in a Christian parish through the liturgical year. I don't think anyone who has been brought up in the Church can know what this means to someone who has never known it before. I got to know Christian parish life from the inside and I knew this was for me.

In the spring of 1946 I became a postulant under Bishop Dun. That spring I commuted out to the Virginia Theological Seminary in Alexandria and sat in on a course on revelation taught by Professor Mollegen and one on the Church, the sacraments, and the ministry taught by Dean Zabriskie. In the summer of 1946, not wasting any time, I attended Union Theological Seminary and took courses with Professors Reinhold Niebuhr, Paul Tillich, and John Knox. In the fall I entered the Episcopal Theological School in Cambridge with three of my friends from that group at St. John's.

Since I started from scratch, how did I happen to land in the Episcopal Church and its ministry? In the first place I was drawn to it by the people I happened to meet who represented it, and this was largely a matter of chance. But I was also drawn to it by the deep seriousness in regard to the Christian Faith and life which I found in it everywhere. This seemed to me at the time to be in sharp contrast with much of the sentimentality and irrelevance of the liberal Protestantism I had found in some other groups. Because the Episcopal Church has always been more or less liberal in the right sense of not squinting at any of the results of modern secular science, it has avoided the worst results of theological liberalism. For the same reason the Episcopal

Church never offered any stumbling blocks to my scientific background. Although I did not understand all this at the time, this was a real source of its attraction for me.

Closely connected with this was the fact that the Episcopal Church mediated to me the reformed Catholic Faith of the Christian ages, relevant and yet not watered-down. Without excuse or embarrassment the whole faith of St. Paul and St. John, of Augustine and Aquinas, of Luther and Calvin was given to me in a way I could grasp and make my own. Along with this went that great and rich liturgical deposit which is the Book of Common Prayer. Part of all this was my good fortune in running into some of the keenest minds in the Christian Church today within the short course of a year.

It soon became clear to me that the Anglican Communion was, potentially at least, best fitted to commend the whole Christian Gospel to the world today. This is not boasting, because most of this fitness is still potential, unfortunately. But at least I had a real chance to choose what branch of the Catholic Church I would be a member of, and everything I have learned about the Christian Faith and the Episcopal Church since then makes me deeply thankful that I landed where I did.

12

EMANI SAMBAYYA

Raised as a Hindu and a Brahman, the Rev. Canon Emani Sambayya is now Vice-Principal and Lecturer in Liturgiology at Bishop's College, Calcutta. He is a graduate of Calcutta University (Master of Arts in Mental and Moral Science) and Serampore University (Bachelor of Divinity). He served as Secretary of the Student Christian Movement from 1935 to 1937 and studied for a year at Westcott House, Cambridge. In 1940 and 1941 he served as Assistant Chaplain of Byculla, Bombay. He has been on the staff of Bishop's College, Calcutta, since October, 1941, first as Lecturer in the New Testament. In 1948 he was appointed the Metropolitan's Commissary for Nandyal, ministering to a group of "continuing Anglicans" in South India. Thereafter he studied for the degree of Master of Sacred Theology at Union Theological Seminary in New York City. From there he came to his present post and recently became one of the canons of St. Paul's Cathedral, Calcutta. Canon Sambayya contributed a chapter on "The Mission of the Anglican Communion" to the volume The Genius of the Anglican Communion.

EMANI SAMBAYYA

FROM whatever angle I look at it the conclusion appears to be the same: I am deeply indebted to a number of persons from whom I have learned the more excellent way. The compelling character of Anglicanism is seen in the lives of men, and they have imparted to me something of the faith by which they lived. Let me explain.

It was a large and well appointed Wesleyan Methodist mission station. I was one of the many Hindu masters in the mission school. One or two sharp blows of misfortune put me in a receptive mood. The Book of Psalms which I was reading spoke to my soul directly. All that I wished to say to God was said there in a timeless language.

There was something arresting about the ordered life of Benjamin, whom I used to meet daily on my way to the school. He was a peculiar person of an individualistic type of piety. His simple love of Jesus was arresting. Cultivating his friendship, I used to read the Bible with him, and pray. He was not much of a teacher, yet through him the claims of Jesus on my love and loyalty became inescapable. I cheerfully gave up all to which my birth as a Brahman had entitled me and was made a member of Christ through Baptism.

What my friends call "the great upheaval" in my life occurred when I was barely twenty. I have never found it easy to communicate satisfactorily the experience of my conversion from Brahmanism to Christianity. It was not as though I turned from rank paganism to a life of religious devotion. Even from my school days I was fully aware of the rich heritage of South Indian Brahmanism with its unbending orthodoxy and unique social privileges. I was brought up to perform my religious duties with meticulous care. I was taught the Bible in the Mission School which I attended.

What drew me to Christ in the first instance was His passion and death, and the realization that it was for me and for my salvation. But when I became aware of the call to the discipleship of our Lord there ensued a struggle which absorbed my whole being. As I read the Bible the purpose of God for my life gradually became apparent. It never occurred to me that I ought to make a comparative study of the relative merits of Hinduism and Christianity. The one was so different from the other that comparison seemed hardly possible. The question which engaged my mind for a long period was whether I could not fulfill my call to the discipleship of my Master within the orbit of Hinduism and Hindu society. Hinduism is so amorphous and comprehensive that I thought that Christian discipleship was compatible with membership in the Hindu community.

The relevance of the Church and membership in the Church to Christian profession was not explained to me at the time, though this was to come later in my life. Christianity meant (for me) a personal devotion to a personal Lord whose call was compelling. It was particularly difficult to answer the call by reason of the fact that the bulk of the Christian community in India consisted of outcastes. It seemed utter madness to throw away with both hands all the advantages to which my birth as a Brahman entitled me, and cast my lot with the outcaste Christians. Such has always been the consequence of Baptism in India. The summons to own Christ publicly and come under His rule became so insistent that it was impossible to have peace of mind without submitting to Baptism.

So I launched out into the deep at the bidding of the Master. A storm was brewing ahead. The news of my Baptism reached my folk and caused deep consternation at home. A week later they arrived in force to reclaim me to the bosom of the Hindu fold. I went with them and put myself under their care for a few days. They were deeply hurt at my having brought disgrace upon the family and the community. They generously offered to take me back in the event of my submitting to the ceremony of purification; and assured me that all would be well ere long. I took no advantage of the offer. Then they proposed that I should consent to live with them as "a Christian at heart" with no contacts with outcaste Christians. I would not be dissuaded from my original resolve. All the time I felt that I was being upheld in a remarkable manner; and one day I walked out of the house with my bundle of clothes, saying to myself the Twenty-third Psalm, to the profound dismay of my household.

The years that followed were marked by the growing experience of Christian fellowship, and I learned in an increasing measure the meaning of our Lord's words: "There is no man that hath left house, or brethren, or sisters, or father, or mother, or wife, or children, or lands, for my sake, and the gospel's, but he shall receive an hundredfold now in this time, houses, and brethren, and sisters, and mothers, and children, and lands, with persecutions; and in the world to come eternal life" (Mark 10:29-30).

Yet I was militantly anti-Church. All that mattered to me was my love and loyalty to Jesus Christ. Though my first association had been with the Methodists, I knew precious little about Methodism. I could not make out the difference between a Calvinist and a Lutheran, or between a Methodist and a Baptist. On one occasion I was introduced to a most impressive looking gentleman with a beard, one of the bish-

ops of the Syrian Orthodox Church. I at once concluded
that everyone with a beard must be a bishop. What *is* a
bishop, anyway? I wondered.

A few years later I embarked on the study of divinity at
an interdenominational college. During my first summer
holiday I went to stay with a newly inaugurated religious
community of English priests living in the Indian style. There
my daily delight were the Eucharist and the Office of Compline, notwithstanding my complete ignorance of the liturgy
or the Daily Offices. The Eucharist with full ceremonial had
an irresistible appeal to me. From that time onwards I made
it a point to attend the Anglican church services wherever
possible. For the first time I learned with dismay that I would
not be permitted to communicate in the Anglican Church.
In any case the English-speaking Anglican churches in India
at that time had an air of exclusiveness about them. On two
occasions I was refused admission into the church by the
ignorant verger, who would not take the risk of allowing
an Indian in the national dress to a service which the Viceroy
was attending.

It was during my days as a seminarian that I first saw
and heard the man who was to have a far-reaching influence
upon my life—Philip Loyd, then Bishop of Nasik. Though
I was greatly attracted to him I was afraid to speak to him.
Inwardly I longed to learn many things from him. My spiritual life was poverty-stricken. No one taught me how to pray
properly nor brought home to me the necessity of feeding
the soul on prayer and the Blessed Sacrament.

A little while after my seminary I joined the staff of the
Student Christian Movement. It was an enterprise rich in
friendship; and the constant traffic in personnel and knowledge created by it across national frontiers was most stimu-
lating. The Far Eastern Conference of the World's Student

Christian Federation in Java in 1933 brought me the fruitful friendship of Dr. Visser 't Hooft, the General Secretary of the W.S.C.F. His learning was immense, and his theological outlook robust. As I cultivated his valuable friendship I found myself learning more and more of New Testament theology. I owe my understanding of the Bible as the book of redemption to him and later on to Dr. C. H. Dodd at Cambridge.

My work as the traveling secretary of the Student Christian Movement in North India brought me into touch with two outstanding men in the Indian Church. On the northeastern frontier of India, tucked away among the tea plantations, was living George Hubback, the celibate Bishop of Assam. He had about him a cleansing type of personal holiness which was most attractive. But why was my spiritual life lacking the joy and compelling force of that of this vigorous and holy bishop? To know him was to be deeply dissatisfied with one's life. The other person was Bishop Loyd, whom I approached this time through the good offices of a mutual friend. He was the embodiment of all that was best and beautiful in Anglicanism. His personal charm and infectious holiness were his unfailing weapons; and it spelled disaster to the existing allegiance of any non-Anglican who drew very close to him. I was no exception. He was the soul of charity, and the beauty of holiness radiated from his common life. I have often said to myself that he has been one of the rare gifts which the Church of England had conferred on India. Here I found what I had always wanted—that by which Philip Loyd lived.

About this time Dom Bernard Clements' little book entitled *When Ye Pray* fell into my hands. It opened for me a window into the land of prayer. I felt that I could learn a great deal from Dom Bernard if only he were available; and when I was invited to attend, as a youth delegate, the Ecumenical Conferences of Oxford and Edinburgh in 1937 it was no small thrill to discover that Dom Bernard of All Saints', Margaret Street, was my host in London. When I rang the bell at No. 7 Margaret Street the door opened and I was warmly greeted by an outsized monk in the Benedictine habit, who was none other than my genial host. My three weeks' stay with him was in a real sense like my admission into the portals of Anglicanism. With his characteristic humor and commendable patience my host and friend answered my numerous questions and taught me many things about the Faith in an artless fashion. Was it true that he always prayed in Latin? "Yes, my dear friend, I say the Divine Office in Latin, but when I wish to talk to the Almighty I do so in my mother tongue!" The High Mass on Sundays at All Saints' filled me with strange satisfaction. At first it seemed theatrical, but very soon I found myself being swept into the action of the Eucharist. The influence of Dom Bernard on my life is quite out of proportion to the short period of our friendship in London. The discussions at Oxford and Edinburgh were beyond my depth; but at these conferences I had as it were a kaleidoscopic view of world Christianity. For the first time in my life I perceived how central was the Church to the Christian Faith. When the conferences ended the question of my offering myself to the sacred ministry began to present itself seriously to my mind. It was no longer easy for me to dismiss the suggestion and I needed help and counsel.

During the crossing of the Channel to Dieppe I opened my heart to my dear friend Visser 't Hooft, who always had my welfare at heart. He on the one hand, and Dom Bernard on the other, seemed to be presenting two different confessions of the Christian Faith—one Calvinist and the other Catholic. After listening to me patiently, "Wim" said, "If I were you I should consider ministry in the Anglican Communion, which is much more Church-centered than any other communion; and what is greatly lacking in Indian Christianity at present is the Church sense." The next ten days he and I were engrossed in the Bible study conference of the W.S.C.F. in a small village in the vicinity of Paris. This afforded me an insight into the thought-world of continental Protestantism with its flair for the Bible.

Back in India and with the S.C.M., I found that the call to the ministry was pressing for an answer. The decision seemed difficult as I did not at that time belong to any of the denominations of the Church. In the words of C. S. Lewis, I was like a person who had arrived at the house and had been ushered into the hall. Surely no one can live in the hall for any length of time. I must soon knock at one of the many doors which led from the hall. At about this time I found great satisfaction in saying Morning and Evening Prayer from the Book of Common Prayer daily. I spent three days with Philip Loyd finding out everything about the Anglican Communion. What about non-Anglicans and the Holy Communion? What exactly were the bishops for? Was that cassock really necessary? There could have been no better teacher than Philip Loyd. He talked as one who was grateful to the church of his Baptism.

Sometime in 1938 I wrote and informed the bishop of my desire to offer myself to the sacred ministry under him. I do not fully remember what he wrote at the time in reply. He said something about the nature of priesthood and asked whether I was prepared to be broken as the host is broken at the altar for the sake of the people. It was a disturbing analogy but put me in a right state of mind concerning priesthood. He then handed me over to the Bishop of Calcutta and the Metropolitan of India, the Most Rev. Foss Westcott. I was trembling with fear when I was called for the interview. "I have heard about you," said the Metropolitan, "but I would like to know why you desire to work as a priest in the Anglican Church." This is a question which I had been trying to answer all the while, like the other question as to why I had become a Christian. I was unnerved by the bishop's blunt question and blurted out something to the effect that the emphasis on the sacraments and the life of discipline in the Anglican Communion had attracted me. After the usual preparation I received the Sacrament of Confirmation in the bishop's private chapel.

Ordination had to wait till I received further training. I was sent to Westcott House, Cambridge, to sit at the feet of the late Canon B. K. Cunningham. Before going abroad, while still with the Student Christian Movement, I came into close touch with the Oxford Mission Brotherhood of Epiphany, an English society of mission priests living under solemn vows. As I stayed in the holiday home of the order at Shillong during my travels in Assam, Fr. Strong used to explain to me the purpose of Religious Life, the joy of priesthood, and the supreme privilege of offering to God daily the perfect sacrifice of Christ in the Eucharist. Before I took leave of him, Fr. Strong presented me with copies of his two well-known books, *The Incarnation of God* and *Lectures on Christian Character*. Fr. Strong's excellent teaching, which throughout is based on Scripture, was originally delivered in the form of lectures to the Sisters of Epiphany whose Warden he had been till the time of his death in 1944. His writings and my personal talks with him have gone a long way in establishing me in the Faith.

Cunningham of Westcott House was a legend among priests and ordinands of England. His pupils are legion. There was no doubt that young English ordinands flocked to Westcott House mainly for the privilege of living in the presence of B. K. Cunningham during the important years of their preparation for the ministry. It meant everything for them. The canon was stone deaf and conversed but little, and that too through a hearing aid, but he exercised a profound influence over the young men under his care. He had a soft corner in his heart for the ordinands from India, for he himself had been a lay brother in Cambridge Brotherhood of Ascension, Delhi, before the First World War. His undemonstrative but deep piety, his abounding charity and sober scholarship made a lasting impression on me. Canon Cunningham was yet another person who, under God, showed me the beauty of holiness as nurtured in the bosom of the Anglican Communion. It was said of him that he was the greatest Churchman of his generation.

It was an act of unforgettable kindness on the part of Professor C. H. Dodd to have taken me under his wing and taught me New Testament Theology during my residence in Westcott House. One had to be told that he was a member of the Congregational Church; his writings and preaching were fully consonant with Anglicanism. I spent my vacations visiting some of the leading Anglican religious communities, where I had friends. The Franciscans in their holy poverty, and rendering loving service to the tramps, the Cowley Fathers with their emphasis on contemplative life without overlooking the active aspect, and the Benedictines whose vocation is to offer God a perfect worship—all testified to man's primary obligations with reference to God. I realized what a strength the religious communities are to the Church and how powerful is their witness. I also saw some of the results of the liturgical life of the Church in the shape of the London East End Missions. Some of the parishes in areas like the Victoria docks showed how the stream of life which flowed from under the altar of the temple of God was healing and fertilizing the arid and barren areas of human life.

At the end of two years' curacy in Bombay I was asked to join the staff of Bishop's College, the theological college of the Indian Province. At the time of leaving Bombay I told my parishioners that the two memories I carried with me were the Parish Eucharist which was attended by a large number of the families of the parish, and pastoral visiting. These two were closely connected in my mind.

Serving on the staff of Bishop's College at Calcutta afforded opportunities of numerous contacts, some of which contributed substantially to a deeper appreciation of Anglicanism. Westcott, the celibate bishop who lived an utterly simple life, was an apostle of peace and unity, not only in the household of Faith but in the Indian political field as well. He was most generous with his money as well as his friendship, which he offered without measure. He was in great demand in the peace parleys between the Hindus and the Muslims. His successor, Hubback, was a vigorous personality with a consuming zeal for dignified worship in the churches. Holding the view that in any given situation (in the Church) the clergy were the key, he sought to instill high ideals into his clergy by getting them together and personally teaching them.

My real discovery of Anglicanism began with my study of the Caroline Divines. Here again I learned more from the persons themselves than from their treatises. Nicholas Ferrar of Little Gidding with his entire household given up to the serving of the Lord with the daily round of worship and work—all arising from the dedication of the common life to God—showed me how religion can be integrated into the common life. George Herbert, pastor par excellence, stands forever in my thinking as the ideal of the parish priest; and his book *The Country Parson* sketches the life and work of the pastor which in the main is to gather regularly the flock of Christ and feed them on the Word and the sacraments. Edward King of Lincoln, who is nearer to our times, brought home to us the ideals of George Herbert through his life devoted to the care of souls. His life is a veritable mirror of holiness.

Among the Caroline worthies Bishop Andrewes as the master of devotional life and Bishop Jeremy Taylor as the teacher of morals and spirituality greatly attracted me. Both in his writings and in his prayers Lancelot Andrewes witnessed to a belief in the Catholicity of the Anglican Church and showed a longing to get rid of the obsession with the medieval Western Church and recover the tradition of the undivided Church. His *Private Prayers,* a classic among manuals of prayer, is a treasury of devotion. Here Bishop Andrewes shows us a new dimension of prayer embracing Heaven and earth. All his devotions are cast in the language of the Scriptures and of the early liturgies. From the writings of Bishop Andrewes one can deduce that the calling of Anglicanism is to manifest a Catholicism which is Scriptural and rational. In Jeremy Taylor the Anglicanism of the seventeenth century presented a reliable teacher of moral theology combining authority with freedom. He stands firmly in the Catholic tradition of ascetic and moral theology but with the appeal to Scripture. Further, unlike the post-Tridentine Roman moral theologians, Jeremy Taylor regarded moral and ascetic theology as one science leading to the beatific vision. He discountenanced Puritanism on the one hand and Romanism on the other and was consistently Anglican in his writings. The Churchman's piety in which feasts and fasts, the Daily Offices, the Eucharist, and the ordered system of meditation and prayer have their appointed place is convincingly taught in his devotional classic *Holy Living and Holy Dying*. I gradually discovered that the Caroline Divines returned to the primitive Catholicism of the New Testament in their writings on theology, the penitential system, and direction of spiritual life.

It was when I started reading Hooker that I felt I was getting at the heart of *Ecclesia Anglicana*. Hooker asserted the continuity of the Church of England with the historic Catholic Church, holding the view that to reform was not to sever ourselves. "In the Church we were, and are so still." As the great exponent of the *Via Media* of the Anglican Church, Hooker took the middle way between Rome, which asserted that the seat of authority lay in the edicts of the Pope, and the Puritans, who relied upon the Scriptures for an absolute and all-embracing authority. He taught that neither the word of the Scriptures nor the authority of the Church was to be flouted, but that man should be guided by reason in the reading of the Bible and in submission to authority. So in reaching a conclusion, a man after he has consulted the Scriptures and made use of his reason should rely upon the voice of the Church, if doubt were to persist.

Hooker made Incarnation the center of theology and linked it with the sacraments. On every question of theology he represented a conservative reaction to the excesses of the earlier Reformation and thus paved the way for the fuller recovery of Catholicism by the school of Andrewes and Laud. Every now and again one would come across disturbing tendencies in the formulations of Hooker, but we should go back to the temper of the mind of the Caroline Divines rather than to their literal formulations in order to get at the heart of Anglican Christianity. Theirs was not a cheap compromise between rival dogmatisms but rather a narrow way of suffering and tears marked by a refusal to tread the way of partisanship—a humility which is willing to efface all that is local and particular and which is willing to be judged by the authority of the Christian tradition which is neither in the West nor in the East in their separation. The English reformers were all along appealing to sound learning and to Scripture as understood and interpreted by the general consent of antiquity.

The task of recovering the full Catholic tradition in the Church of England began with Hooker, continued in the Caroline Divines of Laudian School, and found its climax in the life and work of the Tractarians. I learned to look upon Pusey as the greatest of the Tractarians. His life always moved me with strange delight, for in it I saw the fulfillment of my highest ideal of Christian life: sound learning combined with deep personal religion. The massiveness of Pusey's learning and his profound piety are a perpetual inspiration. He brought to bear the force of these two singular gifts on the problems of the Church of his day. The life of Pusey gave me a real insight into the nature of Catholicism, the costliness of its discipline, and the joy it imparted to the soul.

One always remembers with gratitude that it was under the guidance of Pusey that Religious Orders, which were held in abeyance for three hundred years, had been revived in the Church. I had not been aware that the lack of the Religious Life was an impoverishment to the Church till I came to know the Society of St. John the Evangelist and the Oxford Mission to Calcutta. The Religious Life as the answer to man's longing for unbroken communion with God and for a total self-giving to Him is something which I understood only after reading the life and letters of Fr. Benson Cowley. But the most convincing interpreter of the blessedness of Religious Life was Mother Edith, founder of the Oxford Mission Sisterhood of Epiphany, who to my mind was the counterpart of Edward Pusey—only less forbidding and much more winsome. Her writings, which for the most part are confined to meditations and prayers, take after the *Preces Privatè* of Bishop Andrewes.

While serving on the Negotiating Committee of Church Union in North India I became aware of tensions between High Churchmen and Evangelicals within the Anglican Church. It is easy to exaggerate these differences and feel thoroughly depressed. But underlying these party alignments is the deeper unity in the Church based on the historic Faith expressing itself through the Episcopate, and wholehearted loyalty to the Book of Common Prayer. Undoubtedly the strength of the Church lies in its liturgical life and its Bible-centeredness. It is a Scriptural Church. Its services are replete with Scripture. It maintains resolutely and consistently a Biblical religion. The Bible is the foundation of all its doctrine and practice. The Fathers of Anglicanism always appealed to Scripture as understood and interpreted by the general consent of antiquity.

By this time I have participated in a number of ecumenical conferences and have been able to know something about each of the churches which constitute the Universal Church. I am aware of the many sins of omission and commission of my church: our intolerance and pride which have driven people away from our fold; our lack of zeal for preaching the Word of God; and our sense of self-satisfaction which has often made us blind to our own shortcomings. As a reparation (shall we say?) the Anglican Church has been a pioneer in the efforts for healing the divisions in the household of God. This is true at any rate of the Anglican Communion in India. She has partially succeeded and there are hopes of further success. Under God, she is a bridge church between Rome and Protestantism; and she bids fair to be the bridge between the Latin Church and the Eastern Church which is her neighbor and friend on the Indian soil. Today Anglicanism has most to learn from the relatively unexplored treasury of Eastern Orthodoxy.

13

WILLIAM A. SPURRIER, III

Well known as an author in the field of doctrine and ethics, the Rev. William A. Spurrier, III, is Associate Professor of Religion and Chaplain of Wesleyan University. Born in 1916, he is a graduate of Williams College and Union Theological Seminary. He was ordained to the Congregational ministry in 1942 and taught religion at Amherst for two years. During the war he served as an Army chaplain with the 69th Infantry Division in the European Theatre of Operations and was decorated with the Bronze Star. He joined the Department of Religion at Wesleyan in 1946. He is a member of the National Council on Religion and Higher Education, of the American Association of University Professors, and of the Student Christian Movement.

Professor Spurrier is author of Power for Action, *an introduction to Christian ethics,* Guide to the Christian Faith, *an introduction to Christian doctrine, and* Guide to the Good Life, *a text on Christian ethics, published last fall. He has served as a member of the Authors' Committee of the Department of Christian Education, National Council of the Protestant Episcopal Church, and is editor of* The Church Review, *the publication of the Church Society for College Work. He is married and has two children.*

WILLIAM A. SPURRIER, III

THERE are at least two dangers in describing a person's change from one denomination to another. First, it is easy—even unintentionally—to disparage the Church one has left. Or the reader may feel that some experience was frustrating and therefore the writer is bitter. Second, it is also easy to regard one's change as enormously significant, one that every person should make. Or the account may appear to be egoistic, conveying the ideas that one Church was not good enough for me, and the other Church is lucky to have me aboard.

At the outset, then, I should like to try to avoid both dangers. Let me begin by affirming as sincerely as I can, that I have a deep affection and gratitude towards the denomination I left. I was born into and raised up in it, and finally ordained by it. For my nurture in the Christian Faith, I am profoundly indebted to several ministers, and three or four truly great but unsung Sunday School teachers. Later, as a minister in this denomination, it was my privilege to work with other ministers whose dedication, theological knowledge, and insight were most superior. I had no frustrating experiences, no bitter incidents which led to any "sour" feelings about the Church. There was no sudden decision, no traumatic distaste of, nor call away from, this Church. In short, I believe this denomination to be thoroughly Christian and one which contains some much-needed strengths not always found in other denominations. I did not leave it because I thought I was going from the kingdom of Hell to the Kingdom of God.

In the second place, let me also try to make clear that I regard my reasons for changing as strictly personal. I do not believe that everyone should necessarily make the change I did. I do not affirm that my reasons are universal reasons. Nor do I believe that there was anything unusual or powerfully significant in my change. It was essentially a personal odyssey for personal reasons, and I attach no virtue or stature to my change. This account then, from my point of view, can have only the merit of description—an account of why one man changed to the Episcopal Church.

As far as I can recall, my first uneasiness about my original denomination occurred while I was in Seminary. I had been nurtured in an excessively optimistic type of liberal humanistic Protestantism. In college, I added a large amount of German Romanticism. During my senior year in college, however, I had begun to read Brunner, Kierkegaard, and Niebuhr. At Seminary, I majored under Reinhold Niebuhr and so, of course, liberal humanism took a terrific beating! Like so many others at the time, I became "another little Niebuhrean." Though by the senior year in Seminary I became at least a little critical of "Niebuhreanism," nevertheless I had become convinced that I belonged somewhere in "the classical (historic) Christian theological tradition."

My ordination occurred immediately after graduation from Seminary. At the time, I did not see any conflict between my theological position and the denomination in which I was about to be ordained. I remember that I did feel the lack of any theological tradition, or creed, or statement. But the idea of freedom seemed to permit all kinds of theological room. Hence I believed there was room for the tradition I subscribed to. I also remember thinking that my central theological beliefs were much closer to the founders of the denomination than to my contemporaries. But then, I reasoned, perhaps there will be a theological revival someday, and anyway there is no need for just "one party line." Indeed, this is perhaps the virtue of freedom, that there is no one point of view.

I remember quite clearly the statement of faith which I read at my ordination. Or rather, I remember the reaction to it. The statement was essentially a neo-orthodox one. A few of the examiners wondered if I were turning Fundamentalist! A few were a little uneasy about "a return to orthodoxy." The majority, however, were friendly but perhaps just a little surprised at "the conservative view." I was not surprised at the reaction and I regarded the whole ordination process as pleasant, serious, and meaningful.

As time went on, my uneasiness grew. As I came to know the Church and its work, further doubts arose. At the same time, I was acquainted with and often had occasion to take part in the work of the Episcopal Church. And so the inner conflict began and a long period of wrestling ensued. It would be long and boring to try to recount the pros and cons of each doubt and thought that occurred in the four years of indecision. What follows is the conclusion and decision which resulted in the change to the Episcopal Church. For purposes of clarity, the reasons can be divided into separate but not unrelated areas.

1. *Theology.* As I came to know more about the denomination to which I belonged, I became more convinced that it had pretty much sold out to liberal humanism. For me this meant that the prevailing voice of the Church was not the voice of the Gospel. Rather it was primarily a cultural voice, all too ephemeral, but what was worse, all too irrelevant. World War II had begun, the world was in agony. Yet I would read literature and attend conferences on "Building a Better World" *via* education, tolerance, reason, etc. Yet I

also knew that this ironic irrelevancy was not unique to nor confined to this denomination. This virus had long infected most of Protestantism. I also found that I was not alone in my feelings. A few of us started a little theological journal entitled *Christus Victor*. Our purpose was to do what we could towards starting a renewed interest in classical Christian theology. We did not expect much and our little venture ended when we all went off to the wars. But the problem remained. And it gnawed at me. While in the Army, I wrestled with this issue and I came to the conclusion that no theological revival was possible in this denomination because there was nothing to revive. Liberal humanism might eventually wane and neo-orthodoxy become the predominant vogue. But this would not solve the problem because neo-orthodoxy is a transient theology as is liberal humanism. And after this vogue, what?

Further, one was free to believe almost anything or nothing. It seemed to me that freedom had come dangerously close to nihilism. Most of us knew what we were against: dogmatism, narrow sectarianism, ecclesiasticism, etc. But few of us stood, positively, *for* anything. Our Church had no theology and therefore it had no voice. We were so afraid of creedalism and dogmatism that we were afraid to say what we were *not* afraid of; so tolerant we tolerated almost anything. For me, theology is of prime importance, for it is the articulate wisdom of the experience of thousands of Christians. It is the voice of the great company of saints and sinners under Christ—the Church. The Bible is central, but theology is the response to and description of the Biblical Faith in action in the lives of men. I am fully aware of the corruptions and misuse of dogmas, creeds, and theologies, of all the differences and variations, etc. But danger and misuse of a thing does not rule it out as a necessity or value.

I firmly believe in spite of all the corruptions and variations that there is such a thing as "the historic Christian Faith," that this can be articulated and stated, that it is different from all other faiths, and that within this framework there is plenty of room for freedom and diversity. I further believe that the spirit and intent of this Faith can be found in the Bible, Creeds, theology, and traditions of the Church. I also believe that no one denomination has a complete monopoly on the Christian Faith. Yet I believe that some denominations have more than other denominations. For myself, I came to believe that my denomination really lacked theological rootage and foundation. Without this foundation, I feared it would be tossed to and fro by every wind of cultural vogues or theological fads without ever finding its way back to a sure anchorage.

As I looked at the Episcopal Church, I saw that it too had been infected by excessive liberal humanism. And I was aware of its scandalous demise into deism in the eighteenth and nineteenth centuries. Yet I felt that with its Prayer Book and Creeds it always had an anchorage to which it could return, and to which, in fact, it always had. That other future wanderings might occur seemed obvious. Nevertheless, there was a home port, a rock to come back to.

Still, I was uneasy about the theology of the Episcopal Church—and I still am! What bothered me initially and still bothers me is that the Episcopal Church has not yet made up its mind about the Reformation. That is to say, it has not even decided what the Reformation was all about. Of course, some people have very definite ideas. But in general, the Church prefers to duck the issues by smugly saying, "We are both Protestant and Catholic," or "We are the bridge Church" and "We have room for both." This is too easy. It is analogous at points to say that we are a roomy club because we believe that two plus two equals both four and five—so inclusive, you know. While on other matters like Holy Communion and Apostolic Succession, we are often quite exclusive.

I do not expect the Episcopal Church to come up with some master synthesis of the Catholic and Protestant traditions. But there are some who would abolish Protestant traditions altogether, and there are others who would virtually abolish Catholic influences. Both of these groups must be resisted, in my opinion. But my primary concern is the smugness of the middle group who do not recognize the tension in these two traditions. When tension is lost or denied, then we become smug and complacent. When the tension is recognized and honestly faced, then we are alive and there is freedom in the house.

But in spite of these weaknesses and conditions, I felt that the Episcopal Church was closest to my own theological position. Clearly I neither expected it to be nor regarded it as complete. Let me put it this way: I felt that the Episcopal Church was my theological home. It had a tradition, a structure, a form. This structure seemed to me to be aligned with the historic Christian Faith. Yet there was room inside, plenty of freedom, and the possibility of lively and healthy controversy without tyranny on the one hand, or anarchy on the other. To use an analogy: a nation cannot long endure without a constitution. Slavery to the literal words of the constitution results in petrification. To have no constitution invites anarchic decay. But critical loyalty to the spirit and intent of the constitution makes for both growth and stability. The Bible, Creeds, and theology are the constitution of the Christian Church. I believe this constitution is preserved and amended in the Episcopal Church. I also believe this situation exists in the Presbyterian Church, with some minor differences. In short, I felt I could be at home *theologically* in either the Presbyterian or Episcopal Church. But, of course, there were other factors.

2. *Worship.*   As one travels along in his religious pilgrimage, worship usually becomes more central than in earlier stages. Such was the case with me. I became increasingly dissatisfied with the lack of liturgy and architectural symbols. Adoration of organ pipes seemed to me to be bad symbolism. Concentration on the sermon to the neglect of meditation, confession, thanksgiving, seemed out of proportion. I also discovered that the use of liturgical forms without theological content just didn't ring true. Ritual in such cases became theatrics, not worship; a show, not participation.

The Episcopal form of worship attracted me, in the first place, by its balanced structure. It appealed to and evoked all the aspects of religious experience—one's mind and emotions, heart and spirit. The liturgy contained the Law, judgment, confession, repentance. But also petition, praise, and thanksgiving—after forgiveness. The sermon is important, but the service does not stand or fall on whether the minister "scores a hit." Worship is bigger than either the minister or the congregation.

I also found the prayers in the Book of Common Prayer to be unmatched in both literary beauty and religious depth. Knowing that most of the prayers were wrought out of the profound experiences of Christian saints centuries ago testified to the universality of the Faith. I could understand the somewhat facetious remark that "the Prayer Book is the layman's best defense against the Pastoral Prayer." Yet for those few who can deliver a meaningful Pastoral Prayer, there is room for this too.

And of course the service of Holy Communion came to have powerful meaning for me too. I confess, however, that at the first such service I attended I was repelled and disgusted. Some of the phrases seemed archaic and barbarous. The "rush to the rail" was irritating and disconcerting. And some priests and laymen seemed to regard the service as magic. To almost all problems, they seemed to say, "Just go to Communion and everything will work out all right." After a while, I came to see that while some particular churches might misuse the service, there was something historic and deep there. I also discovered that much of my difficulty was due to my own ignorance of what Holy Communion was all about, what was behind the archaic words, what reality the symbols and rites conveyed. So the service grew upon me until it became central in worship.

3. *The Church.* Reared in an atomistic view of the Church, I also became uneasy with this concept. As my theology developed, my understanding of the nature of the Church changed. I came to believe in the historic continuity of the Church, the need for some structure and responsibility of authority. The Church's function seemed to me to be at least twofold: (1) "to preach the Word and rightly administer the Sacraments," and (2) to be the vehicle of Christian witness "yesterday, today, and tomorrow." Again, I could not accept the authoritarianism of Rome on the one hand, nor the anarchy of some of the free churches on the other. The Episcopal Church seemed to me to be the best (but not perfect) "middle ground."

There was also a practical reason for my attraction to the Episcopal Church. Faced with the problem of raising children, my wife and I came to the conclusion that what is most important in religious education for children is not

particular Bible stories or memorization of the Ten Com-
mandments or any other obvious rational education. All
these are necessary and useful. But it is our conviction that
it is the emotional religious atmosphere which is the most
influential and lasting foundation. It seemed to us that the
Episcopal Church with its emphasis on worship offered the
best chance for our children. Further, we could be reasonably
sure that wherever we might move, the worshipful atmosphere and structure would be about the same. This situation
also appealed to my wife and myself. We felt that there was
a sameness in worship and attitude wherever we might live.
And we particularly responded to the attitude that our
loyalty is first to the Church, not to the rector, that it was
really a joint enterprise of both laymen and clergy, and that
for the good of the Church, the rector puts up with our
weakness, and we with his.

4. *College Work*.   An additional attraction in my period
of transition was the Church Society for College Work. I
have always been interested in a ministry which was at least
related to college work. It seemed to me that most denominations at that time had woefully neglected this area. College
people were among the great unchurched of our time. This
was a fertile field for domestic missionary work. All churches
wonder why so many young people grow up in their Sunday
Schools, go away to college, and never come back to the
Church. Of course, there are many complex reasons. But one
of the causes is the failure of the Church to go to college with
its young people. It seemed to me that the Church Society
saw this problem and was really trying to do something
about it. As far as this part of my vocation went, I had to
decide whether I would spend a major portion of my time
trying to arouse my Church to this need (and some of us

tried to do so), or whether I could devote more positive energy through an organization already alive in the field. The latter opportunity seemed best for me, especially since I do not believe I have much gift for organizing an organization!

I have tried to state what were the chief reasons for my joining the Episcopal Church. In addition to the above description there are a host of other influential factors. But they are often so subtle, subjective, and personal that it is hard to articulate them clearly. For example, there is no doubt in my mind but that the personal friendship and influence of several Episcopal friends had much to do with my change. This does not mean that I abandoned my other friends or that other denominations are lacking in men of stature and appeal. It means that one's friends are often accidental; one just happens to be in a job where he meets a variety of people. Yet the fact remains that our friends do have a pervasive and subtle influence upon us.

I would not want to close without also affirming that my wife played no small part. Our change was a joint pilgrimage and we talked and prayed and considered the issue for several years, and finally arrived together.

Lastly, there were many other smaller influences of a subjective nature such as personal aesthetic preferences, geographical location (if I were going to live in Holland, it would be difficult to follow through in attending an Episcopal church!), and many other minor influences—the sum of which would probably be classed under personal idiosyncrasies.

In closing, then, I wish to say again that perhaps the best summary of my reasons for joining the Episcopal Church is to say, simply, that I felt more at home there than in any other Communion. At the same time I want also to reaffirm that I believe I did not come in blind and rapturous. The Episcopal Church is not perfect; it does not have a monopoly on God and Christian saints. It may not even be the best church for everyone. This account has been written almost entirely from the subjective attitude of why I joined the Episcopal Church, and it appears as if I stood, at times, in judgment on the Church and asked, "What's in it for me?" This is true, but it is also true that the Church has since judged me constantly, and offered a creative discipline and criticism. It is a home where freedom and discipline are welded together in what is for me a creative structure. So now I am sure that this is where I belong and am grateful for the many influences which led me on the pilgrimage.

14

EDUARD HEIMANN

Economist and sociologist who has taught on two continents, Dr. Eduard Heimann has been since 1933 Professor in the Graduate Faculty of Political and Social Science of the New School for Social Research, New York City. He received his Ph.D. from Heidelberg and the honorary degree of Dr. rer. pol. from Hamburg, where he was Professor of Economic and Social Sciences from 1925 to 1933. He has lectured in England, France, Switzerland, and Holland, and in 1948, 1950, 1953 and 1955 was Visiting Professor at the Universities of Göttingen and Hamburg, and at the Free University of West Berlin. Since 1950 he has been a lecturer at Union Theological Seminary. He was a consultant to the Commission on Social Reconstruction of the Protestant Episcopal Church.

Dr. Heimann is author of a number of books in German and English (some of which have been translated into German, Italian, Japanese, and Spanish), including Communism, Fascism or Democracy? History of Economic Doctrines, *and* Freedom and Order. *His two most recent works, which were published in Germany in 1954 and 1955, are* Wirtschaftssysteme und Gesellschaftssysteme *(Economic Systems and Social Systems) and* Vernunftglaube und Religion in der Modernen Gesellschaft—Liberalismus, Marxismus und Demokratie *(Faith in Reason and Religious Faith in Modern Society—Liberalism, Marxism, and Democracy). He is married and has two children and two grandchildren.*

EDUARD HEIMANN

WHEN I was baptized into the Church of Christ a number of years ago, I had not yet given thought to joining any particular denomination, except that it seemed clear, for reasons to be mentioned below, that I would not become a Roman Catholic or a Lutheran. I was not only doubtful as to which denomination to join but whether to join any at all. I did not then, and do not now, believe that the words *Extra ecclesiam nulla salus* are valid unqualifiedly, if they refer to one or the other of the churches rather than to the whole Church of Christ. Love exceeds justice; else nobody would be saved. But then I am unable to imagine that God's loving mercy should fail those who, while denying Him in thought, may be nearer Him in their actions than many a professing Christian. One may be able to argue that they are justified by their faith expressed in their actions; this would exclude the hypocrisy of mere "works." I am convinced that Abraham Lincoln, who did not belong to any church, was a man far more profound in genuine Christian insights, far more moving in proclaiming them, and far more true to them in the midst of tragedy than any other Christian layman known to me, with the possible exception of William of Orange. Nay, I was somewhat leaning toward a negative answer to the denominational question on the positive ground of a longstanding, deep, and deepening devotion to the Ecumenical Movement, which cuts across all such divisions and thus confirms, on the institutional or half-institutional level, the layman's impression that to his life those divisions mean far

less than they naturally do to those ordained by those denominations. And after all the Church of Christ is for the
layman as well as the clergy.

I present these reflections here because I still consider them
valid. In other words, they were not refuted by my asking
Dean Pike to arrange for my reception into the Protestant
Episcopal Church some years ago. The reasons for membership in a particular church, in my opinion, are on a somewhat secondary level—valid for me but not necessarily for
everybody—compared with the reasons for being a Christian.

I wonder whether it is an acceptable motivation simply to
say that the periodic pause in all other engagements and
activities, the sitting down in quiet so as to listen to the
message, the exposure to the ancient, ever new, and never
exhausted key words so as to relate them to recent private
problems and troubles, the participation with many others
in the same simple motions at the common recital of the
Creed or the mention of the Holy Trinity—all this is an invaluable help in attaining a deeper understanding and discipline. I do not include the sermon in this enumeration of
comforts derived from worship services. I have indeed
received much education from the profoundly moving sermons of the great preachers of Union Theological Seminary
at whose feet it has been my privilege to sit for many years.
But to go to Sunday services for unique preachers would
not be going to service but to those preachers. And the service
would still be the service even if it is on a more modest
level, as it must normally be; what is required is a respectable, not an exceptional, level of sermon. It is the more or
less fixed form of the service which matters, not the varying
sermons, although I am the last to deny their possible contribution. I for one was led precisely by the frequent at-

tendance to exceptional sermons to the gradual realization of the effect on me of the service itself, sermon or no sermon. A sermon may be weak; the service cannot be weak.

(I wish I could include here another varying element of the service, the hymn-singing. I am fond of singing, and I heartily enjoy the powerful chorales of the old and great hymns. The trouble is in the far too many hymns mediocre and sentimental in words and music alike, which disturb me rather than help me. I definitely feel that a hymnal reduced to one tenth of its present size would be far stronger both in religion and music and would still offer abundant variety.)

I have tried to suggest how I gradually discovered the help to me of more regular attendance of services. This at last brings me to the topic, If a church, why the Protestant Episcopal Church? The answer is implied: because it is the most churchlike church. The preacher does not appear in professorial garb; he appears as priest and is one. The congregation do not sit stiffly in their seats when praying but assume the posture natural to worship. Most important, they are not mere onlookers of the Sacrament being received in the distance by a man of higher religious rank; nor do they receive the Sacrament sitting immobile in their pews through the hands of deacons and from individual cups of guaranteed hygienic trustworthiness. They move forward to kneel at the altar and drink from the same chalice offered them by the priest as he repeats to them the sacred words—a true communion, and neither a mere spectacle without participation nor a mere parallelism of individual motions. Twenty-five years ago in Germany I had begun to wonder about these questions, from afar, and became interested in what I learned about a movement for liturgical reform (*Berneuchener Bund,* now *Michaelsbund*). The Episcopal Church does not basically need a movement for liturgical reform; it represents among the Protestant churches the sense of form and tradition.

This blend of Protestantism and tradition, naturally, is seen not only in the liturgy but in the entire spirit of Anglicanism as shaped by its unique reformation. If it is certainly true that even Luther did not want to be anything but a mere reformer instead of becoming a dissident and church founder, how much truer is it that the Church of England, divorcing itself from Rome for a bundle of good and less good reasons, has always remained the least anti-Catholic of the reformed churches, the protestant church of Catholic tradition, both in form and doctrine. We all are proudly aware that the Book of Common Prayer is the unique achievement; it is because of its use of the good wherever it could be found. One of the reasons which made the achievement possible is the humble recognition of the fact that there are diverse types of piety, and that no one person or group of persons can claim to know everything about piety. The miracle is that the eclectic method thus proclaimed still produced a fully balanced, harmonious whole, suggesting that Cranmer's gentle and scholarly hand was not without its own constructive strength.

So much the more, however, is it true that the Episcopal Church and her mother Church have been uniquely blessed in not having at their origin an overpowering religious genius of the Aquinas or Luther or Calvin types. Without their creativity the Episcopal Church would certainly not be what she is, but under their absolute claims she could never have developed her own sense of humility, moderation, and balance. There are in our Father's house many mansions, more mansions than the intellectual clarity of Thomas and the burning zeal of the great Reformers could concede;

their sharply drawn figures in the sharp light of their inspiration cast a sharp shadow. The reverse side of our blessing clearly is that eclecticism is not a constructive principle, much less a prophetic quality. Preservation is not creation, and the Church of England could never have led the Reformation. But let the sons and daughters of the Lutheran and Calvinist Revolutions not boast too loudly of the creative power of their founding fathers; it could easily turn into a fetter of docility for the children. If their fathers were creative, are they themselves anything but preservers? Nay, is it not precisely the task of a church to preserve, and trust that the wind will continue to blow where it listeth?

To me personally one point in our Church's sense of tradition is of prime importance: the continuity of social ethics. Whether more typically Anglican, or more inclined toward Thomism, as in Temple and Demant, the elaboration and application of Christian principles for institutional life has to this day remained a matter of religious dignity directly and is thereby opposed to the procedure in the Lutheran and Calvinist churches, where justice is the duty of the state, that is, of the world, and is thus below religious dignity. This dichotomy proved a disaster because it institutionalized, as it were, the Protestant tendency of concentration on one's own salvation, the religious parallel and sanction of the rising philosophical and social individualism: am I my brother's keeper? This is not to deny, of course, the effectiveness which the religious emphasis on the social responsibility of government has shown, most conspicuously in Lutheran Germany under Bismarck in the enactment of social security as early as the 1880's. But the responsibility of government for social justice is something different from the salvation of the individual soul through faith and the Christian virtue of love among the faithful: justice is divorced from love and relegated to a lower plane, it is not a topic for sermons, it is of a material nature, having to do with the distribution of material goods, while love is a spiritual relationship between souls.

That such a doctrine should have been dominant in a branch of the Church of an Incarnate God for many generations, no matter whether it could legitimately refer to the Founder or not, kept this descendant of the Jewish prophetic tradition from joining the German church as long as he was in his native Germany. Returning there after the cataclysm one finds a thoroughly changed scene, of course, in the center of which the Evangelical Academies testify to the strong social concern of clergy and laymen, and to the response which their sincerity and intelligence meet among the churchless people of industrial society. But it must be suspected that this honorable about-face has far less to do with an autonomous development of Lutheran orthodox thought than with the gradual infiltration of the long-frowned-upon teachings of religious socialism with which I had been associated during the twenties, under the influence of Paul Tillich (who certainly is of good Lutheran breed but was not in the best standing as far as his philosophy of history and society is concerned).

Against this background my first personal contact with the Episcopal Church, several years before I became a member, was bound to make a deep impression upon me. Bishop William Scarlett invited me to serve as a consultant to the Joint Commission on Social Reconstruction, of which he was chairman at that time. The Commission, of course, was a new venture, but certainly not a revolutionary one, since the Catholic tradition of the mother Church had preserved, by and large, the proper balance between the social concern and that religious individualism which dominated the other Protestant churches. (One can say that it is the tradition of community and social concern in the Church of England which is responsible for the striking social and emotional stability of that country in the turmoil of the last years, in contrast to the wild and sometimes dangerous emotional fluctuations in this country; that tradition has democratized, not liberalized, the monarchy and has thus balanced the liberalism of the Free churches.) The important and to me surprising point, when joining the Commission, was to find that it was an officially constituted church agency, whose regular members were five bishops, four other clergymen, and four laymen. Hence the private conversations even more than the discussions revealed the deep concern of the members and their real familiarity with the problems that were troubling me. All this I found crystallized in the figure of the chairman, a flaming sword of Justice in the hands of Love. No wonder that my dream of pursuing my studies at Union Theological Seminary to final ordination culminated in the hope that it might be this bishop who would ordain me.

The dream had to be given up, for a number of reasons, and I shall live and die a social scientist. But if it does not sound too arrogant to say it, instead of seeking ordination I made myself a missionary to the infidels, the most provocative kind of infidels, namely, my colleagues in the social sciences (with the exception of the New School, where I have never found anything but generous encouragement). I am deeply convinced that academic education, and particularly that in the social sciences, is a key position with which Christian strategy has so far not come to grips. If John Dewey was no doubt right in complaining, a few years before his death, that in the twenties and thirties one could be confident that America was now securely pursuing her course toward the light, but that now everything seemed to be clouded by a new obscurantism symbolized in Reinhold Niebuhr, then the one bastion which Niebuhr and his cohorts have not so far breached is the social sciences, which preach increasing specialization on techniques of psychological, sociological, or economic control without historical or philosophical, let alone religious, background. This is called the autonomy of science, whether or not the practitioner realizes that it implies a far-reaching unverifiable assumption as to man's nature as a composite of separate predictable and controllable processes without an underivable core of personality, freedom, and responsibility. The more man's consciousness of his however limited freedom can be discouraged, the better will the theorems on scientific control be verified; hence the authors of the hundreds of elaborate textbooks, the many thousands of social science teachers and researchers, and the tens of thousands of their students have a vested professional interest in denying God, man, and love. The clergy, of course, have a similar vested interest in religion but do not know how to fend off that insidious attack on the minds of the young, particularly since they themselves have imbibed too much of the same intellectual poison into their own mental organism. Hence the task is to validate the Christian understanding of man and society by demonstrating that here alone the real and profound problems of social life become accessible, while conventional science blocks the access. *Credo ut intelligam.* But I know of no ground from which a social scientist can better pursue such studies than the Protestant Episcopal Church, into which I have been received in my advanced years.

15

MICHAEL ALLEN

In August, 1954, Mr. Michael Allen was a department editor of Look *magazine; in September, he was a junior in the Episcopal Theological School in Cambridge, where he is now a middler. He was born in Paris in 1927 of American parents. He had his early education at the Friends' Seminary and the Riverdale Country School. After his freshman year at Harvard he volunteered for the Army, and by the age of eighteen was commissioned as a second lieutenant after training in an engineer electrician's school and the Engineer Officers Candidate School. After a year's service in Japan he returned to Harvard, graduating* cum laude *in history, a field in which he did graduate study at the Sorbonne. He joined the staff of* Look *in 1951. He is married and has two young sons.*

MICHAEL ALLEN

WE HAVE all suffered too many defeats. Our nation, our whole civilization, our very beings have seen too many victories for all the things we hate. And we recoil in horror.

But can we afford despair? We could, but then life itself would be lost. We can't let that happen. At least I can't. So I have turned to the Episcopal Church where I have found an answer. Defeat can indeed be turned into victory.

I look back and wonder. Haven't we all known good men, men with fine ideals, who died too soon? Not the death of the body. This we can bear. Rather the far more horrible death of the spirit cut down too soon. I have known such men.

I knew men who fought to preserve the freedom of the Spanish Republic. Here were men who lived an ideal of democracy, freedom, opportunity. They saw a vision of a new Spain. And then Spain fell and with it their dreams. With the dreams were destroyed their lives.

I was a small boy when that war was fought. Perhaps then the memory is stronger. My mind was less cluttered. I saw tragedy more clearly, so death was more vivid.

Then there were those who sought to awaken America to the threat of Hitler's fascism. They loved this country too much to see it betrayed to sordid fears and petty ambitions. They saw that our borders lay on the Rhine and that our hopes were centered in Paris as well as Milwaukee. But they too went down. Premature anti-fascists they were called.

Today there are men who fight to preserve us from the double danger of Russian communism and home-grown fascism. Perhaps too clearly they see that freedom cares not who quenches her. No matter the source of its destruction, the lost freedom is just as irrevocably gone. When their ideals perish, these men will be destroyed too.

The ideals were majestic and so were the lives dedicated to them. But when the ideal falls, he whose life is centered in it must inevitably fall with it. Because I lived this, I know it. Spare me from this defeat!

But there are other defeats, too. Our hopes need not be shattered alone with the loss of a war. They can as well be crushed with the loss of a wife, a husband, a child. Even an opportunity destroyed bears its defeat. And the little sorrows and petty losses can well accumulate into death for the spirit.

There are so many of us who suffer on in jobs we hate, living not for today but a distant tomorrow. Yet in our hearts we doubt that tomorrow can ever come.

Perhaps I felt this way myself. Certainly I knew others who nursed the sorrow of crushed ambitions and blunted goals. These were men who watched their most cherished desires disintegrate piece by piece. They watched with a sardonic smile—a poor substitute for the pain they truly felt. And when they laughed I hurt inside.

But can we, can they, afford defeat? We want so much from life. We want the joy, not just the pain. Can we ever accept small desiccated lives, eaten with hate, envy, malice? Not when we know something better can be had.

And so what is the answer? Let us find the ideal which cannot be vanquished. In the wild and tossing sea which is life give us a mast we can tie on to. We can stick it then. Many a seaman survived just so. Surely our salvation lies therein.

Yet perhaps the greatest defeat our civilization has suffered is this: our ideals themselves have foundered. The great world systems have proved devoid of meaning.

I think of the French Revolution, a field I concentrated on in college. Here I saw the problem if not the answer. Christianity in the form of Roman Catholicism was forever destroyed for too many men. The Church betrayed not only its people but the nation. When foreign nations sought to destroy the revolution—and perhaps France as well—Rome gave her blessing to the enemies of France and freedom. Is it any wonder that Rome can offer no appeal to the Frenchman who cherishes the France of the revolution? Or is it any wonder it can offer no appeal to those of us who have read what happened then and ever since then, when men sought to widen their horizons? Can we ever accept the defeat Rome now and always has inflicted on her own very best?

Yet, tragically, the alternative to Roman Catholicism perished too. And we have been sitting in on the wake ever since. The great ideals of the Enlightenment, ideals that promised new hopes and at last happiness to men on earth, were diminished with every new stroke of the guillotine.

It seemed so obvious that thinking men could reorganize society. People had just never tried it before. But when those men of 1789 tried they failed forever. For every new reform brought with it new chaos. And with the defeat that is the French Revolution the human mind lost some of its lustre. So imperfect did the instrument now seem.

So now we have the puerilities of the modern novel, the despair of young men who fear to give up their freedom to the Church but distrust more deeply the capacities of the human mind. A whole new generation is raised on the psychoanalyst's couch, turning inward for fear of turning out to a life we cannot face.

Thus we give ourselves up to iron men: Hitler, Mussolini, Stalin and his successors, Franco, McCarthy. Let someone else do the thinking. Let someone else take the responsibility. Let me trust and let me follow.

I write this way because the French Revolution became very real to me. I saw mirrored in 1789 the revolutions of our time. I saw there my own doubts and fears and the tragedy of our own present.

I grew up in a dedicated home. My father was a journalist who breathed the air of Spain until it became his country too. Loyal to his second nation and all her hopes, he fought for the Spanish Republic. At a very early age I saw the fullness of life reflected in my own home—the fullness that comes alone from dedication to some ideal beyond our limited beings.

And I knew France. Perhaps that is my second country. I was born there and I grew up there while my father covered Europe for his American newspaper. The ideas and needs of Frenchmen became real to me. And when I finished Harvard and studied at the Sorbonne, they became a part of my own life.

Do you know the problems of French youth? The young Frenchman can find little hope. Nowhere does he find a satisfactory ideal, a decent goal. He can of course delude himself and for a while accept something less than the truth. Many do, but it doesn't last, and then they see no way out.

Perhaps this is a depressing picture of life. But I think it is a real picture of the life without God. We are untrue to ourselves if we deny the experience we have had. We deny reality if we pretend we have never seen misery and injustice. Yet too many of us do deny our experience. Perhaps we do this because we can no longer face the truth.

So, as I grew up I looked around, searching for my goals and my ideals. I saw my father, whom I respected deeply and still respect. I saw our family friends, men of talent, integrity, stature—men to whom I could look up. But I couldn't help but feel that they were unhappy, unbearably so.

In college I continued the search for identity, for goals that offered hope. And I had to see those goals working through another man's life. But no sooner did I find the man of stature than I saw that he was as lost as I.

But I never looked to the Church. Perhaps because I grew up among people who were still living the effects of the French Revolution, I distrusted the Church, which to me was all the same, Catholic or Protestant. After all, those men whom I must respect hated the Roman Catholic Church for what it had done to France, to Spain, what it was trying, they thought, to do to America. And they disdained Protestant churches for all they had failed to do.

The very few ministers I had ever known seemed less well equipped for life than the already downcast men I knew. Or they were too busy. They were too busy to cope with the problems of a young man who hardly knew what his problems were.

Failing to find an answer for the present, I turned to the future. When I went to work for a magazine, I did so for the future goal. Someday I could be editor, if not of it, then of some other magazine or paper. This ambition nourished me, but not very well. This is what consumed the hours and days I spent working my way up the ladder. Sometimes I felt that I was constantly climbing, but never arriving.

I felt a stranger in New York because today didn't matter, only that future day when I finally arrived. Too many people feel the same way, adrift because they have found no mast to cling to. Searching for an ideal they can never find, their despair remains intact and deadly.

Certainly the answer is not to practice the stoic way, to withdraw from life, tasting but a little that we may suffer less. For to do this is to abdicate the beauties that transcend the sorrows. The answer is not to endure life, but to dare it.

The answer is to find something to hang on to in the storm. I remember a storm at sea when I was going overseas. The waves were crashing over the bow, leaving buckled plates and smashed stanchions. I was one of the officers assigned to clear the decks of men. I could have been afraid, but I was not. And I loved the storm. Somehow the beauty of those angry waves overshadowed their fearful destruction. And in the blackness of night this awesome spectacle became a gigantic game, and I played my part.

To enjoy the storm is perhaps more worthy than merely to endure it. But we cannot enjoy the prospect of permanent human defeat. So we cry for hope and the very Creator of the universe offers us more than we can ever desire. Here is the wholeness of life, not just a part. He is above defeat, this One who created us and the world we live in.

I wish I could say this answer had come to me in a moment of clarity and vision, but it did not. It came to me slowly as I groped through college and those first few years I worked. And it came to me through another human being, many human beings in fact, but one in particular.

One day I met a minister who had suffered the same disillusionments and fought the same battles. But he was alive, completely alive and happy. He did not endure life. Rather he—and I have since found so many more men like him—faced life, accepted its inevitable shortcomings, and rose above them. He had faith in an unshakable idea. And through him I found a promise: Jesus Christ said, "I am come that they might have life and that they might have it more abundantly."

Here was an alternative I had never seen. I need not bend to blind authority on the one hand nor cling to beaten hopes on the other. But I can be free as I have never been free before.

We can all find Christ for ourselves. And we can take to heart His promise. It was meant for us. We can nourish our lives with His strength. Here is the mast. We can face the storm with our manhood intact.

Now I can search out life's beauty. Far from being cut off, I have entered into life as never before. I can indeed drink deeply.

Certainly defeat confronts me at every turn. Battles can still be lost. No matter. Jesus Christ suffered the greatest defeat of all only to rise to victory. He showed us the way. Can we reject the hope He offers us?

If we believe in Jesus Christ, we can never keep our faith hid. Rather this new faith burns within, and I want to shout it out that I have found an answer. So I study for the Episcopal ministry—my postulancy following quickly on the heels of my Baptism and Confirmation.

Now I look back and what was dark before is light. It all seems so obvious now. I was meant to embrace this faith from the beginning. Why did I wait so long? For now I feel what the psalmist once said: "For a day in thy courts is better than a thousand. I had rather be a doorkeeper in the house of my God, than to dwell in the tents of wickedness."

16

ENRICO C. S. MOLNAR

Raised a Moravian in Czechoslovakia, ordained a Methodist minister in the United States, and a priest of the Episcopal Church since 1954, the Rev. Dr. Enrico C. S. Molnar is at present rector of St. Timothy's Church, Compton, California. Born in 1913 in Frankfurt-am-Main, he attended primary and secondary schools in Prague, engaged in Arabic and Islamic studies at the Oriental Institute in Prague, and after further study at the University of Redlands entered the Pacific School of Religion at Berkeley, California, from which he graduated magna cum laude. *He completed the degree of Doctor of Philosophy at the Iliff School of Theology, his doctoral dissertation being on* Anglo-Czech Reformation Contacts.

. .After his ordination as a Methodist minister in 1946, Dr. Molnar served Methodist churches in California, except for one year as pastor of the St. John Hus Methodist Church in Slany, Czechoslovakia. He is author of a book (in Czech) on the monastic republic of Mount Athos and of articles in American and Czechoslovakian theological reviews. He is familiar with twelve languages and has painted a number of church murals, including an altar triptych for the church in Ramona, California, where he served as vicar for one year. He has ecumenical interests and has served as a member of the Board of Trustees of the San Diego Council of Churches.

ENRICO C. S. MOLNAR

THE LANDSCAPE of my spiritual pilgrimage appears to be composed of high Alpine peaks and deep Waldensian valleys of Switzerland and Piedmont, rolling hills of Hussite Bohemia and verdant Moravian plains, roseate Umbria blessed by the saints of Assisi, mystic penumbra of Byzantine shrines in the monasteries of Mount Athos, the serene loftiness of Anglican cathedrals and the simple dignity of Episcopal churches in sunny California. Continents, geographical and historical, compose its setting, and eternity provides its frame. Where earlier I thought of myself as an aimless wanderer, now I know, from the perspective of time, that I have become a pilgrim. The change was not due to any merit of mine, but to the guidance of Someone who provided me with a sense of direction. I rejoice in the pilgrimage.

Lest the above paragraph sound melodramatic and cryptic, let me explain myself in factual terms. My mother is a Waldensian. From her I learned to respect the integrity of the Waldensians, their heroic attachment to their faith in the face of a ruthless Inquisition. My grandfather, a pastor in Torre Pellice in the Cottian Alps of Piedmont, led me to tragic precipices, from which the *sbirri* of the Inquisition used to hurl heretical mothers and their children to a certain death. As a youngster I often heard John Milton's words,

> Avenge, O Lord, thy slaughtered saints, whose bones
> Lie scattered on the Alpine mountains cold. . . .

I was brought up in Prague, Czechoslovakia. My father was a Moravian. His father represented Czech Protestants at the Imperial Court of Austria-Hungary before World War I.

He was a poet and a scholar. From him I learned to love the Church and her history. Often he took me to St. Vitus' Cathedral dominating the spectacular Hradčany Castle of Prague. There we stood before the tomb of St. Wenceslas, patron saint of Bohemia—and subject of an English Christmas carol—who died a martyr's death in A.D. 929. In the ambulatory we saw the tombs of the rulers of Bohemia; we stayed longer at the sarcophagus of the Hussite King George of Podiebrad, bathed in the azure light of stained windows. And I heard my grandfather tell the story of the Bohemian Reformation. Way up in the clerestory masons were chiseling out details in stone. Once outside, I often wondered why so many of our modern Protestant churches were so bare and cold. I found the answers as I grew older.

As I gradually delved deeper into the Reformation story of Bohemia, I became proud of the fact that Holy Communion was celebrated in both kinds for the first time in several centuries by Jacobellus, a Hussite priest and professor of Prague University, in the little Church of St. Martin-in-the-Wall, on October 28, 1414. This sacramental act became the birthday of the Utraquist Church of Bohemia. (In Germany, Luther introduced the chalice for the first time in 1521; in Switzerland, Zwingli reintroduced the cup in 1525; in England, Cranmer's Order of Communion of 1548 contained the first rubric reinstating the communion in both kinds.) I discovered that the Bohemian Reformation really represented an attempt to restore the spirit of the primitive Apostolic Church, while preserving at the same time the orthodox structure and tradition of the pre-Reformation Church. I felt that this catholicity of the Bohemian Reformation has been ignored or explained away by later church historians. That tendency persists to this day among most Czechoslovak church historians who in the past Calvinized and Lutheranized, and most recently Marxianize Hus and the Hussite movement.

When I finished my secondary schooling, my Waldensian godmother offered me a glorious "grand journey" through Italy. I saw many places, sacred and profane, but none left a deeper imprint on me than Assisi in picturesque Umbria. I had planned to stay there three days—and I was still there at the end of the third week, imbibing the spirit of the Poverello of Assisi. There, whether it was in the monastery of San Damiano, or in the Carceri, or wherever Saint Francis left the impact of his radiant personality, I discovered the strength of disciplined piety. Some four years later, a variation on the theme produced a powerful effect on the mind and soul of the wanderer: I was sojourning among the Greek Orthodox monasteries of Holy Mount Athos in the Aegean Sea. While recording on canvas various vistas of cloisters, cypress-shaded cupolas, and wayside shrines, I savored the richness of Orthodox devotion. Beneath the stones I found the secret of the springs. While the monks chanted their ancient office in the darkened church lit by tapers, I heard my first call to the ministry. But Eastern Orthodoxy did not find a convert in me, only a friend and an admirer.

Presently the landscape darkened with war and rumors of war. The so-called Munich Crisis was thrust upon us, and with it came nightmarish goose-stepping days, concentration camps, hasty farewells, and escape to the free West. Assisted by Methodist friends, I went to America. There I studied theology and was ordained into the Methodist ministry in 1946. I shall always be grateful for my "Methodist years," the insights into the social implications of the Gospel, and the many cherished friends in that denomination. However, I grew increasingly restive for having to harbor mental reservations. I could not bring together that Church's inconsistency of practice which, on the one hand, tolerated a secularized humanism that virtually denies the relevance of Christ, while on the other hand, it equally tolerated escapist revivalism and fundamentalism which lays stress on Biblical literalism and outward observances of behavior rather than inner disposition. With others, I have observed what seemed to me a progressively evident departure from the creedal and sacramental basis of the Church as understood by John Wesley, Methodism's Anglican founder.

It was these disturbing signposts which led me to question the direction of my own spiritual pilgrimage. In order to avoid making hasty decisions, I withdrew to the Iliff School of Theology in Denver, to survey the scene as objectively as possible, and from the larger perspective, as it were, of the calm milieu of a theological seminary. However, the questing spirit led me always to the same conclusions, and the seminary only expedited the moment of decision. It proved an adventure which changed the wanderer into the pilgrim. Led by historical interests, I gathered data on "Anglo-Czech Reformation Contacts" for my doctoral dissertation. The research connected with this theme led me into the fascinating region of medieval history, and I spent much time with John Wyclyf, Fitzralph of Armagh, John Hus, Peter Payne, Jacobellus, Comenius, and the patristic literature of the undivided Church which was their common source of spiritual nourishment. And the pilgrim rejoiced, for he discovered that the ground on which he was treading was holy ground. Was it possible to be Catholic without being Roman Catholic, and logical without being astrological?

I may say that I arrived at my decision to become an Episcopalian through a second gradual conversion brought about by a careful study of the history of the Church. And so, after returning to California, one evening in May, 1952, I read in the First Methodist Church of San Jacinto my Statement of Resignation which I began with this paragraph:

> From his very first day in Paradise, man was set before the necessity of exercising his freedom of will. It is impossible to have a moral life without the freedom of choice. And there come times when man, prompted by the Spirit of God, has to make a choice that will of necessity take him from one pattern of life to another. For every such decision man has to pay the price; it may be in losing some friends, in incurring hostility and misunderstanding of some, or in false motives attributed to his decision. My friends, this hour of decision has come for me and, even though I am willing to pay the price, I pray that it be none of these three possibilities. . . .

Soon thereafter I was confirmed, together with my wife, in St. Paul's Cathedral in Los Angeles. We withdrew from the Methodist parsonage, stored away our possessions, and lived for a year in our house trailer while attending an orientation course at Church Divinity School of the Pacific in Berkeley, California. It was a glorious and busy year. I discovered that I did not have to give up a single one of my former beliefs, but that much more had been added in depth, in height, in width, in warmth, and in devotion. While studying the liturgy of the Church, my wife was helping me with the final revision of my dissertation. I thanked God that He led me to choose the particular theme of the thesis.

When the solemn day of my ordination to the diaconate came, and the bishop laid his hands upon me, the pilgrim heard for a fleeting moment distant echoes from Mount Athos, recalled the triple spires of St. Vitus' Cathedral and the penumbra surrounding the shrine of St. Wenceslas and the tomb of the Hussite King, felt the coolness of the Waldensian valleys and the warmth of the hills of Assisi . . . And it all made sense. It made great sense. It all pointed toward this moment, when my bishop would lay his hands upon me.

And the vistas of my past pilgrimage were again vividly present when I was ordained to the priesthood. I have not become a member of yet another denomination, of another organized form of human speculation, but a very member incorporate in the mystical Body of Christ, the One, Holy, Catholic, and Apostolic Church, with its outward and visible signs of inward and spiritual graces, spanning all times and all places. And more than that: the bishop said, "Receive the Holy Ghost for the Office and Work of a Priest in the Church of God . . . And be thou a faithful Dispenser of the Word of God, and of his holy Sacraments. . . ." The landscape has become meaningful, sacramental.

In the beginning, some of my friends used to ask the question (but they do not ask it any more), "Aren't you sometimes a bit sorry that you turned into an Episcopalian?" And I always answered, "No. I have not regretted my decision for a single minute." And the statement is not an exaggeration. Becoming an Episcopalian has, for me, opened doors into a new—and yet so old!—world in which being a Christian is an adventure where saints are partners and sinners are forgiven.

Let me list a few reasons why I like the Episcopal Church (and my answers are not necessarily in the order of their importance):

1. I like the Episcopal Church because, teaching the sacramental principle that all physical matter is the instrument of spirit, the Church believes that spiritual healing is a

natural part of her ministry. We believe that God is really present in the sacraments. They are not just a memorial to us. We do not presume to explain when and how God is present, for in presuming to explain this mystery we would place ourselves on the level of the omniscient God.

2. I was a professional artist before studying for the ministry. The artist in me likes to worship God in a meaningful "beauty of holiness," in a place where the accumulated treasury of ages of Christian experience is expressed through a shorthand language of color, symbol, gesture; in a place where, in short, everything suggests that I am not in an ordinary house, but in a House set apart for worship. And there is something of the artist in every one of us. Beauty is the visual language of heavenly mysteries. To me, it is most eloquent in the Episcopal Church.

3. I like the Episcopal Church because the kind of temper which marks her tradition is a spirit of ordered liberty and self-disciplined freedom. To be sure, there are various parties in the Church. However, we are, to quote the Archbishop of Canterbury, "attempting, for the good of the universal Church, the most difficult of all its internal problems, the due combination of order and freedom within the Church —and attempting it, not by running away from the tensions thereby created, but by meeting them in the spirit of Christ."

4. In this connection, I like the Episcopal Church because she is free from the narrow denominationalism which mars so many Christian organizations. Since the Church sees no conflict between religion and science but fully accepts scientific methods, fundamentalism can hardly exist in our Communion. We consider revivalism an unfortunate emotional aberration from the historic expressions of the Faith. We also eschew the other extreme of converting the Church into a

shallow liberalistic society for the fellowship of do-gooders only, where the supernatural aspect of life is minimized.

5. I like the Episcopal Church because she does not consider the Scriptures verbally infallible, an assertion which, by an objective test of modern archeology and higher criticism, could hold no water. Was it not Erasmus of Rotterdam, perhaps the greatest mind of the Reformation age, who observed that "by identifying the new facts of learning with heresy, you make conservatism synonymous with idiocy"? We do not have to believe that God's revelation begins in Genesis and that He stops revealing Himself in the last verse of the last page of the Book of Revelation. We believe that God continued revealing Himself through the succeeding centuries of the Church down to our own time. That is why we are wary of rejecting post-Biblical insights. The Scriptures are an integral part of the development of the Church.

6. There is something in my temperament which responds quickly to Anglican objectivity and its shying away from extreme positions. It is this objectivity which has led Anglican theologians to speak of the *Via Media*. This means also that, being both Protestant and Catholic, preserving the best from the pre- and post-Reformation Church, we are in a unique position when it comes to problems of ecumenical relations. It is not without significance that the Episcopal Church was for a long time vitally interested in the Ecumenical Movement, giving it outstanding leadership. I am proud to belong, in a humble way, to a Church which took such strong ecumenical initiative at the 1954 assemblies in Minneapolis and Evanston. I was in both cities, quite unofficially, just having an Anglican and ecumenical vacation, but what I saw filled my heart with joy and my mind with challenge.

7. I suppose many others writing for this symposium will mention the centrality of the altar. I like to worship in a place where the altar is the center of attention, and not the pulpit. This is important to every Churchman. For where the pulpit is at the center, that by itself symbolically indicates that the most important feature in worship is instruction, sermon, man's interpretation, man's subjective importance. We Episcopalians agree with Eastern Orthodox, Roman Catholic, and those historic Protestant Churches which place the emphasis on an objective worship, altar-centered. The altar is a visible symbol of an invisible Grace, the Presence of God. I sense that same objectivity in the music of the Church, which unites me, through her chants, with the early Apostolic times, and with the faithful saints of the cathedral age, and with every age.

To sum it all up, to my mind our Communion most fully expresses the marks of being the "extension of the Incarnation." In my library in the vicarage I have, beside books in the English language, Czech books documenting the story of the Bohemian Reformation, the sermons and writings of Hus, Comenius, Chelčický, and many others; French and Italian books on Peter Waldo, the Huguenots, the Curé of Ars, Francis of Assisi, and others; German and Russian books about Luther and Loukaris, by Barth and Berdyayev, and so on. None of them need be relegated to a hidden shelf, just because I am an Episcopalian. There is no Index! For in the Anglican Communion there is most fully expressed the basic Christian belief that God reveals Himself through history, not in an esoteric abstract speculation, but in history, "in events through which we event," in a St. Francis, in a

St. John Hus, in the Celtic Saints. This is the genius of the Judeo-Christian faith. The Word became Flesh. The Spirit sanctifies matter. God's redemption of man in history is a reality. That is why, as a Christian, I chose the Episcopal Church.

17

HOXIE NEALE FAIRCHILD

A distinguished authority on English literature (especially poetry) of the eighteenth and nineteenth centuries as a reflection on the history of ideas, Dr. Hoxie Neale Fairchild is Professor of English at Hunter College, New York City. Born in 1894, he graduated from Columbia College in 1917, a member of Phi Beta Kappa. In World War I he served in France as a Second Lieutenant in the Infantry. Injured in combat, he was honored with the Silver Star, the Croix de Guerre with palm, Chevalier (1st class) and Order de la Couronne (Belgium). He returned to Columbia as an instructor in English, serving as William Bayard Cutting Fellow in 1925-26 and receiving his Doctor of Philosophy degree there in 1928. Thereupon he was advanced to Assistant Professor and served as Associate Professor from 1934 to 1940, at which time he assumed the present professorship at Hunter College.

Professor Fairchild has been active in the leadership of the Modern Language Association in America and is author of The Noble Savage, An Approach to Literature, The Romantic Quest, *and* Toward Belief *(an approach to Christian apologetics chiefly for college students). His major work has been the four-volume* Religious Trends in Modern Poetry, *completed this year. He served as a member of the editorial committee and one of the authors of* Religious

Perspectives in College Teaching, *sponsored by the Hazen Foundation. He is Vice-President of the Board of Trustees of the Church of St. Mary the Virgin, New York City, and a founding member and the first president of the Guild of Scholars in the Episcopal Church. He is also a Fellow of the Conference on Science, Philosophy and Religion. Dr. Fairchild is married and has had two children.*

HOXIE NEALE FAIRCHILD*

I AM NOT at all sure that the story which I have to tell deserves to be included in this book, for it does not concern any one illuminating moment. Things never happen to me in that catastrophic way. Even the conscious, climactic period of my religious conversion occupied a whole summer. Nor does my "case," though very important to me and, thank God, to God, offer anything unusual to a student of the varieties of religious experience. Furthermore, I do not wish to use the term *conversion* without observing that I have been a Christian all my life, for I was baptized in infancy. One could present a respectable theological case, if perhaps a slightly technical one, for regarding the moment of my Baptism as the real turning point of my personal history. But a person who was baptized in 1894 and confirmed in 1934 is something of a procrastinator, and there is a great difference between receiving grace and trying to use it. Every minute of those forty years must have done something to retard or advance the final outcome, but this little essay is not an autobiography. My Baptism was largely a concession to the proprieties: nobody took it very seriously except God. I do not blame my parents for giving me practically no religious teaching or guidance as a child. The blame lies rather with the nineteenth-century sentimentalism which made them liable to the fallacy that the truly spiritual person is he who refrains from believing anything in particular.

* This essay, which appeared in 1954 in *The Hour of Insight* (Harper), is reprinted with the permission of the author and of the Institute for Religious and Social Studies, the copyright owner.

How many of the young people who are supposed to lose their faith in our "godless" colleges had any faith worth mentioning when they matriculated? The boarding school which I attended for five years was intellectually and ethically sound, but spiritually as sterile as an operating room. When I entered Columbia College in 1912 I knew practically nothing about religion, and had no religious beliefs whatever. Already conditioned to regard all problems from a secularistic point of view, by the end of my sophomore year I was not only unreligious but rather aggressively antireligious—an atheist of the good old-fashioned nineteenth-century materialistic type.

I remember very clearly the opinions which I held in those days, but the feelings which lent force and color to those opinions are now so deeply buried that I cannot drag them up to the surface of consciousness. So far as I can recall, I was quite at ease in my unbelief and supposed that I was living a reasonably happy life. As regards moral conduct, I have nothing lurid to report for the reader's edification or entertainment. There was very little active evil and practically no good. Being a shy, sedentary, bookish youngster who had been decently brought up, I did nothing quite base enough to arouse the remorse that might have pushed me toward religion.

In the First World War, I commanded an infantry platoon in France, had several narrow escapes from death, killed three men with my own hands, and lost a leg as the result of a wound received in action. None of these experiences gave me the faintest glimmer of a feeling that I wanted God or that God wanted me. It is not true that there are no atheists in foxholes: I was one of them. I went through the amputation exactly like a fox who escapes from a trap by pulling off the caught foot.

On my discharge from the Army I married and began teaching at Columbia. My wife was a liberal Protestant, as she still is; but in those early days the relation between her religious beliefs and her beautiful moral character was vaguer and more tenuous than it has since become. At first she would argue with me a little, but at that time her only real arguments were feelings—feelings which I did not possess. We soon agreed to disagree on these matters, and left them in silence.

The 1920's went by without any awareness of God. Where was the need of Him? I was very happily married. Our little daughter, growing up beautifully, was a great joy to us. We had very little money, but lived comfortably enough for people of simple tastes. My war injury was no great handicap in my profession. I loved my work as teacher and scholar, and I was fairly successful in it. In short, there was simply nothing to threaten the illusion of self-sufficiency.

One slight change may be worth mentioning. Although I scorned religion as much as ever, my academic specialty, the study of literature in relation to the history of ideas, compelled me to learn something about it. I did not become a real expert in the philosophy and history of religion (nor have I become one since), but almost against my will I gathered a certain amount of knowledge which was precious to me later. In a coldly objective way, I knew what religion had meant to other men long before it meant anything to me.

In 1930, I hit rock bottom for the first time: our seven-year-old daughter died of pneumonia. Without one thought of God, without one hope of immortality for her or for me, I sat by her bed and felt her hand growing colder, until at last the useless oxygen pump was unplugged and whirred to a stop.

But during the bitter months which followed, obscure subterranean currents began to move. The courage and goodness with which my wife rose to confront this tragedy made me wonder whether after all she did not know something of which I was ignorant. I was still far from sharing her opinions, but I thought a little wistfully of those spiritual resources which seemed to grow deeper and stronger in her with her increasing need of them. I had always been a rather coldly self-centered person with no real enemies but very few real friends. Now, in my sorrow, I found that although I had been so unloving a great many people stood ready to offer me love. Their sympathy made me feel a little ashamed of myself. It softened my cynicism and rendered me less cocksure about many things.

But I was not yet ready to make religious use of those better feelings which pain and love had given me. Instead, I was caught for some time in what I now regard as the most treacherous of all snares—the humanistic notion that the mind of man possesses autonomous power to create those values which are essential for the good life. The feeling-tone of this theory was of course richer, more elevated, if you like, more "spiritual" than that of the drably negative positivism which I had formerly cultivated. But that was precisely where the danger lay: it made me suppose that I had found an adequate substitute for religious belief.

Three years went by. I felt serene and happy when my wife and I went off to our country home for the summer vacation of 1933. We had completely adjusted ourselves to the loss of our child. A second daughter had been born to us, and our faces were turned toward the future. I was so well satisfied with my humanistic-values philosophy that I decided to set it forth in a series of semi-popular dialogues —a sort of literary scholar's holiday, very ripe and urbane and quietly contemptuous both of the crass materialist and of the bigoted supernaturalist. With three whole months ahead of me, I should easily be able to do it.

But when I began to write I found myself in a ridiculously embarrassing position: I could not complete even the first page. I wanted to affirm the creativity of the human mind. This power could hardly exist unless man possessed some measure of free will. But although I no longer actually thought of the universe as an automaton, I believed in no principles from which to argue that it was anything else. If the universe were an automaton, how could it grind our human freedom? If it were not, how could it be described without any recourse to religious concepts? There seemed to be no earthly reason for believing in the values in which I already did believe. Could there be some *un*earthly reason?

Haunted by this question, I gave up my precious dialogues and began to think about God as rationally as I could. Of course I also began to desire God with my emotions. My thinking was certainly wishful, but I doubt if it was more wishful than when I wished to believe that the universe was a mechanical gadget, or when I wished to believe that man could make spiritual values without divine help. If there are wishes that corrupt reason, there are also wishes that guide reason into truth. That without which reason is impossible must somehow be reasonable.

My first step was to insist that if nature included me it must include the *whole* me—not merely the mechanisms of my body but all the powers and aspirations and potentialities which distinguish man from the lower animals. A universe thus stretched to include the human imponderables could no longer be symbolized by a machine. It seemed more rational to think of it as a fabric of thoughts proceeding from a divine creative Mind—not *my* mind. But I could not conceive of divine Intelligence without divine Wisdom, and how could there be divine Wisdom without divine Love? Moving onward in this direction I found, not without surprise, that I believed in a divine spiritual Personality who was the source and giver of all values.

Then gradually arose a deeply painful sense of the awful apartness and differentness of this divine Personality, together with a strange feeling of kinship with Him—broken kinship, but real kinship nevertheless. By about the middle of the summer I was trying to pray to this God. Perhaps my first attempt to pray was the moment of which I have been asked to write. But it was not a moment of *discovery* —to this day I have had nothing that could be called a mystical experience. It was rather a moment of attempted self-surrender, the first willed act in a long struggle against pride which is still going on in me, and must go on until I die.

As I prayed I seemed to receive no answer at all, except for a slowly growing assurance that I was praying to an objective reality and not to a projection of my own feelings. But obviously my prayers *were* answered—otherwise I should not be writing as I am today. The great change which took place in me that summer was no accomplishment of my own. Apparently it was demanded that I make just one contribution to the process: I had to say that I wanted to find my way home. The grace needed for saying that had always been in my possession. Once I had said it, my Father saw me coming a great way off, and ran to meet me.

What remains to be said will not, I hope, be interpreted as an attempt to argue with any reader about religion. I am simply describing what happened in my own mind, without any implications as to what might happen or should happen in other minds. My beliefs are so precious to me that I can realize how precious the beliefs of other men must be to them. I have never found that the definiteness of the position at which I finally arrived has made for intolerance. On the contrary, it has drawn me into friendship and working alliance with all men who profess a positive religious faith.

Both my efforts to reason and my efforts to pray opened up the whole problem of Revelation. With religion as with everything else, I reflected, all real truth must be concrete and specific; we talk in vague abstractions only when we do not know. Would a God of love leave us completely in the dark as to the one subject which matters most for man's life? Surely He must have employed some means of showing us His nature and His will in order to enable us to draw closer to Him.

Some readers may feel that I should have been content with my initial shapeless belief in an unknowably transcendent Spirit of Love. But I found that I could not firmly believe in this without believing more than this. I must either go further or relapse into subjectivism and romantic self-worship. Once I dared to think about these matters at all, I must think onward to some objective commitment. I must never forget that I might be wrong, never presume to judge my fellow men. But, right or wrong, I must "take the leap"; I must impose my trust if I was to live at all. Merely saying, "Well, I suppose there must be Something," was intellectually spurious and emotionally impotent. In short, I saw no way of being fruitfully religious without having a religion.

By the end of that summer I regarded myself as a Christian, but I was still very hesitant to commit myself to any particular expression of the Christian Faith. I felt rather superior to "mere creeds and forms." I was proud of what I had accomplished during the summer (I thought *I* had accomplished it!), proud of my new-found humility, and I was inclined to think myself the only real Christian in the world.

But during the academic year 1933-1934 I continued to think and read and pray. More importantly and rather surprisingly, I condescended to worship God in the company of other Christians. In my sharp reaction against humanistic subjectivism, I found myself powerfully drawn toward a religion of sacramentally mediated grace. I desired to be touched *from the outside* by the redeeming energy which had been set going in the world of space and time by the Incarnation. To be brought into contact with that historical event would be the closest approach to union with God that I could hope for on this side of the grave. A hostile critic of Romanticism in my personal scholarship, I was suspicious of any reliance upon an Inner Light which was not kindled and constantly rekindled from the great Outer Light. A professional rhetorician, I preferred a cult of symbolic actions to a cult of words. I felt, as I still feel, grateful to all devout and eloquent men who expound the Gospel and show us how to apply it to our own lives. But what I thought I needed even more than that was a sacramental extension of the Incarnation, a Church which inherited from Christ through His Apostles the power and the right to say to me, "*Behold* the Lamb of God! *Behold* Him, that taketh away the sins of the world!"

On the other hand, I felt that I could never guarantee absolutely unconditional obedience to the authority of the Visible Church, much less to any one of its functionaries. I believed that it was indeed guided by the Holy Spirit, but not to the exclusion of human error (and hence to the exclusion of human free will) in matters of faith and morals. It seemed to me that any uncertainties and inconsistencies in this position were inevitable characteristics of religious belief in this mortal life, where we see through a glass darkly and know only in part until that which is perfect is come.

For several months, in pursuance of these ideas and feelings, I had been attending Masses at the Church of St. Mary the Virgin, one of the Anglo-Catholic parishes of the Episcopal Church. Of course I did not receive Communion—that would have been dishonest. But by May, 1934, I knew that I could no longer be a mere spectator. I must either share in it or go away. And it had become absolutely impossible for me to go away. Hence I made a profession of faith to Father Granville Williams of the Society of Saint John the Evangelist, who was then rector of St. Mary's. Under his guidance I prepared for Confirmation. I was confirmed and a few days later received my first Communion in the Advent season of 1934, just forty years and two months after my Baptism. I had wasted a great deal of valuable time. No wonder my favorite parable is that of the vineyard!

For many people who are likely to read this book, what I have had to say is an old familiar story. Probably I should not further labor the obvious by telling them what they already know about the changes which are produced in a man's life when he moves from secularism to a positive supernaturalistic religion. Excluding matters too deeply private to be spoken of in print, so far as I am concerned the great difference may be summed up in the word *integration*. When I was an unbeliever, my life was an incoherent jumble of conflicts, but since 1934 I have held a clue which makes sense of everything. A single set of principles now focuses and harmonizes my intercourse with other men, my worship, my political and social views, my philosophy of man and nature, my interpretation of history, my teaching of literature, my personal scholarship.

My application of these principles has been abysmally inadequate. Nevertheless, the mere recognition of them as goals to be striven toward gave my life new meaning and new direction before it was too late. At least I think I know what St. Paul means by *newness of life,* and as I begin to grow a little elderly I draw deep peace from the knowledge that *newness of life* and *life everlasting* are one and the same.

18

WILLIAM H. BAAR

Not long ago Minister to Lutheran Students at Yale University, the Rev. Dr. William H. Baar is now Episcopal Chaplain at the University of Chicago and Director of Brent House, international students' center. He was born in 1919. After graduation from Carthage College and Chicago Seminary, he did graduate study at Yale University, receiving his Master of Arts in historical theology, and the degree of Doctor of Philosophy in the field of Church history. During the war, Dr. Baar served first with the Marine Air Force and then as Chaplain of the Fourth Submarine Squadron aboard the U. S. S. Howard W. Gilmore.

As a Lutheran pastor, Dr. Baar was pastor of Emmanuel Church in New Haven for five years and editor of two national publications, Una Sancta *and* Sursum Corda. *After his ordination to the Episcopal priesthood he succeeded the Rev. Canon Bernard Iddings Bell in his distinguished work at the University of Chicago. Dr. Baar is married and has three children.*

WILLIAM H. BAAR

I FIRMLY believe, prevailing fashion to the contrary, that the goal of life on earth is life with God in Heaven. This means that life is a journey of the soul to God. From God we came and to God we return, and as St. Augustine observed, we shall never find our rest until we find it in Him. Although the journey of life has many aspects, and is involved in numerous complexities, the most important aspect of my journey has been the search for my true spiritual home.

Now most people find their spiritual home in the Church into which they are born. They receive its sacraments, pattern their lives according to the ideals which it presents, and live as much as possible within its discipline. They receive the nurture, encouragement, and assistance which their Communion offers and are in general spiritually satisfied. For some people, however, this search for a spiritual home is not at all so simple. It is not an easy accommodation to the religion of their fathers, the prevailing temper of the times, or the general practice of their home environments. For some this search will always involve a long, perhaps agonizing, quest.

It is a well-known fact that among earnest seekers for religion, many finally come to find their spiritual home in the Anglican Communion. Thus the question at once arises, "Why this Church?" I cannot answer this question for the many, but I can answer for myself. Reviewing the development of my own life and thought, I can now see how I have been led on my journey into paths which I did not plan for myself or foresee. Although I would hesitate to generalize on the basis of my own experience, there may be those who will find that the long and dusty road they are trying to travel parallels mine.

My early training and experience was such that even as a child I took religion very seriously and had a very deep interest in the Church. As far back as I can remember, all I have ever wanted to be was a minister of God. Living in a metropolitan area, where there were many churches, I took advantage of the opportunity from my earliest years to acquaint myself with the worship of other denominations. Once I had fulfilled my obligation of singing in the boys' choir at an early service in my own parish, my parents allowed me to go to any church I chose. The churches I usually attended were Roman Catholic or Anglican. If they were Lutheran I usually chose ones that were more advanced liturgically than my own parish. Somehow the quiet and beauty of these churches drew me into their worship. To this day I seldom pass a church without stopping by for a few moments of quiet, and I still feel that same indescribable sense of mystery and awe as I enter.

As this interest in the worship of the Church matured and I began reading about the history of the liturgy, I learned that liturgical worship was as much a part of the Lutheran tradition as of the Roman or Anglican. Thus all of my years within Lutheranism were spent in work and prayer that the truly great traditions of Lutheran worship and piety would be revived in our day. I studied liturgics deeply and wrote voluminously to this end. However, my real interest in the Anglican Church had, I think, very little to do with these childhood experiences or this study.

My real interest in the Anglican Church arose not out of an interest in liturgics, but through my study of the history of doctrine and Church history. Passing through several years of careful and serious consideration of the history of doctrine, especially the teaching of the Fathers, through the Athanasian struggle, through the many heresies and schisms of the ages, the picture of the true, visible Church began to penetrate my consciousness. I came gradually to realize that the Church of God was not merely a general fellowship of the faithful, but a definite entity in history. I saw the Church as having a definite organization as well as a definite theology, a definitely sacramental worship as well as a definite canon of Scripture.

This discovery on my part came very slowly, as it contradicted a great deal of what I had been taught. The general conception of the history of the Apostolic Church that had been conveyed to me was that of an informal fellowship proclaiming the Gospel. Its worship was generally informal and its organization accidental and inconsequential. I also had the impression that the Scriptures were the Church's one and only guide in worship and practice. When I had the opportunity to study on my own, I learned what should have been obvious, that the early Christians did not have as a Bible only the Old Testament, that their worship was liturgical, and that considerable care was taken in the formulation of its organization. I learned that the Eucharist was celebrated at least weekly by the first Christians and that anointing the sick with oil was an Apostolic practice. My whole conception of the early Church was at first demolished and then reconstructed when I began to interpret the Scriptures and the facts of Church history for myself.

The second interesting development in my thought came from a reading of the history of heresy and especially that which resulted in the formulation of the Nicene Creed. The early history of the Church is full of the struggles of saints and theologians in their attempts to formulate and present a rationale of Christian Faith. There were no doubt many possible hypotheses put forth by theologians about which we have never heard. These theories were probably discussed in the Christian community, found to be unsatisfactory or inconsistent, and were consequently abandoned by their authors. However, occasionally a theologian regarded himself as committed to his theory, and it was upon such occasions that the bishops and scholars of the Church had to meet to formulate the proper statement of the Christian Faith. Through the titanic and humiliating struggles of the Church with Arius and Nestorius, the truth was finally vindicated. Many times it seemed that heresy had become firmly rooted, but in the end it was always put down. Sometimes the Church lacked as clear a formulation as we might desire. There are likewise times in Church history when the condemnation of heretics seems unduly severe. Yet, cost what it might, the Church set herself against the storm. Against popular or imperial opinion, her proclamation of the Holy Gospel went on.

After each decision of the Church there were defections of those who preferred their own interpretations of the Faith. In the story of the early Church we read of the constant growth in her numbers. Sometimes we fail to note that there was also, at the same time, a constant attrition in her membership. The fact remains, however, that whatever power sacred or secular there may have been in the ranks of the heretics, their numbers soon diminished, their organizations splintered to pieces, and thus they faded into history. Rival theologies and rival polities were in their times powerful enough to threaten the existence of the Church, but they died out one by one. The Catholic Church remained, and only the Catholic Church remained! Thus the first great decision I made on my journey was that I must find my home within the Catholic Church.

I believe in the Anglican Church, therefore, because, in the first place, I found it to be not Anglican but Catholic. It is a part of the Holy Catholic Church founded by Jesus Christ and continuing throughout history. By the Catholic Church, I mean precisely the Church of history.

We know from the New Testament how after Christ founded the Church His Apostles brought the faith and worship which He ordained to the great cities of the world. St. James continued the work of the Church in Jerusalem, St. John went to Alexandria, St. Peter went to Rome, and St. Thomas may have gone to India. In every place in which the Church was established, we observe four important elements constituting the visible aspect of her existence. The Eucharist was celebrated and the Scriptures, so far as the early Church had them, were read. The celebrant at the Eucharist was the bishop. Entrance into the Christian Faith was through Baptism and every baptism included a formula which later became the nucleus of the ecumenical Creeds. In the first few centuries, as now, men were bewildered by the myriad groups and varied sects which claimed to represent Christianity. They wondered, as I wondered, how a man can know the true Church. Throughout the first thousand years of its history the Church had been recognized by four clear signs. The Catholic Church was the Church of:

1. The Holy Scriptures
2. The Creeds
3. The Sacraments
4. The Episcopate and Priesthood.

The crucial question is not the problem as to when each one of these signs became a recognizable mark of the Church.

The real question is whether, whenever these developments occurred, they were legitimate developments. The liturgy and sacraments, the priesthood and the episcopate all preceded the acceptance of the canon of Scripture and the formulations of the Creeds. Nevertheless, the time sequence is not essential. The Church throughout its history regarded these four signs as marks of the true Church and their development, therefore, not only as legitimate but as inspired by the Holy Ghost. It is a fact of history that rival polities and theologies could have survived, but it is equally a fact of history that they did not. (The Nestorians have survived more as a sociological than an ecclesiastical phenomenon.) He who would look to Anglicanism for the four marks of the visible Church, will find that the Anglican Church is constituted in the same way as the Church of history. I took the verdict of history, therefore, to be that the Anglican Church is a Catholic Church.

The second major insight that led me to the Anglican Church was that although the Anglican Church is Catholic, it does not claim to be the only Catholic Church. Church history makes very dubious any claims to the exclusive possession of Catholicity on the part of any one Christian Church. The first few centuries of the Church's life indicate some very interesting developments along this line. Two important events determined the alignment of Christian forces from the early centuries until our own times. The great centers of Christianity were Jerusalem, Rome, Alexandria, and Antioch. In all of these centers the Church was doubtless of Apostolic foundation. When the tide of Mohammedan invasion swept over the Near East, all of these centers with the exception of Rome were overwhelmed. The Churches in these occupied cities were very greatly hampered in their development. Their large constituencies were lost, and their very existence was at the mercy of dictatorial Mohammedan rulers. Of all the great Churches of the early centuries, only the Church of Rome enjoyed both freedom to determine its environment, and a large and determined constituency. The great historic centers of Christianity in the East continued as they do to this day, but their best days were over.

The second great event in early ecclesiastical history was the fall of the secular government of Rome. Although the fall of Rome antedated the Mohammedan invasions, its real significance in the life of the Church took longer to be felt. Yet the whole development of the papacy was determined by this event in 410. The ecclesiastical organization of the Roman Empire paralleled that of the secular. When the secular government broke down, the Church of Rome was the only power capable of continuing the functions of secular government. Thus the Roman Church became to a large extent both the sacred and secular ruler of the Western world. Blessed with enormous generosity and incomparably great leadership in this black hour for Western civilization, the Church of Rome emerged as a militant and powerful defender of religion and order. The whole Western world knew how great was its debt to the bishops and Church of Rome. Thus it was that when later on in history all of the other great centers of Christianity fell to the Mohammedans, Rome emerged as the one vital hope for the Christian Church. Practically all Christians were willing to recognize the bishops of Rome as among the greatest leaders in Christendom. However, as Rome was more and more successful in her exercise of both sacred and secular power over the Western world, the East realized that here was a development far beyond the ideal of the Church in Apostolic

times. The East, as always, had a spirit of its own, both
theologically and liturgically. The bishops, Eastern and
Western, could remain in communion with each other,
however, because of their essential unity, and because there
was not too much strain in the relationship. However, as
the papacy developed and Rome began to claim for itself
spiritual power over all Christendom, the Eastern Churches,
suffering so much persecution and holding the Faith at such
great cost, became exceedingly resentful. In spite of their
terrible losses in numbers, Eastern Christians knew that
their Churches were of Apostolic foundation. They regarded their bishops as equals of the bishops of Rome. Thus
Eastern and Western Christianity were disjoined, and the
Body of Christ was broken over this jurisdictional dispute.

Our Church views this schism sympathetically because,
though she is Catholic, she does not think of herself as the
only Catholic Church. The tragedy of the division of East
and West is taken more seriously in the Anglican Church
than in any other because of her close historical ties with both
contestants in the dispute. To a unique degree the whole
Church tradition, Eastern as well as Western, belongs to
the Anglican Church. This synthesis of Eastern and Western
tradition goes back to the very beginnings of the Church
in England.

The earliest days of the Church in England are shrouded
in mystery. Legend says that Joseph of Arimathea brought
the Christian Faith to England. However, this cannot be
proved. It is reasonably certain, nevertheless, that it was
through Eastern sources that Christianity first came to
England. The Church of England, dating almost from the
time of the Apostles, gained its orders from the East, probably by way of Gaul. The Church of England sent three

bishops to the Council of Arles in 314 and, though probably poor, was certainly flourishing at that date.

Considerably later, when the Roman Mission came to England under St. Augustine of Canterbury, the Church was reorganized, and the remnants which had suffered from the barbarian invasions were gathered together once more. The Church of England therefore owes a tremendous debt both to East and to West. She views the Eastern Orthodox Churches and the Roman Church with a great deal more love and sympathy than they view one another. Though the Anglican Church is largely Western in its type of Catholicism, it has an appreciation for the East unexampled among the other bodies of Christendom. Here I found an attitude and a tradition which I thought I could trust.

At the same time, I came to realize that the Anglican Church has no fear whatsoever in examining and re-examining the traditions and attitudes she has inherited. One cannot read the history of the Anglican Communion without recognizing the fact that here is a body in constant reformation. At the time of the sixteenth-century Reformation, the Church of England, having grown weary of centuries of papal dictation, threw off, as the Eastern Churches had done previously, the burden of Italian rule. The Church of England reformed itself in many respects, but it was most conscientious in retaining historic polity, worship, and doctrine. The denominations which had their inception in the sixteenth century tend to think of reformation as something that happened once and for all. They spell Reformation with a capital "R." They are proud to call themselves after Reformation leaders. The Anglican Church, on the contrary, does not look to any particular Reformation leader for its inspiration. It is a matter of record that the Church of England has tended to diminish the importance of individual leaders. Though it has produced a St. Patrick, a St. Anselm, an Andrewes, and a Keble, it has never followed its leaders slavishly. The Church of England was affected by the Reformation, but it was not produced by the Reformation. Anglicans believe that throughout the history of the Church there have been many reformations. It might well be that the Benedictine reformation much earlier has been every bit as important for the Church and for Western civilization as "The Reformation" of the sixteenth century. History has not yet delivered its verdict. Further, our Church sees herself as engaged in a series of reformations. Sixteenth-century extremes have been corrected in the nineteenth century, just as medieval errors had been corrected in the sixteenth. Retaining an appreciative but discriminating attitude toward tradition, our Church regards reformation as a chronic part of its activity. Reformation Churches speak of the Church as under judgment. Anglicanism would remind all of non-Roman Christianity that "The Reformation" is also under divine judgment.

The Church of England owes its foundation to the Eastern Church, its practical organization to the Western, and its vivid sense of divine judgment to the Reformation. Our Church takes very seriously the command of Christ to proclaim the grace of God. She knows, however, that grace comes through means of Grace and therefore holds the sacraments and the word of God as in a unity. I mean specifically to say that the Anglican Communion is thoroughly Catholic and thoroughly Evangelical at the same time. This is why our Church can view the Protestant Communions as well as the Catholic with so much understanding and sympathy.

The fact that the Anglican Church is right in the middle of the whole Christian tradition is the key to the Anglican way of looking at things. Take the Anglican attitude toward history as an example. All of the great Churches look back to some special time in history as the glorious age of Christendom. The Eastern Churches tend to look back upon the first four centuries as the time of real, spiritual splendor. The Roman Church tends to locate its time pathos in the thirteenth century, the "age of faith." Most Protestant Communions look to the sixteenth century as the age of the Church's glory. I believe in the Anglican Church because it has no special time pathos. Anglicans look to all of the ages of the Church's greatness. Anglicanism also has a deep consciousness of the time of the Church's humiliation. With Protestant, Roman, and Orthodox Churchmen alike, Anglicans share the full joy and the full sorrow at the picture of the Church as she has made her way through history. But we do not depend upon any age for our inspiration; we do not believe that at any time the essential message of the Church was ever totally obscured, and we look to the future with as much veneration as others look to the past.

Another interesting example of the Anglican way of looking at things is found in the problem of authority. When the question, "What is the authority in the Church?" arises, Eastern Orthodox theologians tend to say that Church authority resides in tradition; the Roman Church centers its authority in the deliberations of its scholars and, more recently, in the expressed statements of the Bishop of Rome. Orthodox Protestants locate authority in the Scriptures; liberal Protestants stress the authority of experience. The Anglican Church bases its authority, on the other hand, on four things having an affinity with all of those held in the other traditions: (1) the Scriptures, (2) tradition, (3) reason, and (4) experience. All of these witnessing in harmony become the center of authority for Anglicans. Here again the richness of the whole Christian enterprise throughout history is evident.

It is not an easy task for the earnest pilgrim to make his way among the sects and denominations that claim to be Christian. Almost all of the Christian Churches believe themselves to be universal, yet, generally, they exclude one another. The names of the Churches in themselves contradict their claim to universality. They have to distinguish Roman Catholicism from Eastern Catholicism. These very titles are contradictions in themselves. An even more obvious contradiction, of course, occurs when Churches claiming to be Catholic name themselves after one person or one doctrine or form of polity. The brokenness of the Body of Christ is never so evident as in the simple listing of the names of Churches. No one who believes in the existence of the Catholic Church can rest easy in this situation. Upon practical or theological grounds, no one has been able to defend to the complete satisfaction of all the exclusive existence of his Church. The history of the Church is a long one, according to human calculation, but in the eyes of God it may still be in its infancy. At all events, no Christian can fail to hope that the present state of the Churches, with their divisions and differences, is not a permanent one. Certainly, the time of exclusively Protestant witness should, under God, someday pass. Likewise, divisions based on geography can have little to do with the Lord of the Church to whom there is no East or West. I believe that the Anglican Church, in the center of all the great Christian traditions, is in a position to be used by the Holy Spirit in the healing of the breaches in the Body of Christ and in the perfecting of her doctrine, worship, and polity.

Finally I have come to believe in the Anglican Church because it allows freedom within the Catholic tradition. Perhaps a rather interesting example of the Anglican position in this regard is illustrated by the various attitudes of the Christian Churches toward clerical marriage. In large sections of the Eastern Church, canons require that the priest be married. If the priest's wife dies, he is required to leave his parish and to live in a monastery. The Eastern Churches would seem to believe that in a parochial situation a married man can work most effectively. Within the Latin Church the priest may not be married, the consensus of opinion being that a single man makes the best priest. The Anglican Church, looking at the history of this question and able to appreciate both sides, allows but does not require its priest to be married. It leaves up to the individual priest the question of the state of life in which he can best perform his priesthood.

Another example of freedom within the Catholic tradition as found within Anglicanism is seen in the attitude of the Church toward private confession. Our Church insists, as do the other Catholic Communions, on proper preparation for the reception of the Holy Eucharist. Fully realizing the great benefits to many individuals of auricular confession, our Church provides and in many cases encourages penitents to confess privately to the priest. However, realizing the differences in people's needs and the harm that can come about through the use of undue duress in spiritual matters, our Church does not force private confession upon individuals. She teaches that if a person is truly sorry for his sins, God forgives through priestly absolution whether the confession is said privately or in public as in the General Confession in the liturgy. This attitude takes both the experience of the primitive and medieval Church into consideration. This is an example of freedom within the Catholic tradition.

I hope and pray, as I have said above, that the divisions in the Church of Christ as we know them today will not be permanent. The anxiety which the divisions in the Church cause to the earnest seeker for a true spiritual home is for many almost too much to bear. Certainly the Catholic Churches place a great burden upon the consciences of their constituents when they emphasize their differences. The earnest Christian who wants and needs above everything in the world to be a Catholic will not find perfection in any of the Christian Communions that he finds around him, but I have found my spiritual home in the Anglican Church for the reasons noted above and summarized below:

1. It is a Catholic Church but does not claim to be the only Catholic Church.

2. It takes the idea of reformation seriously, but does not bind itself to sixteenth-century forms.

3. It allows freedom within the Catholic tradition.

4. While being loyal to its Anglican traditions, it can function in love and charity with Eastern, Roman, and Protestant expressions of the Christian Faith.

19

MICHAEL BUDZANOSKI

Of Ukrainian stock and raised as a Roman Catholic of the Greek rite, and a coal miner by calling, Mr. Michael Budzanoski has given distinguished leadership in both the United Mine Workers and the Episcopal Church. Born in 1915, he graduated from the Centerville, Pennsylvania, High School with honors, then went to work in the mines, serving as an officer in the local union of the U.M.W. During the last war he began as a private in the Engineer Corps and rose to the rank of major. While an enlisted man, he took up boxing and participated in fourteen fights. Mr. Budzanoski returned to the mines after the war and in 1947 was elected a member of the executive board of District No. 5 of the U. M. W. He has been re-elected twice to this office, and at present has eleven local unions under his jurisdiction, his primary work being the settlement of disputes which cannot be resolved on the local level.

Mr. Budzanoski is on the vestry and parish council of St. Mary's Church, Charleroi, Pennsylvania, and teaches in the Church School. He is a member of the Standing Committee of the Diocese of Pittsburgh and serves on the Diocesan Council and in the Department of Missions. He was a delegate to the last Synod of the Province of Washington and was a delegate representing the Episcopal Church at the World Council of Churches Assembly at Evanston in 1954. He was a deputy from the Diocese of Pittsburgh at the General Convention in Honolulu last fall. He has written for the Church press on the Church and Labor and on the Evanston Assembly. He is married and has three children.

MICHAEL BUDZANOSKI

O NE OF THE most important and very satisfying decisions I have ever made was that which caused me to leave the Church of my fathers and to become a member of the Protestant Episcopal Church in the United States. In some ways this change was of a minor nature but in one way it was a drastic step. I was born a member of the Russian Greek (Uniat) Catholic Church. This Church is allied with Rome and under papal control. Many elements influenced me in my decision and it is difficult for me, even in retrospect, to evaluate properly the importance of these factors. In this short attempt at autobiography, I will wrestle with this evaluation.

As I look back across the years, my early religious training at home brings only the happiest memories, whereas the recollections of my religious education in the Church are extremely unpleasant and even quite painful. At home it was my father, a man of little formal education, who was the teacher. He had learned to read in the Polish language and laboriously read a Polish Bible. He learned to read the Polish language instead of his native Ukrainian because the Polish alphabet was much simpler than the Russian. I feel that he was a remarkable person in certain respects. He had a natural ability for telling stories to us at home in a most interesting manner. Then, too, he was completely tolerant and he had an almost brittle, undeviating devotion to what he believed to be the truth, right, and fairness. I readily recall many a pleasant evening at his knee along with my brother and two sisters, while he told us in his interesting and completely untheological manner the lessons he found in the Old and the

New Testaments. I can still picture him on many a Sunday afternoon diligently poring over his Polish Bible and then in the evening giving us the benefit of his laborious reading.

The Church which we attended, in my youth, had no Sunday School. The religious education of the children, however, was not neglected, since during the summer vacation period from public school the children attended a Church School. This was a daily school from 8:00 A. M. to 4:00 P. M. except on Saturday, when noontime signalled the end of the school day. Of course, there was no school on Sunday. It is not my intention to be derogatory and I presume that the situation which I knew was strictly local, but I now realize that my early religious training was deplorable. The educational efforts to instruct the children to read and to write the Russian language, to memorize the Catechism, and to read and discuss the lessons of the Bible, were made by a thoroughly unqualified and incompetent teacher. The Church Cantor was the superintendent. His education had been limited to grade school in Europe. Without a doubt, he was a man of good will, but he knew nothing of the intricacies of the teaching profession. The school facilities were wholly inadequate and the discipline was atrocious. Lessons had to be learned or extreme punishment was meted out. Some children—particularly those who showed any evidence of rebellion—were horse-whipped. Many were forced to kneel for long periods of time upon a rice-strewn wooden floor for failure to grasp the teachings of the Cantor. A minor punishment was the striking of the fingertips with a heavy ruler while the pupil held his fingers bunched together, palm upward. It became a daily ritual for a majority of the students to be punished, since it was impossible to learn the lengthy lessons assigned in a language of which most of the children had only the most rudimentary knowledge. To attend this

crude and rough summer school was one of the most unhappy experiences of my life. It is entirely possible that this
early period of my religious training irrevocably prejudiced
me against my boyhood Church.

When I reached manhood, I found myself with a very
liberal attitude toward Christian Churches of all denominations. Although my mother was shocked at my thinking, my
father, in his tolerant way, gave tacit approval to this de-
monstration of my feelings for religious freedom. On occasion, especially on Sunday evenings, I would attend services
of various Protestant Churches. I frequently attended tent
revival meetings and particularly enjoyed the hymn singing.
Often I became enthralled by the down-to-earth evangelizing
at these meetings. I could not understand the antagonisms
that these gatherings seemed to engender among people of
my own Church. It was at this stage that I began seriously to
question the validity of Roman claims and the seemingly
incongruous position of the Greek Uniats within the Roman
Communion.

Although the Greek Uniat Church submitted to the authority of Rome, there are great differences in Church law
and in Church custom. In the Uniat Church, married parish
clergy have been the rule, whereas Roman clergy are celibate;
the liturgy of the Church is entirely in the native tongue,
whereas the Roman liturgy is in Latin; Holy Communion
is administered in the Uniat Church by dipping a spoon
into the chalice and extracting a spoonful of bread and wine
(the bread is immersed in the wine during the ceremony of
consecration) and placing it in the mouth of the recipient,
whereas the Roman Church uses the wafer and has dispensed
entirely with the wine; and there are other minor differences
too numerous to mention. It occurred to me that the union
of the Greek Uniat and Roman Church was a marriage of

convenience as far as the Roman Church was concerned and that principle could be compromised as long as papal infallibility was accepted and allegiance to the Bishop of Rome recognized.

Papal domination in modern times, which I firmly believe runs contrary to Holy Scripture, to Church history, and to Christian common sense and logic, was a prime factor in my decision to leave the Church of my youth. As I will try to indicate, I could not believe that papal infallibility was the most important and fundamental doctrine of Christianity. Further study into the history of the Papacy before departing and since leaving the Roman Communion has convinced me that I have come out of man-made error into the truth of God. The foibles of man are frequently evident in papal history and preclude any real assurance that the Pope is the only Vicar of Christ. Bishop William Shaw Kerr in his *Handbook on the Papacy* dwells to some extent on the actually heretical teachings of certain Popes. It is common knowledge, even among well-read Roman Catholics, that certain Popes were consecrated before adulthood and that others were unworthy of consecration even from the most charitable viewpoint. The fact that the great Italian scientist, Galileo, was subjected to the vicissitudes of a vicious Inquisition because he contended for the Copernican theory of the earth's rotation around the sun illustrates plainly the weakness of papal infallibility. Popular church teachings of the time maintained that the sun rotated around the earth. Popes continued to condemn the theory of Copernicus and it was only in comparatively recent times (A.D. 1831) that the Roman Catholic position on this matter became untenable and Pope Gregory XVI finally changed it, thereby acceding to truth and reality.

Shortly after World War II began, I entered the armed forces. I attended Church services with regularity while in the United States Army. On the post the choice of attending Protestant services or Roman Catholic services was strictly with the individual. Although most soldiers were loyal to one or the other, I attended either service with equal regard. Usually the determining factor with me was the time set for the service and its convenience for me. I attended these services with an inward intolerance for others who were not sufficiently liberal in their thinking to do likewise. But I always liked the Protestant services better because I found these were in English and they usually involved a greater degree of "audience participation."

During the war years I attended the services of many Protestant denominations while at army posts. Likewise, Sunday mornings, while on pass, I went to churches of the Baptist, Lutheran, Methodist, Presbyterian, and Congregational denominations. I will never forget the services in Nashville, Tennessee, where I attended the Church of Christ with some regularity and was impressed by the genuinely friendly atmosphere that I found there. Neither before nor since have I found congregations as friendly as the churches of this denomination. Not being of this denomination, however, I could not participate fully in their devotions and I could not approve of a number of their basic tenets.

I also enjoyed my visits in various Baptist churches primarily because I found that the Baptists are such vigorous hymn-singers. It seemed to me that Baptist congregations sing as if they really mean every word they are singing, and the enthusiasm they engender makes a visitor feel as if the singing holds the actual primacy of their service.

In England, where I was stationed before the Normandy invasion, I attended services in both Roman Catholic and

Anglican churches. The first Anglican service that I attended was at St. Lawrence's in Reading. I was very favorably impressed by this first visit to an Anglican church. To me, the liturgy in the Book of Common Prayer was very easy to follow and the resemblance to my own Church was striking. The Anglican Church appeared to me to possess all the Catholic principles of historic Christianity, and at the same time it seemed to have cleansed itself of the aspects of religious authoritarianism which I could no longer, with conviction, wholly accept.

Almost of equal importance to me, however, was the liberal attitude of the Anglicans toward private confession before Holy Communion. I have always believed that, in some cases, it is psychologically beneficial to confess privately to a priest, particularly if some troubling sin plagues the mind and soul, but I could never accept the rigid requirements impressed on me during my youthful years. Although I submitted to the law in order to receive the Host, I was always skeptical of the necessity of such almost automatic confession, and I questioned the authenticity of it from a Biblical standpoint.

Church government in the Anglican Communion appeared to me to be at a happy medium between the rigid extreme as found in the authoritarian Roman Church and the loose, liberal democracy as found in some of our Protestant Congregational Churches. Then, too, I found the organ music as a background to participation in the service a very definite asset. It seemed to energize the sanctity of the religious service. In the Church of my youth, organ music or the music of any instrument except chimes or bells is forbidden by Church law. This is also in contradiction to the practice of the Latin Church.

After the war in Europe was over, I received a furlough for my coming marriage in England. My wife is of Irish-English extraction and had been reared in the Roman Catholic faith. Although she attended Roman parochial schools in later life, she too had found Roman teaching unacceptable. After due consideration, we decided to be married in an Anglican church in Bristol, England.

Upon my return home from Europe, for family peace I renewed my attendance at my old parish church, but the day of decision soon arrived. The parish priest called on me shortly before my first Easter at home and explained to me that I could not receive Holy Communion unless I confessed that I had grievously erred in getting married in a heretical Church. He maintained that I would have to be married all over again. Unless I did this, the Church would look upon me as living conjugally in sin and therefore not eligible for the Sacrament of Holy Communion. I looked with both amusement and disdain upon his demands because I realized that to accede to them would be an admission to his contention that I was living in sin. It would be a repudiation of my honest beliefs, thereby branding me as an outright hypocrite. I asserted that I felt fully married in compliance with God's law and that I would not make a sham of Holy Matrimony in order to appease any Church that I was convinced was narrow, constricted, and even subscribed to error. Thereafter I attended church rarely but I could not take the Holy Communion.

The fact that I was not participating in the Lord's Sacrament of Love in compliance with His admonition eventually affected me adversely. I became embittered by the thought that any Christians could deny other Christians. Rapidly I drifted into a state bordering on agnosticism. I ceased going to church entirely. For several months I remained in a state of religious confusion. In the meantime, we had our first child, and after due consideration we decided to have her baptized in the Protestant Episcopal Church. The Rev. Joseph Wittkofski, rector of St. Mary's Church of Charleroi, Pennsylvania, whose story is found elsewhere in this volume, was a tremendous help to me during this period and upon my return to God. For several months after my first daughter was baptized, we attended the Episcopal Church very infrequently. I constantly felt guilty in the eyes of God from morning to noon on Sunday, but as a result of family pressure for the old Church, I refused to allay this guilty feeling by regular church attendance. I was glad that the nearest Episcopal church was twelve miles away and used this as an excuse in my mind for non-attendance. I had certainly drifted from the sheepfold of our Saviour.

One morning I got up rather early and, thinking it was Saturday, I strolled into the garden for a bit of fresh air. It was a glorious spring morning with an unusually warm sun shining out of a cloudless sky. The grass was still covered with a heavy dew and the stillness of the morning was broken only by the frenzied warbling of some itinerant bird. I reflected upon the wonder of nature, and it occurred to me that this was a true reflection of the glory of God. Suddenly the stillness of the morning was shattered by the tingle of church bells in the distance. For a moment, I wondered why the bells should be ringing, and then it came to me that it was actually Sunday and I had totally forgotten it!

During my high school days my class was assigned, on one occasion, the creative chore of writing a parody upon some famous poem. I chose to write a parody upon Edgar Allan Poe's remarkable poem "The Raven." As I listened to the church bells on this wonderful morning, the words of the parody came flooding back to me even though I had no written record of it nor had I recited it since my high school days.

> Once upon a morning cheerful,
> While I wandered, free, unfearful,
> O'er the lovely lanes that lurk
> Within my garden wall;
> While I sauntered softly singing
> Suddenly there came a tingling
> As of church bells gently ringing
> Ringing in the morning lull;
> " 'Tis the Sabbath!" They reminded,
> Church bells in the morning lull,
> Church bells calling, calling all!

A feeling of great guilt swept over me that morning as I stood in the garden in deep thought. This feeling was shortly overwhelmed, however, by a feeling of determination and exultation. I had resolved that the next time I heard the call of the church bells, it would be from a pew inside a church. My wife and I discussed the subject of regular church attendance and we decided to attend St. Mary's Church of Charleroi. The next Sunday we were in church, and from that day seven years ago we have attended church with absolute regularity.

Within the Episcopal Church I have found deep religious peace and serenity. The Rev. Joseph Wittkofski has been of tremendous assistance in instructing me with Episcopal principles, Church canons, and Church teaching. His kindly understanding and ever-willingness to help me could only have been God-sent. I have found that the Episcopal Church stands for beliefs that I have always possessed. I have found the position of the Church on dogmatic principles supported by Scripture and amenable to reason and logical thought. Recently I had the great honor and undeserved privilege of representing the Episcopal Church at the Second Assembly of the World Council of Churches, which was held in Evanston, Illinois, in August of 1954. In my preparation for this Assembly, I carefully studied the points of theological difference between various major denominations that were to be represented. The Assembly itself, for me, was a theological education. I am convinced that the stand that the Anglican Communion took as expressed in the Lambeth Quadrilateral is a true measure of Catholic belief. The principles of the Quadrilateral are (1) the Holy Scripture is the Word of God; (2) the Apostles' and the Nicene Creeds make up the rule of Faith; (3) the two Sacraments of Baptism and Holy Communion are generally necessary for salvation; (4) the historic episcopate ought to be the source and structure of the Church's ministry.

The Anglican Communion, of which the Protestant Episcopal Church in the United States is a part, must be called a true Catholic Church under God. In this I believe I can find a way to eternal life.

At the World Council of Churches Assembly, a report was presented by the section on "The Laity" which stated: "There is a need to change the atmosphere which strikes the newcomer so forcibly in many churches, the atmosphere of an old-fashioned middle class culture, now radically changed in society but surviving in the Church. A tendency to choose the lay leadership of a congregation from among white-collar workers often prevents others, especially young industrial workers, from feeling at home in the Church." The Episcopal Church cannot be exonerated of this charge. This condition must be remedied if the Church is to have an appeal to the great mass of rural and industrial workers here in the United States. All things considered, I firmly believe that the

Episcopal Church has a great opportunity for evangelization here in America and it is best suited to act as a unifying force among all Churches of Christendom. I am truly happy to be a small part of this great missionary effort of our Church.

20

CHAD WALSH

A distinguished poet and author who began his career as a reporter and linotypist, the Rev. Dr. Chad Walsh graduated from the University of Virginia, and received his Master of Arts in French and Doctor of Philosophy in English at the University of Michigan. After serving for two and a half years as a research analyst in the War Department, he joined the faculty of Beloit College, where he is now Professor of English and Poet in Residence.

Dr. Walsh is author of two books of poetry, The Factual Dark *and* Eden Two-Way, *and of six religious works, including* Stop Looking and Listen, C. S. Lewis: Apostle to the Skeptics, Early Christians of the Twenty-First Century, Knock and Enter, Campus Gods on Trial, *and* Behold the Glory, *and he is co-author of* Faith and Behavior. *He is one of the founders of the* Beloit Poetry Journal *and has published poems and articles in a number of periodicals, including* The Atlantic Monthly, The New Republic *and* The Saturday Review.

In 1949 Professor Walsh was ordained a priest in the Episcopal Church and has been serving as associate rector of St. Paul's Church in Beloit. He is married and has four children.

CHAD WALSH*

WHY I BECAME an Episcopalian is less interesting to me than why I have remained one. It is easy enough to join a Church or get married or begin a career in the flush of strong enthusiasm; but the years that follow must affirm or invalidate the wisdom of the decision. For this reason, I shall move rapidly through the considerations which originally led me to the Episcopal Church.

I suppose the story really begins in the small Virginia town of Marion, tucked in between the Blue Ridge and Allegheny Mountains. I remember it with a good deal more tenderness now than I often felt when I was growing up there. It seemed a constricting environment to me. In particular, the brand of religion that I encountered in playground conversations and in sermons preached during school hours was centered around certain key words, of which *blood, fire, sin,* and *death* are those I remember best. I suppose there must have been a more winsome Christianity locally available—indeed, I now know that this was the case—but I was scarcely aware of it at the time. I got the impression that the Christian faith is a dour, repressed, rather ferocious creed, and that salvation consists in believing the Bible (especially the Old Testament) from cover to cover. At an oddly early age I resolved to avoid churches and Sunday Schools, and I remained faithful to this private vow, with very few exceptions, all through my teens and early twenties.

It was not until I had finished my college work and taken a couple of years of graduate work at the University of

* This chapter is in part based upon my pamphlet *I Chose the Episcopal Church* (revised and enlarged edition, Seabury Press). Copyright 1953 by the Seabury Press, Inc., and used with their permission.

Michigan that my reaction against this early environment faded enough for me—by very slow degrees, with many hesitations—to be able to look at Christianity through reasonably unbiased eyes. What I finally saw made surprising sense. I began to understand the veiled meanings in even the cliché phrases of my childhood; I also glimpsed some part of what is meant by such words as *incarnation, creation,* and *love.* This did not happen overnight; it was a matter of years and much groping in the twilight.

However, my purpose is not to explain why I became a Christian, but why I chose the Episcopal Church. It is enough to say that by my late twenties I had about reached the point where I believed in God and in Christ as the incarnate Son of God. I was now ready to think about becoming a member of the Church.

But what Church? I was never tempted to be part of the universal Church by meditating in God's green woods on Sunday morning; I was sure that it is better to be part of the fragmented Church than to be a one-man Church. So, in an unsystematic way, I went shopping.

I did not shop along the whole spectrum of possibilities. For one thing, my childhood had taught me what I did not want. I was not seeking a denomination which was overly literal in its interpretation of the Bible, or which insisted that evolution must not be true because then the earth could not have been created in 4004 b. c. Neither was I convinced that tobacco, alcohol, short skirts, dancing, and card-playing were the main challenges faced in the Christian life. In short, I automatically ruled out the more Fundamentalist Churches. I say this now in full realization that I may have been selling them short. I have since come to believe that many Fundamentalists have so great a depth of conviction that it at least partially compensates for their beetle-browed emphasis on matters I consider secondary to salvation; also, I have met a number who are not beetle-browed at all. But I would still make the same decision, despite the mellowness that age, experience, or the Holy Spirit seems to be achieving in me. I was looking for a Church which put first things first.

Fundamentalism was out. So was Roman Catholicism. I must confess I never considered it with complete detachment, though I circled close around it. Perhaps my all-Protestant background in the South had lasting effects at this point. At any rate, when I tried to think about it, I found that much in the Roman Church seemed thoroughly fine to me. I liked the sense of continuity with the past, the effort to worship God with beauty and dignity and a sense of awe and mystery. But I detected also a certain rigidity, as though this Church had crystallized prematurely during the feudal period, and both its social attitudes and its philosophic presuppositions were the sort that rendered awkward any attempt to meet the twentieth century head-on. I shall have more to say about this later.

To conclude the negative part of my quest, I soon found that the more "liberal" or "modernist" Protestant Churches were no solution either. They left me with a feeling of emptiness. I mean those denominations which tended to water down the basic theology of Christianity: which, for example, delighted in distinguishing between "the religion about Jesus" (which was bad) and "the religion of Jesus" (which was good).

The advancing years have again done their work of mellowing. I now see in the whole movement of "liberal theology" a necessary corrective to the literalism and rigidity against which it was reacting, and I know from a study of Church history that many of the liberalizers deserve special

credit for their fine work in sensitizing the social consciousness of their fellow Christians. But I still feel as I did: that
Christianity is far more than a system of Golden Rule ethics,
that its unique core is that cluster of doctrines—the Incarnation, Atonement, Resurrection—centering around Christ,
and that any denomination which preaches these truths in a
muted voice is muting the transforming power of the Gospel.

But enough of negations. What I was fumblingly seeking
was a Church true to the basic affirmations of Christianity,
as I could best understand them; one not inclined to go off
on extreme tangents; one which had a sense of continuity
and fellowship with the Church of the Apostles; one which
worshipped with beauty in such a way that I could participate wholeheartedly and unself-consciously with my fellow
members.

I found all this in the Episcopal Church. Even during that
transition period when I was learning my way around in the
Book of Common Prayer, and often standing when I should
have been sitting—and vice versa—I still had a feeling of
being at home. Thus it was that soon after I came to Beloit
in 1945 I asked Father Johnson, the rector of St. Paul's
Church, to baptize me, and I was confirmed the next spring.

So much for why I became an Episcopalian. A few years
later I was ordained to the diaconate and then to the priesthood, and have since served as a week-end assistant at St.
Paul's, here in Beloit. I now have a chance to see the Episcopal Church from the sacristy and the sanctuary as well as
from the nave. If I had any inclination toward disillusion-
ment, I suppose my present status as a clerical "insider"
would accentuate it. I do not feel that inclination.

I went into the Episcopal Church with my eyes open,
knowing that even though it is part of the universal Body of
Christ, it would also be composed of human beings as limited

and distorted as myself. I did not expect to be transported to a fellowship of stained-glass saints, but rather to take my chair in a club for struggling sinners.

My expectation turned out to be accurate. There is everything possible wrong with the Episcopal Church, precisely as there is with faculty meetings, family life, and political parties. But all these shortcomings are the "accidents," generated by human imperfection and sin. The "essence," the inner reality of the Church, has that rightness which comes from Christ and the indwelling Holy Spirit. I do not see any eternal obstacles, within the nature of the Episcopal Church itself, which can stop God from His painstaking and continuous work of cleansing and revitalizing it.

Whatever appealed to me in the Episcopal Church ten years ago still does—though in some cases I think I see the appeal in closer focus—but there are other aspects which I did not notice then and which now loom equally large. However, I shall not try to be too pedantic about separating "early" and "recent" insights; that would be to make the whole thing too schematic.

As I sit here thinking about it, it seems to me that one of the most precious traditions of Anglicanism is its intellectual flexibility. By this I do not imply a kind of jellyfish thinking. Anglican dogma is clear and firm enough in its central affirmations. But by intellectual flexibility I mean a freedom in interpreting and expressing the central dogma—a freedom not evident in many denominations. Look at the Roman Catholics, who appear to have contracted a lasting alliance with St. Thomas Aquinas, so that their categories of thought are anchored in the mind of a thirteenth-century thinker. Now if one must marry one human mind, there are few better choices than that of Thomas. But great as he was, he only partly transcended his century, and too exclusive a reliance upon his categories of thought can become a strait-jacket, albeit a more comfortable one than most.

The Fundamentalists find themselves in a similiar predicament. They have a way of singling out some particular strand of the Reformation or later pietistic tradition, and then defensively building walls around every jot and tittle of its verbal formulations.

However, this overly permanent alliance between the eternal Gospel and transient philosophies and modes of expression is not confined to the more conservative Churches. I have known liberal Protestant thinkers tied down in equally deadly fashion by what were "the latest ideas"—of the nineteenth century.

Now it seems to me that Christians make a mistake when they sign a permanent treaty of alliance with *any* philosophy. Philosophy and philosophers, even the towering St. Thomas Aquinas, come and go. They serve a useful function for their particular periods of history, but if they are regarded as final, they can mummify the Gospel. God's mighty acts and their meaning are beyond the power of words to categorize with definitive clarity; the most that words can do is to offer broken hints and clues and flashing signal lights, all pointing toward the God back of every other reality.

I like the eclecticism of Anglican thinkers. Some find the insights of Aristotle peculiarly useful; some are Platonists; many revere and read Hooker; there are Thomists aplenty; others have turned to Whitehead or Marx or Freud and extracted surprising illuminations. This seems to me as it should be. Certainly, when I am talking with someone who does not understand Christianity, I don't want to be obliged to put him through a basic course in Aristotle before I can speak of the Gospel. I want to feel free to start from whatever philosophy he has, even though it is nothing more than God Bless America and Keep the Communists from Crossing the Ocean; then we can explore and determine whether even the most primitive categories of thought may not at least partially express that Gospel which defies Thomas or Kant to express it adequately.

I don't know which is cause and which is effect, but this intellectual flexibility is closely connected with another Anglican quality which I can best describe as *balance*. The Church of England and its daughter Churches throughout the world seldom go off too far on any one tangent. There seem to be in-built checks to prevent fierce extremes from having comparably fierce consequences. It is true that when one particular school of theology gains temporary ascendancy in many denominations, the Anglican Communion moves somewhat in that direction—and indeed contributes its sturdy share of theorists, zealots, and leaders. But the swing in one direction is rarely as violent as in many other communions. For example, the theological liberalism, which steadily gained ground in the early twentieth century until neo-orthodoxy rose to counter it, had a strong impact on Episcopal thought—but even at the height of this period, Episcopalians still recited one of the Creeds each Sunday, and the Prayer Book remained stubbornly Trinitarian and Incarnational. There were the built-in checks, making for balance.

Then, when the seminaries began to speak with a Swiss accent and started mass-producing fiery-eyed young ministers to preach judgment, sin, and original sin, the Episcopal Church also started re-exploring these relatively neglected aspects of a faith that was in danger of becoming shallow and too sunny. Much of the best neo-orthodox leadership has come from within the Anglican Communion. But again the swing has not been as violent as in many denominations. Even the most austerely neo-orthodox Episcopalian still reckons with such a word as sanctification, and unashamedly uses it in public.

The Anglican Communion has never been given to monolithic thinking. From the first moment when the Church of England recovered its independence from Rome, it combined ways of thinking which can be roughly described as "high," "low," and "broad." One should also add a fourth category, "composite," for the numerous communicants who have always tried to merge the best insights of all factions. At any rate, the various groups have had long practice in living under one roof. You do not see them today shaking the dust from their heels and going off to found new Churches. This is to me one of the most splendid things about the Episcopal Church. Its factionalism can be pretty bitter and unchristian, but it keeps its family quarrels within the family. No picture is turned to the wall, though libelous cartoons are sometimes hung next to the family portraits.

This family solidarity is one of the main reasons for the balance and moderation of the Episcopal Church. It does not employ a mere balloting to decide controversies, though on paper it may appear to do so. Before any ballots are cast, the sensibilities of all the members of the family are taken into consideration. There is an unspoken tradition that no one's honest convictions should be outraged too violently.

The result is that a fantastic variety of people find themselves happily domiciled inside the Episcopal Church. People often speculate on what a united Church would be like. They can find out for themselves by studying the Episcopal Church. Every temperament and outlook from the Congregational to the Roman is found within it—under one roof.

This leads me to what I value perhaps most of all—
the feeling, which grows stronger all the time, that the
Anglican Communion is indeed a family. It holds together
as a family does. Each bishop is a kind of father; his authority is not so much in the Canons as in his own character and
the traditional relation with his people. A good priest is a
local father. The members of the Church are brothers and
sisters, uncles and nephews, aunts and nieces. This is not to
suggest that all is sweetness and harmony. Family antagonisms, like civil wars, are peculiarly dreadful. But it does
mean that the bond of unity is a kind that is deeply rooted
in familiar human experience. It is not a unity based on
"social contract," any more than the unity of parent and
child is. Nor is the unity primarily an intellectual one,
sealed by signing on the dotted line beneath a fifty-page
statement of belief. It is something both simpler and deeper.
It is the unity of people who share the same family customs
(habits of worship) and who regard themselves as being
linked not merely with the other worshippers in a parish,
but with their fellow worshippers in other places, and with
the men and women who for long centuries have met together for worship not too dissimilar from that which you
will find in any Anglican church today.

I suppose this same family feeling may exist in many
Churches; it is not my purpose to evaluate them in this regard; indeed, throughout this whole discussion I am dealing
primarily with the positive values I find in the Episcopal
Church, rather than with their presence or absence elsewhere.
But back to my point—I do recognize the family feeling very
strongly in the Episcopal Church, and it seems to me a more
meaningful way of binding people together than any social
contract or coldly intellectual agreement on all the fine type
in some doctrinal exposition. I like to think that I can step

into an Episcopal church anywhere, be at home in its worship, and share the same assumptions and household talk with the other people. I have never been disappointed.

I come now to another thing which is a precious gift of the Anglican tradition. It knows how to deal wisely with "the world." By the world, I mean human activities in general, and the physical universe in which we find ourselves. There are many denominations which regard "the world" as hopeless and fit only for some cosmic rubbish heap. Others make the opposite mistake and confuse its finite values with the infinite reaches of the Christian hope. The right attitude is a subtle one, though I think it consists in taking "the world" seriously but not too seriously; of reverencing it as in part God's creation and in part His theatre of operation; of working to infuse the spirit and insights of the Gospel into "the world" so that the latter becomes more and more a vehicle for God's purposes.

One result of this outlook is the relatively mellow position that Episcopalians usually take, for example, toward drinking and dancing. It is hard for them to believe that the processes of fermentation and distillation, made possible by the kind of universe God created, are inherently evil; it is even more difficult for them, remembering that God created the body as well as the soul, to rule out the innocent joys that the body is granted by God to know.

At its best, the Anglican tradition also emphasizes an all-embracing social concern, a desire to work in politics and every other human arena to make the world of human relationships a closer approach to the Kingdom of God. I emphasize the fact that I speak of the Anglican tradition at its best; there are plenty of Episcopalians who regard their Church as a center for the right people who happen to have a taste for kneeling. But every organization should be judged by its best, by its passionate and growing edge.

Closely allied to the attitudes I have been discussing is the Anglican view of the sacraments. There are very few denominations which take them as seriously. To the Anglican, the two major sacraments of Baptism and Holy Communion are like twin Everests; the five minor sacraments are also very high mountains, though not as high as the first two. However, less defined but sensed, the sacramental landscape includes other mountains of medium height, and countless foothills. Looked at this way, the sacraments—the traditional ones—are intense and dramatic expressions of something which underlies and overarches them: the creative and indwelling presence and purposes of God throughout the whole of His created universe.

This sense of an all-pervasive sacramentalism leads naturally to the Anglican attitude toward the arts. Here one finds a warm appreciation and sympathy. A lack of artistic grace is not considered essential to worship and salvation. I have noticed how many writers and artists of all sorts, as well as persons who do not practice the arts but love them, find themselves drawn toward the Episcopal Church. I can bear personal testimony here. Whatever I most deeply want to say—whether "secular" or "sacred"—I can best express by writing a poem. It means a great deal to me that I belong to a Church which has nourished a long succession of great poets, not the least of whom are the living T. S. Eliot and W. H. Auden, and that the general tone of the tradition is one that makes me believe the writing of poetry can be a true act of love to God and neighbor.

This cluster of considerations, all arising from the Anglican attitude toward "the world," is of more than casual importance. Men are always seesawing back and forth between extremes. When they are not living and dying for two-car garages, they are running off to the desert to become hermits. But in the Anglican tradition I find a clue to how we can learn to function as whole beings in the wholeness of God's universe. I do not believe He intended us to despise any part of the potentialities He has built into us, or to scorn one stick or stone of the cosmos He has extended through space.

I have much to be grateful for. Christianity itself is too good to be true; therefore it is true, for its goodness is a kind that merely human minds could not have invented. And in the Episcopal Church I have found a place where the goodness comes alive for me, so that I can begin my basic training for the "fullness of time" which God has already revealed and has promised to all who will accept it.

21

HOWARD A. JOHNSON

A leading Kierkegaard scholar, the Rev. Howard A. John-
son is Canon Theologian of the Cathedral of St. John the
Divine—the first American priest to hold such a canonry—
and is Adjunct Professor of Religion at Columbia University.
Born in Iowa, he was graduated from the University of
California at Los Angeles and the Virginia Theological
Seminary. After his ordination, he served as vicar of St.
Andrew's Mission, Elsinore, and as curate of All Saints'
Church, Pasadena, in the Diocese of Los Angeles, and was
Assistant Chaplain to Episcopal Students at Princeton Uni-
versity, while enrolled there as a graduate student in philos-
ophy. This was followed by three years as Assistant Minister
of St. John's Church (Lafayette Square), Washington, D. C.
Under appointment as a Fellow of the American-Scandi-
navian Foundation, he next spent two years studying philos-
ophy and theology at the University of Copenhagen. Re-
turning to this country, he enrolled at Union Theological
Seminary, which awarded him the degree of Master of Sa-
cred Theology, summa cum laude, *in 1949. Then followed*
four years, first as Assistant, later as Associate Professor of
Theology at the School of Theology of the University of the
South.

Every summer Canon Johnson returned to Denmark for
additional research, save the summer of 1952, when he lec-
tured on Kierkegaard at twenty-two universities and colleges

—Christian, Buddhist, secular, and Shinto—in Japan. His last post before becoming Canon Theologian of New York Cathedral was that of Visiting Fellow at St. Augustine's, Central College of the Anglican Communion in Canterbury. He has written on the thought of Søren Kierkegaard for Theology Today, The American-Scandinavian Review, *and* The Anglican Theological Review.

HOWARD A. JOHNSON

IN CANTERBURY itself I sit as I essay to tell the story of my own "Pilgrimage to Canterbury." The study from which I write opens on the one side to a splendid vista of Canterbury Cathedral, three hundred yards distant. By universal human consent, it ranks as one of the noblest buildings in Christendom. From the windows on the other side of my study I see, but a stone's throw away, the ruins of the great Norman Abbey Church, built in the time of William the Conqueror and splendid enough to rival even the Cathedral. Here was created a Benedictine center, second only to Monte Cassino, which endured until it was demolished by order of Henry VIII. The monastic buildings Henry saved for himself as a palace, but the church disappeared—except for one section of the nave wall which that athletic monarch left standing to serve as a backstop for handball! And that was the end, temporarily, of "the Mother-University of England," which could boast that it was "the seat of letters and study, at a time when Cambridge was a desolate fen, and Oxford a tangled forest in a wide waste of waters."

This, then, is St. Augustine's, the Central College of the Anglican Communion. If I tell the story of this College, I shall be telling, obliquely, the story of why I became an Episcopalian; for St. Augustine's College exhibits those characteristics of Anglicanism which I first learned to know not in Canterbury but in California—characteristics which (to use a much misunderstood term of another St. Augustine) I had found *irresistible*: continuity with the Catholic past, constant ability to critize herself and reform herself, openness to new truths coming from any quarter whatsoever, missionary zeal, ecumenical concern, delight in God and in all that He has created. Of me, of my personal history, something more a little later. Far more important is it, and far more interesting, to tell first of Canterbury and its unique College—both the symbolical and the actual "end" of my pilgrimage, although, as I shall attempt to show presently, the end was somehow in sight almost from the beginning.

When St. Augustine, as friend and emissary of St. Gregory the Great, landed on the shores of Kent in 597, he found the Church already there. En route to Canterbury, seat of the Kentish kings, he passed St. Martin's Church, where already the Queen of Kent was worshipping and had a bishop as her chaplain. Impressed by Augustine and his forty companions, Ethelbert the King soon applied for baptism. Shortly thereafter, removing the Court from Canterbury for political reasons, Ethelbert gave to Augustine the site of his palace for a cathedral, together with a large tract of land lying between the palace and ancient St. Martin's for the building of an abbey. Within sixteen years of Augustine's arrival, both cathedral and abbey were in being. In rivalry sometimes bitter, sometimes friendly, the two institutions grew side by side. They rapidly became Britain's chief center of intellectual learning and of missionary enterprise.

Being half-Danish myself, I prefer to skip lightly over the grim Danish days which followed. These were replaced eventually by the brighter days of William the Conqueror, during which the Saxon buildings gave way to magnificent Norman structures, and St. Augustine's Abbey flourished as one of the richest and most influential religious foundations in Britain.

The importance of medieval Canterbury as a favorite goal of pilgrims is too well known to need recounting. Nor is it

necessary here to say anything about the complex causes of
the decline and fall of monasticism in England. Nine centuries of existence as a monastic center ended for St. Augustine's when the great church was torn down in 1538. Adjacent buildings were spared, as I have indicated, and were
used as a royal residence by Henry, Elizabeth, and both
Charleses. From royal hands the estate passed to noble and
then to commoner hands. By the early nineteenth century
such buildings as remained had suffered the indignity of
being used as a warehouse, a brewery, and a tavern. Pigs
rooted in the Tudor Garden. The court was given over to
cheap-jack shows. The refectory, where once the pilgrims
of Chaucer had been entertained, became an arena for cock-
fighting.

To J. Beresford Hope, a devout Churchman of the 1840's,
it seemed criminal that so great a foundation had come to so
ignoble an end. He bought the buildings—what remained of
them—but had not the slightest idea what he would do with
them until a master at Eton, the Rev. Edward Coleridge,
came and told him of his dream of founding a college where
English ordinands might be trained for service overseas in
the rapidly expanding British Empire.

These men issued a great public appeal to which the response of the public was great. Endowments were received.
Buildings were restored. A Royal Charter was granted, and
in 1848 the College opened. Thus was reborn the work begun
by Augustine. Books were again read and written where for
three centuries there had been only desecration and decay.

In the century that followed, the new St. Augustine's
trained and sent some eight hundred Englishmen on mission. Their names and the faraway places to which they went
may be read engraved in the walls of the Lower Chapel. The
modern Canterbury pilgrim is put into strange mood by

seeing how brief the lives of most of them were and how many of them fell as martyrs.

This phase of the College's existence met disaster when, in the blitz of Canterbury in 1942, a bomb intended for the Cathedral hit St. Augustine's instead. Apparently this was the end.

But then, at the Lambeth Conference of 1948, by unanimous resolution of the entire episcopate of a world-wide Church, St. Augustine's was for the second time raised from death. Here was to be established a new college—continuous with the old, yet different. Not now was St. Augustine's to be a place for the training of Englishmen to go overseas, but a place where representatives from the Younger Churches, born of English missionary endeavor, were to be summoned "home" to drink at the wellsprings of Anglicanism.

The need of such a Central College was everywhere apparent and insured its immediate acceptance. Rebuilt and reorganized, the College opened again in the autumn of 1952. Since then priest-students from twenty different lands have prayed and studied together at St. Augustine's—and have entertained the citizens of Canterbury by turning the narrow streets into an international fashion show, from turbans to ten-gallon hats! Rich in potentialities, though also bristling with inevitable difficulties, the College has made such progress in the first two years of its new existence as to win from the Archbishop of Canterbury commendation as a major contribution to the unity of the Anglican fellowship.

Anglicanism is committed, of course, to the principle of autonomous national Churches, with indigenous clergy, and with the liturgy "in a language understood of the people." In intention and in fact, our Communion is a family of self-governing Churches, all of them bound to the See of

Canterbury in affection and loyalty, yet none of them bound by Canterbury jurisdictionally. Such a family quite obviously requires links of personal knowledge and friendship if it is to be held together in unity. The Warden and Fellows, in describing the purpose of the Central College, put the case exactly: "It is vital that those who are likely to be leaders in various kinds of work in the Younger Churches should have access to the riches of thought and devotion in the longer-established Churches of the West. It is equally important that those in the Older Churches should share the fresh understanding of the Gospel into which the Younger Churches (in their 'New Testament' situations) are entering. All stand in need of greater knowledge of each other, and, as the number of national Churches and self-governing provinces grows, the provision of means for preserving a common approach to matters of worship, faith, and order becomes more urgent."

Here I have lived for one year, enjoying the remarkable experience of worship, study, parley, and play in a community that is international, interracial, multilingual, Anglican. At this moment, within view of my room, a croquet game is in progress on the lawns of the Tudor Garden. A priest-student from Hong Kong has just made a wicket and is cheered from the side lines by a priest from Louisiana. His glee is shared by an archdeacon from Nigeria, whereas a canon from Australia looks depressed over the way the game is going. On the far side of the court a presbyter from the Church of South India is locked in debate with a bishop of the Mar Thoma Church, a priest from the Syrian Orthodox Church, and two of our clergy from Ceylon. Are they discussing croquet or ecclesiastical polity? At this distance I

can discern only, from gesture and play of countenance, that
—whatever the subject—they are in deadly earnest.

I think back over the events of the day. We began this
morning with Matins, conducted by a priest from Toronto.
This was followed by a half-hour of corporate silence and
then by the Holy Communion, the celebrant being a Japanese. Yesterday a bishop of the Upper Nile, vested only in
rochet and chimere, took the northward position for the
celebration. The day before that the Indians and the Singhalese, in glorious array and with incense, celebrated the Holy
Mysteries in accordance with the Bombay Rite. So it goes.
Every day a different celebrant, a different liturgy, and a
different language. If you live one year at St. Augustine's
you will be able to come in on cue with appropriate responses to any curious combination of versicle sounds!

The breakfast is unmistakably English. Then follows a
morning of lectures. Any trained auditor will at once be
struck by two facts: here is scholarship, but here is no ordinary theological school. The curriculum has been carefully
constructed to meet specific needs. There is, for example, a
heavy emphasis on liturgical studies. The Prayer Books of
each Church and the proposed revisions thereof are examined
critically, historically, theologically. It is right that each
Church should revise its liturgy, its rites and ceremonies, its
vocabulary, and its architecture, in order to speak the Eternal
Word more relevantly in the diverse portions of the vineyard. But would it not be a tragedy if, in this way, we were
to become strangers to each other? Hence there must be
steady conversation among the brethren to inform each other
of local developments, to enrich each other mutually, and
to correct each other, by going deep into the wealth of our
common tradition and by sharing the new insights gained
from being out among the highways and hedges of the

Church's mission. Yet no intelligent criticism of the liturgical evolution is possible unless it is grounded, on the one hand, in Biblical and Patristic studies, and grounded, on the other, in accurate and up-to-date knowledge of the situations actually obtaining in each culture and country where the Church is at work. For this reason, the accent falls at St. Augustine's on the Holy Scriptures, which are examined in the light of their traditional interpretation and in the light shed by modern criticism and the revival of Biblical theology. Equal stress is given to an examination of the contemporary scene. This involves such subjects as the comparative study of religions, the history of Christianity in Asia and Africa, the political and social patterns of various lands, and the whole modern climate of opinion. This means, for example, knowing something about Mohammed and Marx, Hinduism and Freudianism, Singhalese demonology and empirical science. The special task, in other words, is to train men in the skills of apologetics and evangelism. At the same time, St. Augustine's has learned from history the lesson that all apologetics and all evangelization, in their zeal to speak persuasively and to convert, have sometimes been guilty (usually unconsciously) of rewording the Faith in such wise that it is no longer quite the Faith one intended to commend. And this is why St. Augustine's expends its greatest labor on theology—Patristic, Medieval, Reformation, and Modern—with especial reference to our own Anglican divines. However difficult it may be to present the fundamentals of the Faith without becoming a fundamentalist, and however exacting it is to speak a contemporary word without becoming a modernist, this is the task, as the Anglican Communion has been given to understand it, and St. Augustine's College exists to set it forward.

The Warden, as is fitting, is an Englishman, and so are most of the Fellows, although ordinarily there is a visiting American Fellow, and the search is on for a permanent American Sub-Warden. A theological professor from Japan is scheduled to teach next year, and future plans call for Visiting Fellows by rotation from every Province of the Anglican Communion. In faculty as well as in student body, the Central College must reflect our geographical, as well as doctrinal, catholicity.

I have been describing a typical day at St. Augustine's. The croquet game is ending. It's time for tea. After that the students will study until Evensong at seven. But because I've been working all afternoon, I intend to use the study period for a walk about the grounds. Passing the Library, which was reconstructed from the ruins of the abbot's banquet hall, one enters a cloister where Norman pipes still supply water for the fountain. Beyond that one comes to the place where the Norman Abbey once stood and where it is possible to see its foundations and the foundations of its two predecessors. And here are the burial places of many archbishops and abbots. Going farther, the path leads to the ruins of three Saxon churches and to the remains of an altar at which there is no reason to doubt that St. Augustine himself celebrated the Holy Mysteries.

At Evensong tonight, this being a Friday, there will be a sermon. Sometimes the preacher is the Warden or one of the Fellows. Occasionally he is a visiting bishop or one of the students. Tonight he is professor of theology from Oxford, who has come to give a series of special lectures. Very frequently we avail ourselves of the brilliant scholarship to be found at Oxford and Cambridge and the other theological centers of the British Isles, and just as frequently we send the men out to visit these centers and to observe whatever is going on in Britain of an imaginative, creative character, whether it be in parishes, in colleges, or in chaplaincies to miners or factory workers. Everything everywhere is grist for our mill. Anglicanism is that big.

After dinner in the thirteenth-century hall we retire to the common room for coffee and discussion. Every Friday evening one of the students is asked to speak candidly about the particular opportunities and difficulties of ministering in his own land. Perhaps no aspect of the College's life is as important as this, save only the mutual conversations of the brethren which take place at all times, where lasting friendships are formed on the basis of knowledge, respect, and concern—the whole enterprise being informed and inspired, of course, by the ever new discovery at the altar of our oneness in Christ.

So there is something about St. Augustine's, Canterbury. And now, as anticlimax, autobiography can begin. While I cannot suppose that anyone is interested in my personal history as such, I cannot deny that I find it agreeable, for a change, to be *invited* to wax autobiographical!

As a boy I was not exactly a frequenter of Sunday Schools and churches. But I sometimes went—because my friends went. Rarely did I have the patience to persevere for many Sundays in a row. I have never won a pin for my lapel. Nor did any member of my family. Neither of my parents, none of my grandparents, and not a single aunt or uncle has had a relationship to organized religion. In both the families which went into my making there was a two-generation lapse from the Church. Only toward the end of her life did my paternal grandmother find her way back to the Baptist Church, of which her father had been one of the founders in Denmark. From my forebears I learned two important lessons: that a wide compass of authentic existence and genuine idealism is possible *outside* Christianity (a lesson which helped to make me a humanist); and that the existence of such people in such numbers is, in part, a judgment on the Church, from which the Church must learn, in addition to sympathy, patience, and tolerance, greater skill in the apologetic arts.

At the age of twelve I had a religious crisis—the reasons for which I remember most imperfectly, and I have no talent for rummaging around in the depths of the unconscious—which resulted in my applying to the Presbyterian Church for baptism. There was emotion, I recall, and some real comprehension of what the step involved. For the next three years I went faithfully to divine worship. During my junior year in high school I imagined myself deeply in love with a Roman Catholic girl. She was well trained in her faith and devout. I started accompanying her when she went to Mass, and here I encountered *mysterium tremendum* (to use Otto's phrase) which I found both fascinating and repelling. This experience started me on a course of study which was to become an all-absorbing interest. I *had* to know how it came about that Christianity had taken so many diverse forms. But this investigation of denominations suddenly widened to include a study of Christianity's rivals in the world market. I had to know about Confucianism, Shintoism, Buddhism, and all the rest.

It would be tedious to tell the whole story—a story whose pattern is not greatly different, after all, from that of so many others—but, to come to the point, such Christianity as I had (and this is not the fault of Calvin!), a Christianity which was little more than ethical idealism mingled with secular optimism and garnished with a few religious overtones, suffered shipwreck on the twin rocks of intellectual doubt and moral incommensurability. The well-known troubles of a collegian in his sophomore year hit me already in the final year of high school, and the freshman year in college only intensified the break. I became a pagan of sorts —but not the happy sort. Although I now doubted the existence of God, I continued to believe—as I have always believed—that without God we are sunk.

Now began the restless quest. Every Sunday of my first two years in college I went to a different church. Always I prepared myself for the visit by reading all I could lay hands on about the history, doctrine, discipline, and worship of that particular denomination. Living in Southern California, it takes at least twice times fifty-two Sundays to visit them all! It was well along in the second year (I was then eighteen) when, for the first time in my life, I entered an Episcopal church. It amuses me now to read a brief journal entry I made at the time: "The robes were wrinkled. If they're going to be a ceremonial church, why don't they do it right?" My other comments were less trifling: "Was especially impressed by the fact that when the minister prays he turns his back to the people." This was perhaps my first insight into the fact that worship has an objective reference and that prayer is something more than a subjective "pep talk." Lastly: "Rev. Smith [Forgive me! I didn't know better in those days] sounds like a man who knows that something of importance has been learned by the human race in the last two hundred years." This marks me as an incurable liberal and, pray God, may I never cease to be that, if liberal be understood in the sense of that wonderful motto of the Virginia Seminary: "Seek the truth, come whence it may, cost what it will."

The upshot of all my ecclesiastical shopping was that I finally decided to become a Christian. Yes, to *become* one;

for although I *was* one by the gift of Baptism, I certainly was not a practising Christian, and in my conscious mind I had called quits. I report this decision calmly enough, but there was nothing calm about it at the time. It was filled with agony. I knew quite well that while salvation is offered as a free gift, it is nonetheless purchased only by selling everything, i.e., by the gift of self which, to a selfish man, looks just as alluring as does the pearl of great price. In becoming a Christian there is no question of a *sacrificium intellectus* (which for me would have been impossible), and yet there is, unavoidably, a risk, a leap of faith. I was not then as much at home as I now am with the vocabulary I am using, but, without then knowing the words, I knew the reality: while Christianity asks us to believe nothing that is *contra rationem,* it certainly asks us to believe some things which are *supra rationem,* things which can be proved, if at all, only by the experiment of life. This means decision and jeopardy. And I now know the reason for this: in His love, God will not take away from us either the dignity or the danger involved in possessing freedom.

With fear and trembling, then, I made the leap. I made it at a time when the prayer I could offer with complete sincerity was, "Lord, I believe; help thou mine unbelief." So that was that. From my reading, however, I knew enough to know that one cannot be a Christian in the abstract. To be a Christian is to belong. Belonging, integration into the company of believers, is essential to the event. The dangling Christian, the believer with no roots in the community, is a Christian deprived of his proper element, a Christian who has not remotely grasped the central fact that the Word became flesh, that eternity has intersected time, that the end of the ways of God, as someone has said, is

These are some of the reasons, at any rate, why I became an Anglican and am glad to find myself resident in a College which displays, as in a microcosm, the macrocosm of the entire Anglican world. Happily, it does not take a whole Communion or a literal visit to Canterbury, its Cathedral and its College, to demonstrate the points at issue. They can be seen in a local parish, in its people and its priest. It is there I found it first, and it is through priest and people that conversions begin, God being our helper.

22

WILLIAM G. POLLARD

Outstanding nuclear physicist and since 1947 Executive Director of the Oak Ridge Institute of Nuclear Studies, the Rev. Dr. William G. Pollard was born in 1911 and after graduating from the University of Tennessee, where he was elected a member of Phi Beta Kappa and Sigma Xi, he did graduate scientific studies at the Rice Institute, receiving the degrees of Master of Arts and Doctor of Philosophy. He was successively Assistant Professor, Associate Professor, and Professor of Physics at the University of Tennessee, serving as a research scientist with the Special Alloy Materials Laboratories of the Columbia University Division of War Research in 1944-45.

Dr. Pollard has served as consulting physicist to numerous large chemical manufacturing corporations. In 1950 he received the Distinguished Service Award of the Southern Association of Science and Industry. He has been honored with Doctor of Science degrees by Ripon College, the University of the South, and Kalamazoo College. Dr. Pollard is a charter member of the American Nuclear Society and a Fellow of the American Physical Society, having served as chairman of its Southeastern Section in 1951-52. He is author of many articles and monographs in scientific journals.

Dr. Pollard was ordained deacon in the Diocese of Tennessee in 1952 and priest in 1954, and is on the staff of St.

Stephen's Church, Oak Ridge, where he had been vestryman and lay reader. He is a member of the Guild of Scholars of the Episcopal Church, and is on the editorial board of The Christian Scholar *(published under the auspices of the National Council of Churches), for which he has written two articles. He is author of two "Faculty Papers," published by the National Council of the Protestant Episcopal Church*: The Cosmic Drama *and* Revelation and Response. *Dr. Pollard is married and the father of four children.*

WILLIAM G. POLLARD

WITHIN the contemporary life of Anglican Christianity there is taking place today a rather remarkable phenomenon. To an ever-increasing extent mature men at the peak of academic, professional, or business careers are being gripped by the call of the sacred ministry. In every Episcopal seminary today are to be found a good many men who have left flourishing and fruitful careers in mid-life to return to school and tackle the arduous scholastic task of preparation for Holy Orders. Outside the seminaries every bishop has a growing list of middle-aged postulants and candidates busily engaged in a heavy routine of home study under various local arrangements for the supervision of their preparation for canonical examinations. It is like an infection of unknown epidemiology which is spreading through our great Communion. Even those who find themselves caught up in the grip of its strange power do not understand the phenomenon. They do not know, in the sense of secular knowledge, where it came from or where it is leading them. It is all very mysteriously wonderful and remarkable. It is quite exciting and thrilling. But it is not at all understood in the sense in which the world at large tries to understand phenomena.

My own pilgrimage to Canterbury is an instance of this general phenomenon. Like a good many other people of my generation, I was early attracted to science and even before entering college decided to make a career of it. After winning a doctorate in theoretical physics I returned to my undergraduate alma mater as an assistant professor to settle down to an academic career of teaching and research. It was a very enjoyable and satisfying career, quite agreeable to the standards of value and achievement of contemporary culture, and I had every intention of making it a lifetime pursuit. Late in the war I was called, as were so many other professors of physics, to do war research. In my case this was on the Manhattan Project at Columbia University, where the basic work on a process to separate uranium isotopes by gaseous diffusion was being done. After a year and a half at Columbia the war was over, and I joined the great exodus of university people from the war projects in the fall of 1945 to return to my professorship at the University of Tennessee with glowing visions of settling down again to the old quiet, unperturbed, academic life.

This, however, was not to be. Almost immediately I was caught up in a move by southern universities to do something about the fact that the war had left behind in our region the great scientific laboratories of Oak Ridge. I shall never cease to be grateful for the special combination of circumstances which resulted in my playing a leading role in this great regional enterprise. Before long the universities had formed a non-profit corporation with headquarters in Oak Ridge, known as the Oak Ridge Institute of Nuclear Studies. I was elected as the first Executive Director of the new organization, and before long it had entered into an operating contract with the Atomic Energy Commission. The enterprise then grew in size and scope with great rapidity until by three years after its incorporation it was a sizable operation including a school in radioisotope techniques, a cancer research hospital, and an atomic energy museum.

This was the state of affairs just six years ago in the fall of 1949. At that time I had no idea whatever of a change in vocation or calling. Ever since I had entered college twenty-one years before, my career in physics had been one of ever-increasing opportunity, growing achievement, and deepening satisfaction. This latest venture had materialized to an extent and scope which none of us had imagined would be possible. At no other time in my career did my choice of vocation seem to have been so right for me, or was I moving with greater momentum in the direction of my chosen goal. To be sure, I had by then become, by comparison with all previous periods of my life, exceptionally active in our growing Oak Ridge parish of St. Stephen's. But any suggestion that the Church might soon come to replace these goals in my life would have seemed to me then not only inconceivable but actually preposterous.

Yet just one year later, in the fall of 1950, I was admitted as a postulant for Holy Orders by the Rt. Rev. E. P. Dandridge, D.D., then Bishop of Tennessee. Something over two years later, on Ember Wednesday in December, 1952, he ordained me to the diaconate. Then a year and a half later, on St. Philip's and St. James' Day, I was made a priest of the Holy Catholic Church. During all of this time the Oak Ridge Institute of Nuclear Studies continued to grow and flourish, reaching by the time I was ordained deacon an operating level of nearly two million dollars per year. There was still no reason at all for a change in vocation. Yet, nevertheless, it was taking place even more rapidly than I realized then. By now, in the second year of my priesthood, this has all become quite clear. There is no question now but that my primary vocation is the sacred ministry. Although I am still happily continuing as Executive Director of the Institute in Oak Ridge and still keep up my interest in physics and even do a little research now and then, it is now evident that all this has become a secondary vocation for me. The great challenges which now excite me, the real enthusiasms which take hold of me, and the new vistas which I see dimly opening up before me are all in theology, not in physics. So there is no longer any question but that my primary vocation has been radically changed.

Even to me this seems an extraordinary outcome. I am amazed that it could ever have happened to me. Here is a radical change in direction; and yet try as I will I cannot point to anything explicit in my own motivation to account for the change. Indeed, as I look back on the events of the past six years, that which is most clear to me is that the person I then was would not have wanted this new estate at all. If I could have seen a vision then of my present situation, it would have frightened me, and I would surely have determined then and there to set myself resolutely against any such outcome. But thanks be to God that it is not given to men to have such visions! Instead there was just the slow silent working of the Holy Spirit who, without my knowing it, was fabricating a pattern of minor and apparently insignificant steps which all together finally produced the outcome.

It has been an interesting commentary on the nature of our contemporary secular culture to observe the reactions of people at large to this transformation. When the news of my intention to seek Holy Orders first became known, the most common explanation for my action interpreted it as a reaction to the guilt of my involvement in the development of atomic weapons. In a world which by and large does not think of religion as real, it becomes necessary to try to find some psychological or sociological explanation for religious behavior. There is the compulsion to try to understand it in naturalistic terms and so dispose of it and explain it away. In the case of an atomic scientist the most obvious explanation would seem to lie in the emotional strain which those responsible for A-bombs must be under. This is reflected

in such headlines as "ATOMIC SPUR TO FAITH" and "A-BOMB-
ING TURNED SCIENTIST TO MINISTRY" which were used at the
time of my ordination to the priesthood. It has been one of
my most difficult tasks to try to make it clear that this motivation was hardly present at all in my case, and that I could
not therefore be explained away in such an obvious fashion.

Another very common notion is that I must somehow have
argued myself into a religious position through my scientific
reasoning. This way of accounting for my action takes both a
positive and a negative form. On its positive side it is an
expression of the hope that some entirely new approach to
religious truth and man's knowledge of God can be found
which will be independent of past revelation in history. How
many discussion groups, conferences, and even new societies
one finds nowadays in which those involved propose to
re-examine religion and morality in the light of modern
knowledge and science, and ardently expect to come up
with some satisfactory modern synthesis of religious knowledge which will replace all the supposedly outmoded historic
religions! In a majority of the lectures which I have given
since my ordination to the diaconate I have been conscious
of an expectation in my audience of just such an approach.
So great is the prestige of science in our contemporary culture
that it is extraordinarily difficult to convince people of the
patent hopelessness of such a quest. On such occasions I am
frequently keenly aware of the astonishment and surprise
in my audience when I speak so emphatically of the God
who has revealed Himself in the history of Israel and in
Christ, and when, instead of presenting ancient Christianity
from the vantage point of modern science, I seek to show
modern science in its true perspective from the standpoint
of the unique insights of our Judeo-Christian heritage. This,
to say the least, is the last thing a modern secular audience

expects to hear when, out of curiosity, they come to hear what an atomic scientist who has recently become a priest of the Church has to say for himself.

In its negative manifestation this interpretation of my religious pilgrimage would suggest that my scientific work may have led me to some kind of impasse from which I turned to religion as the "answer." Our contemporary culture has been dominated by an exclusive faith in the power of science to solve all questions and a sure confidence in its unlimited potentiality in every area of application. Under the spell of this exclusiveness, religion has seemed to be confined to an ever-shrinking domain made up of those areas which science has not yet gotten around to explaining. It is to me one of the saddest commentaries on the low estate to which modern secularism has brought us to observe the way in which so many people long for a positive assurance from scientists that there are definite bounds to the apparently unlimited extendability of science. To them I can only say that a Christianity so excluded from vast areas of human life and condemned to a defensive position in which it could only lose, never gain, territory could hardly account for the power which has so obviously gripped me.

Another characteristic which runs through all of these reactions is the notion that I must have worked out some unique private faith of my own which at last made it possible for me to become religious. Religion has come to be regarded quite generally as a private affair. A man's faith is something which he works out in private between himself and his God. It is valid and acceptable so long as it sustains him through the difficult business of living. The idea of a public faith shared by a great community of the faithful whose reality and power transcends individual tastes and foibles has practically disappeared from contemporary life. A striking example of this situation is provided by a radio series presented by Edward R. Murrow, selections from which have been published under the title *This I Believe*. No more convincing proof of the spiritual bankruptcy of American life has been given than is to be found in this diverse collection of naïve and tragically inadequate professions of the private beliefs of some of our leading public figures. On several occasions I have been asked for a similar personal expression in the form of "The Faith of an American Scientist." To such queries I can only answer that I have no faith of my own. All I would be in a position to supply would be a copy of the Nicene Creed. For that which has taken hold of me is nothing less than the great historic witness of the Catholic Faith. It is a richly rewarding task and a magnificent adventure to be engaged in the process of ever enriching one's responsiveness to this Faith, and acquiring more and more of a capacity to see life and history and reality through its eyes. I would no more think of working apart from the community of witness to this Faith to produce a private faith of my own than I would of working apart from the community of physicists to produce a private science of my own.

The way in which my transformation from a modern pagan to a priest of the Church actually took place is very different from any of these commonly held ideas of how it must have occurred. The story of this transformation has been told fully and sympathetically by Daniel Lang in the "Reporter at Large" section of *The New Yorker* for February 6, 1954.[1] As this story shows so well, that which actually

---

[1] Available in book form in a collection of Mr. Lang's articles on atomic energy under the title *The Man in the Thick Lead Suit* (New York: Oxford University Press, 1954). —ED.

took place was a gradual process, a series of minor and apparently unrelated and unimportant incidents, having very little to do with atomic energy, science, or rational speculation.

I shall never cease to be astounded at the fruits of this process in my own life and the sheer mystery of the manner of its operation. Every time I review in retrospect this remarkable sequence of events, the one feature which stands out most clearly and strikingly above all others is that the man I was when it started would emphatically not have wanted its outcome. That man Pollard of those earlier days had no way of recognizing the prison within which he was confined, no background or experience for understanding the true character of the primary challenge of our time, and no dissatisfaction sufficiently strong to prod him along the path from which he could discover the wide horizons and thrilling vistas of his present life. He was much too happy and successful in his chosen career, and much too completely a victim of the prevailing secular illusion, self-sufficiency, and passion for science of the culture of which he was a part, to have ever wanted to extricate himself from the bonds in which it held him. How amazing therefore is the transformation wrought by the mysterious working of God's grace without his realizing what was taking place! Small wonder that he is so baffled by those who ask him how he found Christianity. For him the great question will always be how it came about that Christianity found him.

I often think in this connection of that magnificent expression of wonder and amazement over the fruit of the work of the Holy Spirit which pours forth from St. Paul in his letter to the Ephesians:

> And you he made alive, when you were dead through the trespasses and sins in which you once walked, following the

course of this world, following the prince of the power of the air, the spirit that is now at work in the sons of disobedience. Among these we all once lived in the passions of our flesh, following the desires of body and mind, and so we were by nature children of wrath, like the rest of mankind. But God, who is rich in mercy, out of the great love with which he loved us, even when we were dead through our trespasses, made us alive together with Christ (by grace you have been saved), and raised us up with him, and made us sit with him in the heavenly places in Christ Jesus, that in the coming ages he might show the immeasurable riches of his grace in kindess toward us in Christ Jesus. For by grace you have been saved through faith; *and this is not your own doing,* it is the *gift of God*—not because of works, lest any man should boast. For we are his workmanship, created in Christ Jesus for good works, which God prepared beforehand, that we should walk in them.[2]

Such is the work of the Holy Spirit in that life-giving and redeeming community in the Lord which we call the Church. With a strange and wonderful power it seizes hold of men when they are dead in the isolation and futility of an autonomous existence and brings them to life together in Christ. From the very beginning one of the great and wonderful facts of the Christian life has always been the realization that the Holy Spirit dwells in Christ's holy Church and does His work constantly among us. Yet the legacy of rationalism and simple ethical idealism left to us from the preceding century has tended to make Christian people lose hold of this great insight and to come instead to regard it as a remote and obscure "doctrine" of interest only to theologians. This tragic impoverishment of Christian life is the penalty we pay for our contemporary fragmentation

[2] Ephesians 2:1-10, Revised Standard Version of *The Holy Bible,* copyrighted 1946 and 1952 by the Division of Christian Education, National Council of Churches. Italics mine.

of the historic Faith into a diverse assortment of private faiths individually fabricated and privately held.

There are, however, many signs on the contemporary scene of the beginnings of a rediscovery of the presence of the Holy Spirit within the churches, and of the power and joy which He gives to the people of the Lord. Nowhere, I believe, is this renaissance more evident than in our own Anglican Communion. Indeed I have often been asked whether this great thing which has happened to me would have occurred if I had been in some other Communion. Although I cannot of course know how I would have been affected in other circumstances, I do know that Anglican Christianity possesses a special power and a unique capacity which I do not sense in my contacts with my brethren in Christ from other traditions. The great challenge of our age is far more radical and revolutionary than the majority of our people have any conception that it could be. For this challenge is nothing less than the rediscovery by Western civilization of its lost Judeo-Christian heritage and a reacquisition at a common public level of the lost capacity to respond freely and naturally to the values and deep understandings of this heritage. Thus that which we of the twentieth century face today is comparable in magnitude to the challenge which faced the West in the tenth century at the beginning of the Renaissance when it first began to recover its lost capacity to respond to the wealth of its Graeco-Roman heritage.

Such a renaissance as this is a radical cultural upheaval whose consequences must of necessity spread throughout all phases of life. Insofar as it begins really to take place, it cannot by its very nature be confined within any one of the many cells into which our present society is divided. Yet it is, like the earlier renaissance, a most delicate and sensitive plant in its early stages which requires a special soil and an unusual nurture in order to take root at all. Among our varied churches and synagogues within which the remaining vestiges of the former glory of our Judeo-Christian heritage are still retained, we must look for the one which provides the unique kind of environment which is required. Just what this is none of us in this early stage of so tremendous a process can know. But I do think we can sense that neither an undisciplined proliferation of private faiths on the one hand, nor a rigorous insistence on traditional intellectual formulations of the historic Faith on the other, will be equal to the task.

There are doubtless in other communions, both Catholic and Protestant, latent powers of which I from the outside can be only dimly aware. From the finiteness of our own several limited situations we dare not presume to render judgments on those whose life in Christ we have not shared. The Lord does His work among us all according to His good pleasure, and we dare not deny Him to any. Yet without judging others, we can cherish and long to share with others the riches which have been given to us. And how great and full a treasure has been entrusted to the Anglican churches! Here is all the fullness of the historic Catholic faith and sacraments, enjoying through the historic episcopate full visible continuity with Christ's Holy Catholic Church down through the ages to the Apostolic Church. Yet here also, side by side with the staunch solidarity of Catholic faith and practice, is to be found in equal strength the humility which comes with the Protestant rediscovery of the ancient prophetic principle that everything human, including the Church, is forever under judgment. This remarkable capacity to preserve in treasured union paradoxical elements which elsewhere have produced bitter and irreconcilable divisions is a unique endowment of Anglican Christianity.

Those of us within this Communion who have been gripped by its great power sense that here is to be had just that combination of stability and flexibility, of loyalty to the fullness of the historic Faith and of freedom to recast its historic formulations which is required for a full response to the great challenge of our age. In increasing numbers men are coming today to a dawning awareness of the emptiness and sterility, the unreality and illusion, of our contemporary secular culture. At the same time they sense the priceless opportunity which this age offers those who are given the grace to recognize and respond to the new rebirth and renaissance just beginning in that culture. Here is a great adventure in which may be found liberation and fulfillment. Here in the United States we in the Episcopal Church welcome all such to seek this grace within our fellowship. It is surely to be had there, as the rapidly growing body of Canterbury Pilgrims from the academic world will testify.

23

JAMES A. PIKE Publisher's Note on the Editor

Since 1952 Dean of the Cathedral of St. John the Divine, the Very Rev. James A. Pike was born in 1913, graduated in arts and law from the University of Southern California, and after admission to the California bar, received the degree of Doctor of the Science of Law at Yale, where he was a Sterling Fellow. For four years he was an attorney for the Securities and Exchange Commission in Washington, serving also on the faculty of the George Washington University Law School. He is a member of the bar of the United States Supreme Court. In the last war he served in the Navy as intelligence officer and attorney.

After his ordination in 1944, Dr. Pike served at St. John's, Washington, as a tutor at the General Theological Seminary (of which he is now a trustee), as rector of Christ Church, Poughkeepsie, and Chaplain to Episcopal Students at Vassar College. He completed his theological studies at Virginia, General, and Union Theological Seminaries. Before coming to the Cathedral he served as Chaplain of Columbia University and head of its Department of Religion, in which Department he still serves as Adjunct Professor, teaching in the seminar on church-state relations at the law school.

Dean Pike is author of books and articles in the field of Federal judicial and administrative procedure, and is author of Beyond Anxiety, If You Marry Outside Your Faith, *and* Doing the Truth, *and co-author of* The Faith of the Church, Roadblocks to Faith, *and* The Church, Politics, and Society. *He has received honorary doctorates in divinity, civil and canon law, and letters. He is President of the Standing Committee of the Diocese of New York and has twice served as Deputy to General Convention. He serves on the Department of Religious Liberty of the National Council of Churches. Dean Pike is married and the father of four children.*

JAMES A. PIKE

IT WAS probably a rationalization for procrastination when I decided to defer writing my essay until I saw the others, on the theory that perhaps I could then usefully "round out" the picture with a coverage on such features of Anglicanism as might not yet have been touched upon. But it may have been an inspired dilatoriness, for actually every factor which played a part in my conversion —from Rome *via* agnosticism—or which has impressed me in subsequent years, has not only been covered, but in fact has been stated better than my talents would permit. Hence I can limit my personal story to a paragraph, and then turn to an attempt at a brief synthesis of the appeal of Anglicanism today.

The beginning of my doubts concurred with the first serious intimations of my vocation to the priesthood—in the senior year of high school. Seeing the religious question to be the foremost one, I gave up a chance to go to Harvard on a scholarship to study with the Jesuits in a small college, since I understood that they would know the most about the faith I had begun to question. My studies in scholastic philosophy and my intellectual difficulties with it paralleled the description in Mr. Marquez's essay, and my difficulties in accepting papal infallibility were grounded in reasons already touched upon in other essays herein. And, in spite of the high calibre of a number of my instructors, the closed-minded dogmatism and the overprotectiveness against "error," also already referred to, were my experience also. So after two years I left the college and the Church and pursued my studies in secular institutions. Very quickly losing my Christian faith (I "threw out the baby with the bath water"), I sought the meaning for my life in career and in a zeal for social reform—more particularly through my eventual association, as an attorney, with the New Deal. The inadequacy of these aims as a total meaning for life increasingly dawned on me, especially during a period of serious personal crisis. At first I was drawn to Episcopal worship by its aesthetic—and, in my case, nostalgic—appeal; when, soon after our marriage, Esther and I decided to give serious intellectual consideration to religion, it was out of an explicitly felt need for a more meaningful basis for our personal lives, for our marriage, and for our social concerns. In our reading we were influenced first by C. S. Lewis, B. I. Bell, and, like John Hallowell, by Professor Fairchild's *Toward Belief*, and then by William Temple and Reinhold Niebuhr. When we had decided for Christianity we turned next to the question, What Church? For reasons shortly to be summarized (some of which were then inchoate), our answer was the Episcopal Church. On my return to the Catholic Church my vocation to its priesthood, long latent, quickly surfaced. Then in the Navy, I was admitted as a postulant in the Diocese of Washington and undertook my studies under the direction of the Rev. Charles W. F. Smith, then Canon of Washington Cathedral, where I was subsequently ordained deacon and priest; and the understanding of the Faith to which Esther and I had committed ourselves was much clarified by him, by Canon T. O. Wedel, by Professor A. T. Mollegen, and by my present brother in the Chapter of New York, Canon Howard A. Johnson, who introduced us to Kierkegaard. Obviously, this process of clarification and deepening—both intellectually and personally —did not end there, nor has it yet. And those who have helped along the way would make a long list indeed.

What is the nature of the Episcopal Church?[1] It is impossible to answer this question analytically; it can only be answered historically, or in terms of what in physics is called "vector analysis." Anglican Christianity as we know it today is principally the result of three historical forces: Western Catholicism, the Renaissance, and the continental Reformation. Thus one would expect to find the Episcopal Church somewhat Catholic, somewhat liberal, and somewhat Protestant. Actually, we can claim much more for our church than this *Via Media* approach suggests. It is thoroughly Catholic, thoroughly Protestant, and thoroughly liberal. More than that: it is more Catholic than the Church which is colloquially referred to by that name; it is more Protestant than the classical Reformation Churches; and it is more liberal than what are generally thought of as the "liberal" Churches. This is a large claim; but here is why we can make it.

MORE CATHOLIC THAN OTHER CATHOLICS

We are Catholic in that we hold entire "the Faith once for all delivered to the Saints" in unbroken continuity, in faith and in order, with the early Church. We are more Catholic than the Roman Catholic Church because of its departures —by addition, subtraction, and distortion—from the Catholic Faith, departures both before and after the reformation in our Church by which we returned to a purer form of Catholicism. In the case of almost every significant difference between us, in faith or in practice, we are teaching it or doing it the *earlier* way (as examples, we can take a few such assorted items as the doctrine of justification; episcopal

---

[1] What follows is based principally on my article "The Episcopal Church— Catholic, Protestant and Liberal" in *The Church Militant* (Diocese of Massachusetts), September, 1952 (used with permission).

versus papal government; married priests; public confession
and voluntary private confession *versus* compulsory private
confession; vernacular liturgy; the doctrine of the real
presence without the later doctrine of transubstantiation;
communion in both kinds; holy unction for healing versus
"extreme unction" limited to last rites). Later doctrines may
be all right, but the burden of proof is certainly on the
innovator. We are "old-fashioned" Catholics.

This aspect of the nature of our Church was well brought
out in the reply of the Archbishops of Canterbury and York
to the Pope's promulgation of the dogma of the Assumption
of Mary. They did not say, "We as Protestants don't like this
Catholic doctrine." They said in effect, "We as Catholics
don't like this unwarranted and unsupported addition to the
Catholic Faith."

MORE PROTESTANT THAN OTHER PROTESTANTS

Protestant means the recognition of the principle that the
Church is under judgment, that all institutions, ideas, or
forms must stand under the ultimacy of Christ Himself,
and that thus the Church always needs reformation. The
Churches of the Reformation are Protestant in the sense
that they arose from the prophetic movement which critically
re-examined the current teaching and practices of the
Western Church. But these Churches adopted confessions
of faith which were detailed systemizations of doctrine, and
which thereafter were to be looked back upon as final tests
of orthodoxy. Then, in a sense, they became no longer
Protestant; they had *had* their reformation. The situation in
Anglicanism is different. There is no particular historical
point which we can label as the English Reformation; it
has been a gradual process in which there have been repeated
prophetic movements. Because we date ourselves from no

great Reformer and because at no point did we adopt a confession of faith,[2] we have been freer to receive new applications of the Protestant principles. There were some reforms under Henry, more under Elizabeth; then the reformations wrought successively by the Evangelical Movement, the Oxford Movement, the "broad-Church" movement; and creative movements in liturgical relevance and corporate redemptiveness in our Church today which are too contemporaneous to label. We are more Protestant than the classical Reformation Churches because we are free from the absolutes of any past period. We are a Church *in reformation* all through.

What is the fixed reality to which we are bound? One thing—the Gospel, the apostolic proclamation, the *kerygma*,[3] the good news of "the mighty acts of God" in Christ for us men and for our salvation. Even the creeds and the decrees of ecumenical councils are accepted *because* we see in them the assertion of the Gospel.[4] And as to the Bible, we look *beyond the words to the Word*. While the Bible is "the best evidence" of the Word (and hence the faithful are protected from any teaching which we cannot back up by it), still the Word stands in judgment on any particular set of words. Our Church is not founded on the Bible, because the Church which already believed the *kerygma* selected what writings it felt well expressed the Gospel, and the

---

2 The Articles of Religion are not this. In no sense a system of doctrine (as compared with the much more elaborate confessions of the Reformation Churches), they represent the reaction of our Church, at a particular time in its history, to Papists on the one hand and Puritans on the other. It was a significant period and a sound reaction, and one from which we have much to learn, but the Articles are not to be considered a confession of faith. They are certainly useful to show our characteristic approach to the Faith and are so cited in this essay.

3 See *The Faith of the Church,* Chap. I (Greenwich: Seabury Press, 1951).

4 Note the approach in Article VIII (Creeds) and also Article XXI of the English Prayer Book (councils).

Church selected so wisely that we can aver that "Holy Scripture containeth all things necessary to salvation"; but "the things necessary to salvation" (i.e., the *kerygma*) are the ultimate, not the Scriptures which express them. Hence we are also more Protestant than those Churches which, while disavowing a confession of faith, do not bring the words of Scripture within the purview of the Protestant principle.

MORE LIBERAL THAN OTHER LIBERALS

Liberal has both a negative and a positive connotation: it can mean "free from" or "free for."

Because we are Protestant in the right sense we are liberal in the first meaning of the word; that is, we are *free* from bibliolatry, free from the absolutizing of any system of doctrines, free from the thought-forms of any particular age. Now it is as illiberal to be tied to the concepts and aspirations of the nineteenth-century optimism about man and his self-sufficiency as it is to be tied to the thirteenth-century concepts of St. Thomas Aquinas, which were absolutized for Roman Catholics in 1950 by the encyclical *Humani generis*. This does not argue for ignoring either set of ideas; quite the reverse—and this leads to the second, and positive, meaning of "liberal": a Church which sits loose to all systems is free to utilize all of them in its task of understanding and communicating the Gospel.

Thus we are open to, and feel a real sense of identification with, the thought of the Greek and Latin Fathers, St. Anselm, Luther, Calvin, Wesley, Kierkegaard, Von Hügel, Barth. I have it from a Lutheran scholar that the Episcopalians more than the Lutherans are the ones interested in the Lutheran Kierkegaard; a Congregationalist scholar tells me that it is the Anglicans more than the members of his own

Church who are now reading the writings of the late English Congregationalist P. T. Forsyth.

This same breadth is seen in the use of form: the expressive arts of all periods beautify our churches and our worship; our décor ranges from the barest to the richest; our words of prayer echo the piety of all the centuries. This is being liberal in the positive sense.

All of this is not merely intellectual or artistic borrowing; it is the natural expression of our feeling for *the communion of saints,* the sensing of the present reality of those who have gone before us in the Faith. For us the continuity of the Church is not merely mechanical or historical; it is a recognition of organic living relationship with the great *cloud of witnesses* with which *we are compassed about.* And we are free to be helped by all of them, the great ones who have gone before, because we are free from final allegiance to the "dated" thought-forms of any one of them, bearing final allegiance only to Him who is the *author and finisher of our faith.*

There is another sense in which we are liberal. We really take seriously the implications of the doctrine of creation: we believe that God meant it when, looking down on all that He had made, He said, "It is very good." This joyful acceptance of the created order marks us off from the American Churches which have been so influenced by the Puritan and pietistic movements with their flesh-rejecting tendencies. (Even the so-called liberal Churches use grape juice for the Lord's Supper, being considerably more abstemious than the Lord!)

A NOTE ON "CHURCHMANSHIP"

It would be naïve to assume that Anglicanism at all times and in all places has fulfilled the description just outlined.

Further, other Churches have often given a better witness to one or another of the aspects of the truth we espouse. However, the Church in its formularies has consistently adhered to these standards, and they have been displayed sufficiently throughout her life to assure us that we are speaking realistically—and not merely idealistically—when we so describe the Church. But while the Church is Catholic, Protestant, and liberal at the same time, this is a good deal for an individual to wrap himself around. Thus there is always the tendency for these elements to go out of solution, and hence the wide variety in the emphases of individuals and in the ethos of parishes. This is inevitable in a Church which seeks to hold together so many facets of the Christian heritage.

Some are more enthusiastic about our Catholic continuity; others are more interested in our ties with the continental Reformation; others, in the spirit of Renaissance man, are more interested in openness toward new truth and responsibilities and fresher communication thereof. Hence "high," "low," and "broad." The solution of the tensions these emphases create is not for some to become less Catholic, some to become less Protestant, others less liberal. Rather the whole Church needs to become more Catholic, more Protestant, and more liberal; that is, the whole Church should become more in actual fact what in principle it most certainly is: fully Catholic, thoroughly Protestant, properly liberal. That this process is actually going on in our midst is the most characteristic feature of our Church's life in this decade. The happy result is that more and more Episcopalians these days bear no partisan labels at all.

Any one teaching, attitude, or emphasis of Anglicanism can be found elsewhere in Christendom, but not so many true, good, and beautiful things can be found together. We cannot claim that ours is the "true Church," but I am convinced that it is the truest. We cannot claim that ours is the best Church, but I am sure that a tradition this sound and balanced has the greatest potential for goodness in the world. All the more is God judging us for the large gap between our potentiality and our actuality. If we perceive this we should as Episcopalians excel in humility!

So our threefold heritage—Catholic, Protestant, and Liberal—should give us *confidence* in the soundness of our tradition, *humility* as to our performance in promoting Christian Faith and life in the world, and *openness* to truth wherever found, especially when witnessed to by our Christian brothers. These together should make us meet instruments for what is most surely the mind of Christ, the restoration of the visible unity of His Church.

DATE DUE